PLANNING AND MANAGEMENT OF MEETINGS, EXPOSITIONS, EVENTS, AND CONVENTIONS

GLOBAL EDITION

PLANNING AND MANAGEMENT OF MEETINGS, EXPOSITIONS, EVENTS, AND CONVENTIONS

George G. Fenich, Ph.D.
School of Hospitality Leadership
East Carolina University

PEARSON

Boston Columbus Indianapolis New York San Francisco Hoboken
Amsterdam Cape Town Dubai London Madrid Milan Munich Paris Montréal Toronto
Delhi Mexico City São Paulo Sydney Hong Kong Seoul Singapore Taipei Tokyo

Editorial Director: Vernon Anthony
Senior Acquisitions Editor: William Lawrensen
Editorial Assistant: Lara Dimmick
Head of Learning Asset Acquisition, Global Editions: Laura Dent
Acquisitions Editor, Global Editions: Vrinda Sharma Malik
Project Editor, Global Editions: Suchismita Ukil
Director of Marketing: Dave Gesell
Marketing Manager: Stacey Martinez
Senior Marketing Coordinator: Alicia Wozniak
Senior Marketing Assistant: Les Roberts
Program Manager: Alexis Duffy
Senior Managing Editor: JoEllen Gohr
Production Project Manager: Susan Hannahs
Media Production Manager, Global Editions: M. Vikram Kumar
Senior Production Controller, Global Editions: Trudy Kimber
Senior Art Director: Jayne Conte
Cover Designer: Lumina Datamatics Ltd.
Cover Art: momente/Shutterstock

Credits and acknowledgments borrowed from other sources and reproduced, with permission, in this textbook appear on the appropriate page within the text.

Pearson Education Limited
Edinburgh Gate
Harlow
Essex CM20 2JE
England

and Associated Companies throughout the world

Visit us on the World Wide Web at: www.pearsonglobaleditions.com

© Pearson Education Limited 2015

ISBN 10: 1-292-07174-5
ISBN 13: 978-1-292-07174-9

British Library Cataloguing-in-Publication Data
A catalogue record for this book is available from the British Library

10 9 8 7 6 5 4 3 2 1
14

Typeset in 11/13 Adobe Garamont Pro by Lumina Datamatics Ltd.

Printed and bound by Courier/Kendallville in the United States of America

PEARSON

Dedicated to the hard working professionals of the
Meetings and Business Events Competency Standards Task Force and
the Curriculum Guide Task Force, without whom this book would not be possible.

brief contents

contents

5

Stakeholder Management 71

6

Accounting and Financial Planning 87

Preface

The meetings, expositions, events, and conventions (MEEC, pronounced like *geese*) industry continues to grow and garner increasing attention from the hospitality industry, colleges and universities, government officials and communities. This book provides a comprehensive view of planning and management in MEEC. It is meant to provide a hands-on or step-by-step method for planning and managing gatherings in the MEEC industry.

Planning and Management of Meetings, Events, Expositions, and Conventions is based on the work of two task forces initiated and supported by Meeting Professionals International: the Meeting and Business Event Competency Standards Task Force and the Meeting and Business Event Competency Standards Curriculum Guide Task Force. This book should be of interest to practitioners, educators, students, and government officials. It is the most up-to-date book on planning and management in the MEEC industry and covers a wide range of topics dealing with those two functions. This book can easily serve as the basis for a college course on the subject, for training sessions for new employees in the industry, and for educational delivery by industry associations. It should meet the needs of anyone interested in knowing more about planning and management in the MEEC industry.

George G. Fenich, Ph.D.

INSTRUCTOR'S RESOURCES

Instructor's Resources include an online instructor's manual, PowerPoints, and a MyTest.

To access the supplementary materials, instructors need to request an instructor access code. Go to www.pearsonglobaleditions.com, where you can register for an instructor access code. Within forty-eight hours after registering, you will receive a confirmation email, including your instructor access code. Once you have received your code, go to the site and log on for full instructions on downloading the materials you wish to use.

Acknowledgments

I would like to thank Kathryn Hashimoto for her unabated support, patience, and encouragement; event professionals for sharing their knowledge; and adult learners everywhere for their interest in the MEEC industry. Also, thank you to the academics and industry professionals who contributed materials for this book.

I would also like to thank the reviewers: Jeff Beck, Michigan State University; Orie Berezan, University of Nevada, Las Vegas; MaryAnne Bobrow, Bobrow & Associates; Suzan Bunn, University of Central Florida, Rosen College; Uwe Hermann, Tshwane University, South Africa; Godwin-Charles Ogbeide, University of Arkansas, Fayetteville; B. J. Reed, University of Wisconsin, Platteville, for their time and helpful suggestions.

Pearson would like to thank and acknowledge Johnny Chiu, Vocational Training Council, Hong Kong for his contribution in making this Global Edition.

Pearson would also like to thank the Global Edition reviewers: Candace Fu, Community College of City University, Hong Kong; Toney Thomas, Taylor's University, Malaysia; and David Yong, Multimedia University, Malaysia.

About the Author

George G. Fenich, Ph.D., is a professor in the School of Hospitality Leadership at East Carolina University. Dr. Fenich worked in the hospitality industry for fifteen years before joining academe in 1985. He teaches and researches in the area of conventions and meetings and has written three books and over forty academic articles. He has presented at over one hundred conferences both in the United States and internationally. He has filled leadership roles in DMAI, IMEX America and ICHRIE. He is the editor-in-chief of the *Journal of Convention and Event Tourism* and sits on the editorial boards of six other academic journals. He is also the principal of the consulting firm Fenich & Associates LLC.

Introduction

CHAPTER 1

© Kheng Guan Toh/Fotolia

Chapter Outline

PLANNING AND MANAGEMENT OF MEETINGS, EXPOSITIONS, EVENTS, AND CONVENTIONS

Meetings, Expositions, Events, and Conventions (MEEC, pronounced like geese) are a part of the larger field of tourism. This is an exciting career area. Regardless of the attitudes and interests of the potential MEEC professional, they should be able to find a satisfying employment niche in MEEC. It is expected that the reader of this book has some knowledge of the MEEC industry. It should be noted that in some parts of the world this industry is referred to as MICE: meetings, incentives, conventions, events. The "incentive travel" aspect of this industry has diminished in magnitude and has morphed to become much more like a meeting or convention, albeit more upscale. Thus, the acronym MEEC seems more appropriate. While there are multiple aspects and theories in MEEC, the operationalization of MEEC falls into only two categories: planning and producing. Planning is considered to be "determining or figuring out, in advance, what you want to do and how you want to do it." Producing, or logistics, involves the actual setting up of a meeting, event, or convention. This book is meant to focus on the **planning** aspect of the MEEC industry. Production of MEECs is dealt with in another text.

THE MEEC INDUSTRY

Components or Elements

The MEEC industry is quite diverse and multifaceted. The following provides some insight into MEEC divisions or segments:

a. Conventions and Meetings
   i. Political National Convention
   ii. National Restaurant Association Convention in Chicago
   iii. PCMA Annual Conference
b. Expositions
   i. Where Suppliers Meet Buyers
   ii. Education
   iii. Entertainment
c. Corporate Events
   i. Holiday Parties
   ii. Annual Dinners
   iii. Company Picnics
   iv. Meetings
   v. Sales Training
   vi. Conventions
d. Festivals
   i. Marketplace of Ancient Days
   ii. Community Event
   iii. Fair (not for profit)
   iv. Festival (for profit)
e. Social events
   i. Wedding
   ii. Anniversary
   iii. Birthday
   iv. Reunion
   v. Bar Mitzvah (Bat Mitzvah)
f. Religious Events
   i. Papal Inauguration
   ii. The Hajj (Mecca)
   iii. Easter
   iv. Quanza
g. Special Events:
   i. Civic Events
   ii. Centennials
   iii. Founder's Day
h. Mega-Events
   i. Olympics
   ii. America's Cup
   iii. Hands Across America
   iv. World's Fairs

    i. Retail Events
        i. Long Range Promotional Event
        ii. Store Opening
        iii. New Product Rollout
            1. Xbox
            2. iTunes
    j. Sporting Events (occurring relatively infrequently)
        i. Super Bowl
        ii. World Cup
        iii. Yacht Races

Along with the above, there are many occupations and industries that, in part, support MEEC.

For example, there is a company called Accent on Arrangements that provides child care and activities for conventions and attendees around the United States. Their employees travel extensively and consist of people with an aptitude for working with small children but who are not interested in being schoolteachers. The company regularly employs college students. Another opportunity is for someone who loves flower arranging to work for a specialty service contractor who supplies floral arrangements for trade show booths. Still another opportunity is to work as a princess or Snow White for special events at Disney. The work and career opportunities in MEEC are endless and are available in every corner of the world.

The individuals who work in MEEC are known by many different names, including: planner; meeting planner; corporate meeting planner; event planner; wedding planner; hotel or conference center salesperson; entertainment/sporting venue sales and services; destination management; service contractors; and more (adapted from Fenich, G. G., 2012). In this book any of these individuals are referred to as **event professionals**.

Definitions

All of the definitions used in this book are based on the glossary developed by the Convention Industry Council and found at http://www.conventionindustry.org /StandardsPractices/APEX/glossary.aspx/. **The APEX Glossary is a product of the Convention Industry Council (Copyright 2011) and is used with permission:** www .conventionindustry.org.

The following are four definitions that the event professional must know:

1. **Meeting:** An event where the primary activity of the participants is to attend educational sessions, participate in discussions or social functions or attend other organized events. There is no exhibit component.
   a. See also: Consumer Show, Convention
2. **Exposition:** Exhibition that is open to the public, usually requiring an entrance fee.
   a. EXHIBITION: An event at which products, services, or promotional materials are displayed to attendees visiting exhibits on the show floor. These events focus primarily on business-to-business (B2B) relationships.
3. **Event:** An organized occasion such as a meeting, convention, exhibition, special event, gala dinner, and so on. An event is often composed of several different, yet related, functions.
   a. Special Event: One-time event staged for the purpose of celebration; unique activity
4. **Convention:** Gathering of delegates, representatives, and members of a membership or industry organization convened for a common purpose. Common features include educational sessions, committee meetings, social functions, and meetings to conduct the governance business of the organization. Conventions are typically recurring events with specific, established timing.
   a. See also: Consumer Show, Exhibition, Meeting, Trade Show

What all of the above have in common is that they must (1) be planned and (2) must be produced. This planning and subsequent production is done by a meeting and event professional, sometimes called a meeting planner or an event professional.

Magnitude of the MEEC Industry

As can be seen above, the MEEC industry is quite broad and diverse. Thus, it is difficult to ascertain the size, magnitude, and economic impact of MEEC. Based on the statistics from the International Association of Professional Congress Organisers (IAPCO, 2010), the estimated economic impact of the events their members plan was 3.431 billion (pound sterling) with an average delegate spend of 1620 (pound sterling) per meeting. According to the *American Express Meetings to Events 2013 Global Meetings Forecast* (MPI, 2012b), Asia Pacific, with its relatively strong economy, is likely to see the strongest growth among regions in both spending and the number of meetings.

The *Economic Significance of Meetings to the U.S. Economy* study reveals that the U.S. meetings industry directly supports 1.7 million jobs, $263 billion in spending, a $106 billion share of the GDP, $60 billion in labor revenue, $14.3 billion in federal tax revenue and $11.3 billion in state and local tax revenue each year. In the MEEC industry in the United States alone, 205 million attendees participate in the nation's 1.8 million conventions, conferences, congresses, trade shows and exhibitions, incentive events, and corporate/business meetings (CIC, 2010).

Trends in MEEC

MEEC is an ever evolving industry. Thus, event professionals must consider trends in MEEC when planning their events. A major trend is the growing globalization of the industry and the blurring of country borders and boundaries: i.e., the formation of the EU. With globalization comes growing concerns about safety, both physical and medical, along with security and worries about delegates. International travel is increasingly risky whether it is delegates traveling *to* places with problems or coming *from* those places. Thus, event professionals must develop contingency plans, risk management strategies, and appropriate safeguards for their attendees. Staff must be trained to be ready to take action in emergencies (MPI, 2012a).

Another trend is the growing recognition that multiple generations are attending meetings and events, including pre-boomers, baby boomers, and Gens X, Y, and Z. With them come very diverse wants and needs, which means event professionals must vary the content and delivery in their events. Compounding the generational issue is that people from wider cultural backgrounds are also attending these events and have different expectations (MPI, 2010).

A third trend, albeit not necessarily new, is that corporate social responsibility (CSR) will be a continuing interest for meeting and event professionals' organizations and a potential differentiator for companies and associations that can demonstrate a strong commitment to effective CSR programs. CSR policies and initiatives within top-ranked, multinational companies have generated an expectation of CSR practice in *all* industries at *all* levels. In a similar vein, clients are expecting more and more environmentally sensitive event professionals and events and a continuing of the "green movement" (MPI, 2012a).

All of the above, and more, impact on how event professionals plan their meetings and events. Only those professionals who stay aware of trends in MEEC can be successful and create satisfied clients.

Evolution and Maturation of the MEEC Industry

It can be said that events and meetings have been around since the dawn of time. The Romans had the Forum where meetings took place and the Coliseum where events took place. Religious pilgrimages have taken place for thousands of years. In America, town hall forums were a type of meeting begun in the eighteenth century. While someone had to plan all of these events, there was neither formal training nor established sets of skills, standards, and abilities for MEEC professionals. However, like other industries, such as law and accounting, as an industry evolves and matures there is an increasing need among clients, employers, and governments to have a codified set of competency standards to which professionals must adhere. Until very recently no common set of knowledge, skills, and abilities (KSAs) existed for events professionals.

This dearth of standards changed in 2011 with the release of the *Meetings and Business Events Competency Standards (MBECS)*. MBECS contain the KSAs required of meetings and events professionals. It builds on previous work done by Silvers along with work by the Canadian Tourism Human Resources Council where standards for special events professionals were put forth. MBECS are the result of almost two years of work by a task force consisting of both industry practitioners and academics supported by the MPI Foundation.

MBECS

The MBECS are divided into twelve domains or blocks with thirty-three skills and almost 100 sub-skills or sub-segments. The domains and skills are listed below:

A. STRATEGIC PLANNING
  1. Manage Strategic Plan for Meeting or Event
  2. Develop Sustainability Plan for Meeting or Event
  3. Measure Value of Meeting or Business Event
B. PROJECT MANAGEMENT
  1. Plan Meeting or Event
  2. Manage Meeting or Event Project
C. RISK MANAGEMENT
  1. Manage Risk Management Plan
D. FINANCIAL MANAGEMENT
  1. Develop Financial Resources
  2. Manage Budget
  3. Manage Monetary Transactions
E. ADMINISTRATION
  1. Perform Administrative Tasks
F. HUMAN RESOURCES
  1. Manage Human Resource Plan
  2. Acquire Staff and Volunteers
  3. Train Staff and Volunteers
  4. Manage Workforce Relations
G. STAKEHOLDER MANAGEMENT
  1. Manage Stakeholder Relationships
H. MEETING OR EVENT DESIGN
  1. Design Program
  2. Engage Speakers and Performers
  3. Coordinate Food and Beverage
  4. Design Environment
  5. Manage Technical Production
  6. Develop Plan for Managing Movement of People
I. SITE MANAGEMENT
  1. Select Site
  2. Design Site Layout
  3. Manage Meeting or Event Site
  4. Manage On-site Communications

J. MARKETING
1. Manage Marketing Plan
2. Manage Marketing Materials
3. Manage Meeting or Event Merchandise
4. Promote Meeting or Event
5. Contribute to Public Relations Activities
6. Manage Sales Activities
K. PROFESSIONALISM
1. Exhibit Professional Behavior
L. COMMUNICATIONS
1. Conduct Business Communications

The list above represents all the KSAs event professionals need to acquire, and be proficient in, during the course of their career. That these are, in fact, those KSAs event needed by professionals was validated when the Convention Industry Council (CIC) adopted MBECS as the primary basis for their new Certified Meeting Professional International Standards (CMP-IS) and for the CMP Exam. The development of these standards marks a milestone in the MEEC industry. For the first time all players in this industry have a common benchmark or point of reference.

Uses of the Standards

The standards synopsized above represent the first time that the base of knowledge in the meetings/events arena has been codified. Thus, moving forward, the industry profession, academics, students, professionals, human resources staff, and so on can work from the same base.

Uses for Meetings/Events Professionals

The MBECS represent the KSAs a practitioner must possess in order to be successful in the field. Industry professionals can perform a personal "skills assessment" of those standards and skills at which they are adept and those that they are not. The resulting "gap analysis" can help guide their professional and personal development. MBECS can also help plot career paths. Being able to provide an assessment that shows a broad mastery of the subject will enhance employability and mobility across sectors and countries. This also allows an industry professional to promote their KSAs to employers or clients.

The MBECS are of great value to employers and managers. The standards can aid in the development of job descriptions and job specifications. This leads to improvements in determining workforce requirements and producing worker solicitations. The standards can also help in developing a sequence of training for employees as well as a basis for performance assessment and feedback.

Uses for the Academic Community

The MBECS provide the internationally accepted basis for developing courses of study and their requisite content. It is up to a given program or institution to determine how the content is delivered: in meetings- or events-specific courses, in business courses, in general education, or a combination. The significant advantage of using MBECS are that it is not prescriptive: One size does not fit all. A companion "MBECS Curriculum Guide" has also been developed (see MPI website). Existing programs can "benchmark" themselves against the standards with resulting global recognition. The MBECS also provide a platform for dealing with governmental authorities and accrediting bodies. Using MBECS, the program can show the relevance of their course offerings and justify the content based on an international body of knowledge. Students can use the standards to develop their educational pathways and to validate their "employability" to recruiters. They could also use the standards to determine which educational programs best meet their learning needs. For academics, the standards can help delineate areas or topics in the meetings/events world that are in need of research.

Uses for Associations

First and foremost the MBECS provide recognition of the KSAs required by the industry. This can then help guide the development of program content and delivery that is consistent with international standards. MBECS can also be used by the members of an association to determine their educational or professional development needs and how the association can best fulfill those needs (Fenich, 2012b).

Translating MBECS into Educational Content

The MBECS are a tremendous resource and reference. However, given that they cover almost eighty pages in an outline format, they can be daunting to comprehend and understand. Thus, after the MBECS task force concluded its work, a Meeting and Business Event Competency Standards Curriculum Guide task force was constituted. Its charge was to translate the content of MBECS into ideas and tools for providing relevant and quality programming for any individual or academic delivering MBECS-based content. This could apply to the faculty in a university, trainers for an association, or CMPs who lead study groups in preparation for taking the CMP exam.

The Curriculum Guide Task Force reviewed MBECS and analyzed each skill and sub-skill in terms of learning outcomes, depth of knowledge, and time to master the skill. The entire set of 100 MBECS skills and sub-skills fell into three categories in terms of depth of knowledge: what someone who is employed at the meetings/events COORDINATOR level should know, what someone who is employed at the MANAGER level should know, and what someone employed at the DIRECTOR level should know. Thus, MBECS can be covered in a sequential fashion that, generally, follow the career path of a professional from an entry level position (coordinator), advancing to management (manager), and ultimately to executive level (director). The task force further determined that the coordinator and manager level skills could and should be possessed by someone graduating from an undergraduate college/university program. The director level skills would be obtained through continuing education and professional seminars.

PLANNING AND MANAGING MEETINGS, EXPOSITIONS, EVENTS, AND CONVENTIONS

This content of this book is based on MBECS. It was developed using the output from the two task forces mentioned earlier. It is assumed that the reader has some basic knowledge of the MEEC industry and MEEC terminology. This knowledge can be obtained through a minimum of one or two years working in the industry or through formal education using books such as *Meetings, Expositions, Events, and Conventions: An Introduction* by Fenich.

With this knowledge in hand, the reader can work through the content of this book. This book contains all of the knowledge related to planning of meetings and events that is expected of people who are to be employed at the coordinator and at the manager level. It does not deal with knowledge of planning that should be possessed by an event management professional at the director or executive level. There is a companion text, *Production and Logistics in Meetings, Expositions, Events, and Conventions* that covers material related to MBECS knowledge regarding putting on or producing meetings and events.

There are 14 chapters in this book. The topics range from strategic management to financial management, program planning, and various aspects of marketing. Each chapter begins with learning objectives and a chapter outline, both of which tie directly to MBECS. At the conclusion of each chapter there is a chapter summary, chapter review questions, and a biography of the event professional who contributed the chapter content. Most importantly there is also a checklist that indicates exactly what MBECS standards and skills were covered in the chapter. Thus, after finishing this book, the readers can compile a self-assessment relative to MBECS standards and skills and determine what they know, and what they do not. It is hoped that this book will provide content that helps prepare existing and potential event professionals.

SUMMARY

This chapter is meant to provide an introduction to the MEEC industry and to the book. It provides insight into the magnitude of the industry and the various career opportunities that exist. The chapter provided a basic underpinning regarding terminology and definitions used in MEEC. It also provided a discussion of the historical evolution of MEEC from the early days through the development of a common set of knowledge, skills, and abilities (KSAs) required of an event professional. There is an overview of the Meetings and Business Events Competency Standards (MBECS) that incorporates these KSAs as well as a discussion of how MBECS can be used. The end of the chapter covered how the content in this book is based on MBECS.

KEY WORDS

Planning   Event Professionals

REVIEW QUESTIONS

1. What is common to meetings, expositions, events, and conventions?
2. What led to the development of MBECS?
3. How can MBECS be used in career development?
4. What is CMP-IS?
5. What is planning?
6. What are the trends in the MEEC industry?

REFERENCES

CIC (2010). *The Economic Significance of Meetings to the U.S. Economy.* Washington, DC: Convention Industry Council.

Fenich, G. G. (2012a). *Meetings, Expositions, Events and Conventions: An Introduction to the Industry* (3rd ed). Upper Saddle River, NJ: Pearson Education Inc.

Fenich, G. G. (2012b). The New Meeting and Business Events Competency Standards. Published proceedings, AHTMM Conference, Corfu Greece.

IAPCO (2010). Over 3.4B€ from Leading PCOs. *The PCO,* 58, 1.

MPI (2010). *Future Watch.* Dallas, TX: Meeting Professionals International.

MPI (2012a). *Business Barometer Annual.* Dallas, TX: Meeting Professionals International.

MPI (2012b). *Future of Meetings.* Dallas, TX: Meeting Professionals International.

ABOUT THE CHAPTER CONTRIBUTOR

Kathryn Hashimoto, PhD, is an Associate Professor in the School of Hospitality Leadership at East Carolina University. She is a prolific writer having authored over ten books on different aspects of the hospitality industry.

Strategic Planning in Meetings, Expositions, Events, and Conventions

CHAPTER 2

Strategic planning is a winding road. Jim Parkin, Shutterstock

Chapter Objectives

Upon completion of this chapter, the reader should be able to:

- Define the strategic planning
- Articulate the purpose of creating a strategic plan for a meeting or event
- Identify four key steps in the strategic planning process

Chapter Outline

INTRODUCTION TO STRATEGIC PLANNING

Strategic planning for an organization and specifically for meetings and events is a critical business activity. This process serves as a road map to achieve the goals and objectives of the meeting or event while aligning with the organizational vision and direction. The purpose of meeting/event strategic planning is to articulate high-level event initiatives and to tie that vision to tactical, operational projects. Often, the strategic plan is too conceptual and it fails to translate into the day-to-day operations of the event team. This chapter will provide insight into the purpose of creating a strategic plan for meetings/events and provide four key steps in crafting a strategic direction.

WHAT IS STRATEGIC PLANNING?

Strategy is simply defined as carefully developing and carrying out a plan of action to achieve a vision or goal. It is sometimes referred to as a road map; a path is constructed to reach an end vision. The most important part of implementing the strategy is ensuring the organization is headed in the right direction and does not steer off the path toward the end vision.

Strategic planning is an organization's process of defining its strategy, or direction, and making decisions on allocating its resources to pursue this strategy. Strategic planning helps the organization to match its resources to its changing environment and, in particular, its markets, customers, and clients, so as to meet stakeholder expectations (Johnson and Scholes, 1993). This planning process is a systemic tool for planning and managing all activities of the organizations, including events, and are aligned to ensure competitive advantage, profitability, consistency of the brand, and many other activities. Essentially, this is planning for good business.

The planning process requires a commitment to personnel time, money, and other resources. According to Schmidt and Laycock (2012), the timing needs to be appropriate and the resources proportional to the task and intended outcome. Strategic planning is important whether the organization's direction needs reviewing, whether its priorities have changed, or whether the means of achieving desired objectives need to be updated due to internal or external forces impacting delivery.

As it relates to the meetings or events of the organization or business, they may be addressed in the strategic planning process or the event professional may have to take the strategic plan and implement an event strategy based on its direction. Most importantly, the strategic planning of the organization must be parallel to the corporation or organizations' vision, mission, goals, and objectives. If the meeting or event's goals and objectives are not tied to the organization's vision and mission, success of the program cannot be guaranteed or measured.

Why is strategic planning important?   There are multiple reasons that strategic planning is important for any organization, business, or event professional. Critical decisions have to be made based on a sound rationale, creditable data, and logic. The strategic plan should aid organizational leaders when daily or difficult decisions need to be made. The plan should be widely distributed, reviewed, and discussed often.

Beyond making decisions, strategic planning should be used to interact with key internal and external stakeholders. **Stakeholders** are individuals or groups that have an interest in the organization. **Internal stakeholders** can range from executives to department heads to mid-level managers and employees. **External stakeholders** can be defined as customers, the local community, vendors, or media contacts.

The strategic plan also ensures that all stakeholders are on the "same page" and have a clear, united direction for the organization. Stakeholders can have differing

---

MCI Strategic Plan

Sebastien Tondeur, president of MCI, posted the company's strategic plan on its public website. He states clearly in his video introduction of the "Painted Picture," (company's strategic plan) that sharing their core ideologies will inspire their customers and serve as a road map for alignment and growth. The MCI board is committed to the success of the "Painted Picture" and reviews portions of the strategic plan at every meeting, and the staff refers to it in retreats and in daily discussions when implementing programming. MCI sees sharing the plan as a way to share their vision to be entrepreneurial and to be thought leaders in the meetings and events industry.

---

views and unique agendas. However, the strategic plan should steer everyone toward a common end goal and build consensus and understanding.

Strategic Planning Process

There are multiple formats and approaches to strategic planning. Depending on the objectives and business circumstances, the process can take one day, several months, or even longer. Like any process, an organization needs to answer:

- Who they want to be involved in the strategic planning process?
- What they want to accomplish?
- Where this strategic planning session will take place?
- When should the process begin and end?
- Why is this important now?
- How are we going to allocate resources to the strategic planning process?

The answer to these questions may drive the format and approach of the strategic planning process. Typically, the scope of the plan is viewed as a process for determining:

- Where is our organization heading over the next year (short-term)?
- What is our organization's direction in the next three to five years (long-term)?
- What should our organization's vision be in ten years? twenty years and beyond?

Whether the approach is answering a long-term or short-term question, the intent of the systematic process is to envision a desired future, translate the vision into a specific goal, and define objectives that detail how to achieve them.

The difference between long-term and short-term strategic planning is where to start the process. In short-term strategic planning, most organizations begin by defining the desired end and work backward to the current state. The focus is on what must be done or changed to reach the desired end in a limited time span. On the other hand, the long-term approach begins with the current status and lays down a path to meet estimated future needs. Long-term strategic planning looks at the wider picture and is adaptable as the organization goes down this path. Two approaches are seen in Table 1.

Regardless of the approach, there tends to be four steps in the strategic planning process:

- **STEP 1**: Where are we now?—Analysis of the situation and feasibility study
- **STEP 2**: Where do we want to get to?—Determining your future direction
- **STEP 3**: How are we going to get there?—Strategy development
- **STEP 4**: How will we know when we have gotten there?—Measuring success

(Johnson and Scholes, 1993).

TABLE 1 Strategic Planning Approaches

Situation-Target-Proposal	Draw-See-Think-Plan
• **Situation**—evaluate the current situation and how it came about • **Target**—define goals and/or objectives (sometimes called ideal state) • **Path/Proposal**—map a possible route to the goals/objectives	• **Draw**—what is the ideal image or the desired end state? • **See**—what is today's situation? What is the gap from ideal and why? • **Think**—what specific actions must be taken to close the gap between today's situation and the ideal state? • **Plan**—what resources are required to execute the activities?

For the remainder of the chapter, the focus will be on strategic planning, managing, and implementing of the organization's events and meetings, as it relates to its strategic direction. The above questions will be answered for first-time and annual events and meetings.

STEP 1: WHERE ARE WE NOW?— SITUATION AND FEASIBILITY ANALYSIS

Determining "where we are now?" with regard to an organization's meetings and events strategy requires a review of a number of different areas. It is important to first gather information on the organization's current state and provide an objective review of the success of its events and meetings. It is also critical that the review includes the entire picture, is realistic, and is transparent. Covering up an issue or areas of existing concern can have detrimental impacts to the organization and its events moving forward. When considering a new meeting or event, a thorough analysis to determine the feasibility of introducing it to the market is essential. Introducing a new event or meeting to the market when it is not needed or poorly positioned can be the recipe for disaster.

Depending on the scope of the analysis, a situational and feasibility investigation of the organization's meetings and events should take place. Below are some areas to consider:

- Using objective data, provide a picture of how the organization's meeting and event portfolio is performing.
  - Are the events exceeding the organization and attendee/customers' expectations?
  - How have meetings and events contributed to the success of the organization over the years?
  - What needs to be changed to contribute to the organization's success and vision?
  - Is there an opportunity for investment in new ideas?
  - Did the organization's event respond to a major trend or paradigm shift?
  - Did the organization's event change the culture or direction of the organization due to an internal or external factor?
  - What external factors need to be reviewed and considered for future events?
- Who are the organization's stakeholders?
  - Which stakeholders are directly involved in the events and meetings?
  - What is the scope of power and influence of these stakeholders?
  - Who are key decision makers?

- Where has the organization committed to allocating resources?
  - Are meetings and events a major priority for the organization?
  - How is the organization performing compared to their peers or competitive organizations?
  - How much staff, time, and money are dedicated to ensuring the events are successful?
  - What is the risk of introducing a new event or meeting?

To answer these questions, the organization may use a number of tools to analyze the current situation and predict the feasibility or future success of the meeting or event. Tools can include a SWOT (Strengths, Weaknesses, Opportunities, and Threats) analysis, PESTELI (Political, Economic, Social, Technological, Environmental, Legal, and Industry) trends analysis, stakeholder analysis, benchmarking, and scenario planning.

SWOT Analysis—Revealing Organizational Performance

To present a clear picture of events and meetings for the organization, a common practice is first using the **SWOT tool** to analyze their strengths, weaknesses, opportunities, and threats (see Table 2). This can be a powerful exercise to critically review the state of the organization's meetings and events. A number of stakeholders should be asked to complete the matrix, so as to ensure inclusion of multiple perspectives and organizational insight. This process will hopefully reveal the areas the organization does well, areas of improvement, new areas of investment of resources, and roadblocks that need to be addressed. Here is an example of one organization's SWOT analysis. Discuss the implications of these SWOT analysis findings on the event and meeting strategy.

PESTELI Trends Analysis

Another popular tool is **PESTELI trends analysis**. This exercise explores the organization's meeting and events looking at the external environment. PESTELI stands for Political, Economic, Social, Technological, Environmental, Legal, and Industry. Looking at each of these areas may provide additional insight on the SWOT analysis

TABLE 2 SWOT—Internal Look at the Organization

Internal forces	External forces
Strengths: *What are we doing well?* - Delivering high-quality education and training opportunities - Offer multiple opportunities to connect with peers	**Opportunities:** *Any outside forces or trends that would be beneficial for us to take advantage of it?* - New sponsors or donors interested in contributing - Offer programming in other regions of the world
Weaknesses: *What needs to be addressed or changed?* - Did not make revenue projections for three of five meetings - Did not use electronic marketing mediums to promote event - Staff cut to three full-time meeting planners	**Threats:** *Any outside forces or trends that we need to be able to defend ourselves from?* - Participants do not have financial or managerial support to travel more than three days for a meeting/event - Popularity of virtual or hybrid events

TABLE 3 PESTELI—External Scan of the Environment

Political	Increase tax rates on hotel and rental cars Health insurance changes that may affect hiring of new employees
Economic	High unemployment rate Corporations cutting travel and professional development funding Concern with consumer confidence
Social	Meeting and event attendees are connecting differently Impact of social media and mobile technology Different generations in the workforce Different expectations of those attending meetings and events
Technological	Power of social media on marketing Introduction of new technology products to assist planning and project management Effect of mobile technology
Environmental	Importance of sustainability Introduction of best practices in green meeting and events Change in sourcing and procurement selections based on supplier commitment to environment
Legal	Changes in pharmaceutical meetings and events based on regulations
Industry	Emphasis on the value of meetings and events based on outside drivers

providing an explanation of the strengths, weaknesses, opportunities, and threats. See Table 3 for a few examples of external forces.

Benchmarking

Benchmarking is the process of comparing an organization's performance and best practices to itself and other like-organizations. Event professionals can both perform internal and external comparisons to assist in strategic direction and planning.

Internal benchmarking allows an organization to compare itself to its own historic patterns in specific areas, while an external benchmarking strategy compares data to outside but similar organizations. In order to be considered a valid external benchmark study, the similarities between the organizations should be identified. There are several questions that should be posed to evaluate if this is a meaningful comparison, such as:

- Are the cultures of our organizations similar?
- Are the priorities of the organizations significantly different?
- How does the organization communicate the value of meetings and events?
- Are we similar enough in organizational size, number of meetings and events, budgets, other key areas?

Scenario Planning

Scenario planning can be a powerful way to analyze future or potential situations that the organization may face. Traditionally used by the military, scenario planning is now commonly used by large corporations or associations to craft possible or uncertain situations and discuss the complexity of that situation to the organization. This tool may generate role playing exercises, simulations, or "games." It is a unique approach to tackling uncomfortable potential organizational problems to explore if the organization is prepared in the instance of a major change. Use of scenario planning may be for simple tactical issues or as a way to approach strategic planning. Paul Schoemaker, professor at the Wharton School of Business, commented that scenario planning is both an art and a science and must be carefully crafted both in process and content to achieve good results.

STEP 2: WHERE WE WANT TO GET TO?—FUTURE DIRECTION

Determining the future direction of the organization involves clearly identifying the beliefs and values that drive the culture and priorities of the organization. This direction serves as a framework for decision making by organizational leaders and must be reflected in the goals and objectives of the organization's meetings and events. Therefore, to define the future direction for an organization their vision, mission, goals, and objectives must be constructed, widely distributed, and accepted by the organization's stakeholders. The following are important definitions for determining the future direction of an organization:

A **vision statement** outlines what the organization strives to be in an intended future state or an idealized view of the world. It may be driven by emotion or inspiration, and it concentrates on a "perfect" future. This statement may be very difficult, even impossible, to achieve. The key to a good vision statement is that it is tied to the organization's core values and beliefs. Without this connection, the vision becomes meaningless to the organization's stakeholders and outside publics.

For example, Gleaner's Food Bank in Indianapolis may have a vision statement that reads something like *Our vision is a city without hunger—fighting the crisis in Central Indiana every step of the way.* This statement is lofty, but clearly articulates the futurist nature of the work this organization provides to the poor, unemployed, elderly, battered women, victims of disaster, and single partners in need throughout Central Indiana.

The **mission statement** defines the fundamental purpose of an organization, clearly describing why the organization exists and what it does to achieve its vision. The mission outlines the purpose, values, standards, and sometimes competitive strategy of the organization.

Notably, many organizations and individuals combine the vision statement with the mission statement or use the terms synonymously. However, the two statements are meant to be very different, with the vision being a descriptive picture of a desired future state and the mission being a statement of a business rationale, applicable *now* as well as in the future. For an organization's vision and mission to be effective, they must become assimilated into the organization's culture (Schmidt, 2009).

Goals

Goals are typically broad statements that indicate an anticipated outcome and serve as a guide for tactical action planning. An organization may have short-term goals and long-term goals. Typically, short-term goals can be achieved fairly easily, while long-term goals may or may not be achievable. It is important that the many business units of an organization communicate their individual goals, so synergies can be explored and conflicts identified. The goals of the meeting/event team should reflect the goals of the marketing, finance, and other administrative teams. Additionally, all of the goals of the organization must be aligned with the organization's vision and mission.

The special event division of Gleaner's Food Bank has several events that support the organization's goals including a "PUTTing" an End to Hunger golf outing, "Ride Your Can Off!" motorcycle ride, and their annual Harvest Moon Gala. The goal of each event is to raise money to support the food bank's mission to feed the hungry.

Objectives

Objectives are detailed, measurement statements of overall desirable achievements and should be written using the SMART principle. **SMART** stands for specific, measurable, achievable, relevant or realistic, and time-bound. Objectives provide definition and direction and specify how to achieve the short-term and long-term aims. Clear objectives should be written for each individual event or meeting. Objectives can be categorized as programmatic, logistical, financial, or others based on the organization's structure or the nature or purpose of the event or meeting. Below are some examples of objectives for each of Gleaner's Food Bank signature events. Again, many of their objectives will be based on achieving their fund-raising goals to support the organization's mission and vision.

"PUTTing" an End to Hunger Golf Outing

- Register X number of golfers for the event
- Secure X hole sponsors
- Limit expenses of the event to $XXX
- Raise X percent more next year
- Sign up XXX volunteers to assist with the event

Ride Your Can Off!" Motorcycle Ride

- Register X number of golfers for the event
- Secure X hole sponsors
- Limit expenses of the event to $XXX
- Raise X percent more next year
- Sign up XXX volunteers to assist with the event

Harvest Moon Gala

- Register X number of golfers for the event
- Secure X hole sponsors
- Limit expenses of the event to $XXX
- Raise X percent more next year
- Sign up XXX volunteers to assist with the event

STEP 3: HOW ARE WE GOING TO GET THERE?— CONCEPT DEVELOPMENT

The third step in the strategic planning process requires the stakeholders, or a core team, to implement the future direction. This is a detailed action plan outlining how the organization will achieve the SMART objectives. This step is not possible without stakeholder "buy-in" of the vision, mission, goals, and objectives of the organization.

Most organizations identify the entire meeting/event series or portfolio (current and proposed events) and then start addressing each program as it relates to the organization's direction. As the team considers new and reoccurring programs for the future, it is important to return to steps one and two to review the analysis of stakeholders, benchmarking results, and internal and external driving forces. The group must also continue to question "how will this event contribute to the overall success of the organization and tie directly to the vision and mission of the organization?"

A formal project plan on the organization's meetings and events should be presented. This may entail involving other divisions, setting up committees or task forces,

> **ACTIVITY #1**
> Rewrite these meeting objectives to meet the SMART test. Circle the words that make the statement not specific, measurable, attainable, realistic, and/or timely.
>
> - To offer an excellent educational program.
> - To serve the industry by hosting the best research conference in the Midwest.
> - To increase attendance and participation at the conference.
> - To have attendees leave the conference satisfied with the program contact and networking opportunities.
> - To make more money through conference registration to support the association's future initiatives.

or appointment of a core stakeholder group. The format and process of creating this plan varies based on the number of events/meetings, size of the organization, or emphasis of meetings and events to the organization. To determine which events and meetings should be implemented, other methods such as the cost-benefit analysis or a risk assessment should be used.

Each meeting or event should be described in terms of:

- The purpose, goal, or outcome
- The event's specific SMART objectives, as it relates to:
  - Program design (programmatic)
  - Financial philosophy and performance
  - Contribution to alignment with the organizational vision and mission
  - Serving of stakeholders
- Target markets
- Classification: geographic location or type of meeting or event

The event or meeting's **target market**, or the individuals or groups that the marketing efforts are directed to attract attendees, must be clearly defined. There may need to be multiple marketing strategies and channels identified based on the complexity of the target markets' **demographics** (characteristics) and **psychographics** (values).

There are several types of meetings, expositions, events, and conventions (MEEC) and their purposes vary. Events are hosted for educational, social, competitive, business, entertaining, and other reasons. In the meetings category, there are committee, board, symposium, conference, training, and other types under the educational event umbrella. Corporations may host sales training meetings, client education programming, networking and hospitality events. Additionally, associations may concentrate on their annual convention for their membership and/or several smaller conferences in a number of different locations. The MEEC may also be defined based on the geographic scope, such as local, regional, domestic, or international in nature. The classification, scope, and purpose of the meeting or event will ultimately drive the next set of factors (see chapter 1 for a comprehensive listing).

For organizations with multiple events or meetings, it is also important to detail each event's requirements based on its purpose, size, and/or importance to the organization. Again, it is imperative to do a detailed review of the following elements to clearly understand the meeting or event's individual needs:

- potential risks,
- resource needs and allocation,
- the planning cycle with key milestones,
- and a marketing plan.

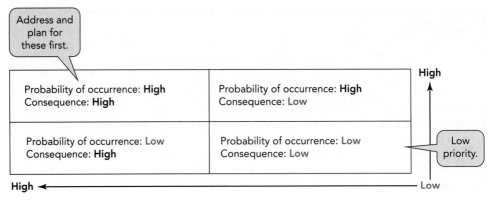

Risk Chart

Potential Risks

The organization should identify, prioritize, and analyze all potential risks to each meeting or event. A **risk** is the possibility that something adverse will occur, not the occurrence itself. Therefore, risk management is really about preventing adverse events from occurring or minimizing their impact if they do occur. To strategically manage risk, each potential risk must be categorized by the probability of the occurrence and the consequence of it actually happening. If an organization's annual meeting is being held in August or September on the coast of south Florida, the possibility and consequence of a hurricane is high, while a delayed flight for one of the breakout speakers may be classified as low possibility and low consequence. For additional information on identifying risks and managing crisis, see chapter 4.

Resource Allocation

Allocation of physical, financial, and human resources should also be carefully detailed. Physical resources include the actual physical space for the events, office or storage space for the meeting's needs. Financial allocation requires an overview of the organization's and event-specific financial position. Depending on the importance and scope of the event, a complete listing on all income streams, as well as expenses may be required for review. The event's income may be from registration, ticket sales, sponsorship, exhibitor, and advertising. Expenses may include facility rental, audiovisual, food and beverage, speaker fees, décor, travel, and many others. Several financial reports can be used to glean insight on the organization's event position. These reports can include an income statement, balance sheet, cash flow statements, break-even analysis, and cash flow. Additional information on the budgeting, accounting, and finance can be found in chapter 6.

Events are staffed by event professionals, full-time staff members, part-time employees, consultants, and volunteers (human resource team). The organization will need to determine which type of team member needs to be assigned to cover the variety of event and meeting tasks. Some tasks are best performed by full-time staff members versus a volunteer, while other tasks are best performed by local temporary workers or volunteers.

Planning Cycle

Constructing a programmatic and financial planning cycle can mean the difference between event success and failure. This exercise requires assembling key dates or milestones and placing them on a time line to measure progress against the event's SMART objectives. The planning cycle can be designed monthly, weekly, or even daily as the date of the meeting or event draws closer. For additional detail on how to construct a time line or establish key milestones, see chapter 3.

Marketing Plan

Without communicating and marketing the event's purpose and objectives, the event has little chance for reaching its SMART outcomes or contributing to the organization's strategic direction. The marketing plan should outline all the marketing, promotion, public relations and advertising strategies. The selected mediums should be attractive to the event's target market and should have some "call to action"—such as registering. For additional detail on how to create a marketing plan and select marketing mediums, see chapter 11.

STEP 4: HOW WILL WE KNOW WHEN WE HAVE GOTTEN THERE?—MONITORING AND MEASURING VALUE OR SUCCESS OF MEETING/EVENT

The final strategic step in the process cannot be overlooked, as it has to do with monitoring and measuring the meeting or event's SMART objectives and the implementation plan. If the event or meeting did not have clear objectives or a project plan to support the implementation of the objective, it is not possible to objectively monitor and measure the success of an individual program, the event/ meeting portfolio, or the overall organizational activities. For instance, how do you objectively monitor and measure this outcome statement: "the objective of this conference is to offer an excellent educational program"? An excellent education program may be measured in multiple ways and have very different meaning to the stakeholders.

Monitoring is an ongoing analysis of the meeting or event to ensure the objectives are being achieved. This review is critically important if corrective action or changes need to be quickly made. The organization should establish key time to review and assess the implementation of the strategic plan. Data on specified indicators should be collected to inform management on progress and aid in decision making for the stakeholders. The process requires that the meeting and event team continually monitor, not only the internal state of the organization, but watch external drivers that may affect the ongoing success of the plan. In April of 2010, a volcanic ash cloud in Ireland paralyzed air travel throughout the northern and western European region. Those meetings and events drawing attendees from Europe suffered significantly, due to their inability to travel. This required some organizations to shift their objectives and plans due to an unforeseen incident. By conducting this ongoing analysis, the organization's implementation plan and even the objectives may need to be modified. The approval process to make changes to an event or meeting plan or the organization's strategic plan may differ based on the organization's structure, bylaws, standard operating procedures, or other factors.

Evaluation is a systematic, objective assessment of an ongoing or completed meeting or event. The evaluation process should include a review of the meeting program, its policies, its design, the implementation plan, and its concluding results. The aim of evaluation is to ascertain the relevance and reaching of objectives, efficiency, effectiveness, impact, and sustainability. An evaluation should provide information that is credible and useful, enabling the incorporation of "lessons learned" into the decision-making process and justification for not meeting or exceeding the event's objectives. Typically, a variety of reports is assembled post-event and customized to the stakeholder audience.

Many organizations use **Key Performance Indicators (KPIs)** to monitor, measure, and assess their progress to reaching the plan's objectives. As it is not the only area to monitor and evaluate, the financial position of the event or meeting is one area most organizations continue to place emphasis. When developing a financial landscape of a meeting or event, be sure to include:

- overall financial position of the organization
- balance sheet
- statement of operational costs
- cash flow statement
- break-even analysis
- projected profits/loss statement

Monitoring and evaluation links the organization's strategy to the measure of the implementation of MEEC goals and objectives. It is a structured approach to continuously keep track of progress using a number of measures identified as being reliable instruments. After this, changes can be planned, implemented, their results observed, and conclusions reached as to the possibility of their wider application. Monitoring and evaluation can only be successful if considered at the beginning of a strategic planning cycle so that baseline data for each indicator has been collected and success can be monitored against these data.

SUMMARY

Strategic planning is a vital, systematic, and *ongoing* process that enables an organization to achieve their vision, missions, goals, and SMART objectives through meetings and events. Most organizations are going through steps of formal situational and feasibility analysis, declaration of future direction, and critical path development, As changes continue on the economic, political, social, technology, environmental, legal, and industry fronts, events and meeting programmatic and operational plans may have to change course. It is the constant monitoring and evaluation of the strategic direction that will ensure the success of an organization's meetings and events.

Now that you have completed this chapter you should be competent in the following Meetings and Business Events Competency Standards:

MBECS—Skill 1: Manage Strategic Plan for Meetings or Event

Sub skills	Skills (standards)
A 1.01	Develop mission statement, goals, and objectives of meeting or event
A 1.02	Determine feasibility of meeting or event
A 1.03	Determine requirements to carry out meeting or event
A 1.05	Develop financial summary

KEY WORDS, ACRONYMS, AND PHRASES

Strategy
Strategic planning
Stakeholders
Internal stakeholder
External stakeholder
SWOT tool
PESTELI trend analysis
Benchmarking

Scenario planning
Vision statement
Mission statement
Goals
SMART objectives
Target market
Demographics
Psychographics

Risk
Monitoring
Evaluating
Key performance indicators (KPIs)

DISCUSSION QUESTIONS

1. Discuss the advantages to a meeting manager and/or event team receiving their organization's one- to three-year strategic plan.
2. Why would an organization NOT want to go through this strategic planning progress?
3. Review a strategic direction of an organization. What surprised you about their vision, mission statement, goals, and objectives?
4. Analyze an event or meeting and list all potential risks. What factors may change the potential and consequences of that potential risk?
5. Discuss the different metrics for events and meetings. What key stakeholders drive the monitoring and measurement process?

REFERENCE

Schmidt, J., and Laycock, M. (2012). Theories of strategic planning. Retrieved August 20, 2012 http://www.healthknowledge.org.uk/public-health-textbook/organisation-management/5d-theory-process-strategy-development/strategic-planning.

Books

Allison, M., and Jude, K. (2003). *Strategic Planning for Nonprofit Organizations: A Practical Guide and Workbook* (2nd ed.). Hoboken, NJ: John Wiley & Sons.

Bradford, R., and Tarcy, B. (2000). *Simplified Strategic Planning: The No-Nonsense Guide for Busy People Who Want Results Fast*. Worcester, MA: Chandler House Press.

Bryson, J. (2011). *Strategic Planning for Public and Nonprofit Organizations: A Guide to Strengthening and Sustaining Organizational Achievement*. San Francisco, CA: Jossey-Bass.

Johnson, G., and Scholes, K. (1993). *Exploring Corporate Strategy*. Harlow, Essex: Pearson Education Limited.

Nolan, T., Goodstein, L., and Goodstenin, J. (2008). *Applied Strategic Planning: An Introduction*. San Francisco, CA: Jossey-Bass/Pfeiffer.

Schmidt, T. (2009). *Strategic Project Management Made Simple: Practical Tools for Leaders and Teams*. Hoboken, NJ: John Wiley & Sons.

Strategic Management/Planning Theorists

H. Igor Ansoff, known as the father of strategic management, is a Russian American businessman and mathematician. He was a distinguished professor at United States International University (now Alliant International University), where several institutes continue his work in strategic management research.

James C. "Jim" Collins, III is an American business consultant, author, and lecturer on the subject of company sustainability and growth. *Good to Great*, his previous book, sold 2.5 million hardcover copies since publication and has been translated into 32 languages.

Peter Drucker is one of the best-known and most widely influential thinkers and writers on the subject of management theory and practice. His books and scholarly and popular articles explored how humans are organized across the business, government, and the nonprofit sectors of society.

Henri Fayol (1841–1925) was a management theorist whose work outlined the prime responsibilities of management, as planning, organizing, command, coordination, and control. He described planning as "examining the future, deciding what needs to be done and developing a plan of action."

ABOUT THE CHAPTER CONTRIBUTOR

Amanda Cecil, PhD, CMP is in her tenth year on the Indiana University's Tourism, Convention, and Event Management faculty. As an associate professor, she teaches several courses in event management and international tourism. Dr. Cecil's professional career started in association and corporate event planning prior to joining the IU faculty. She also spent time working in business travel management, destination marketing, collegiate sport management, and convention and special events planning.

Her research interest involves linking business travel and tourism trends to the convention/meeting market. Additionally, Dr. Cecil has scholarly interests in the development of competency-based curriculum models and the impact of experiential learning, specially service learning pedagogies. Dr. Cecil has consulting experience in instructional design for educational programs in business travel management, strategic meeting management, sports travel management, and event management.

Meetings and Events as Complex Projects

CHAPTER 3

© Ben Chams/Fotolia

Chapter Outline

Chapter Objectives

Upon reading this chapter, you will have been exposed to knowledge about:

- The historical perspective of project management as a business process
- A description of project management
- A comparison of project manager and meeting planner roles
- A definition of the project charter
- A definition of the project management plan
- A detailed description of the project scope and work breakdown structure
- Plans and documents that comprise the collection of data throughout the project's life cycle

INTRODUCTION TO PROJECT MANAGEMENT

Project management is a common international business phrase pertaining to the use of accepted standards and practices that help groups with multiple stakeholders work collaboratively to achieve business goals. From building a bridge to overcoming the devastation of a natural disaster, from planning a religious retreat to managing a product roll-out event, project management is the tool for success across the enterprise.

The practice of project management (PM) has become so widely accepted in business, an international organization for networking, professional development, and organization of the body of knowledge has been successfully undertaken by the Project Management Institute (PMI). That organization, with headquarters in Pennsylvania (USA), has more than 600,000 members and credential holders (primarily the Project Management Professional or PMP) in more than 185 countries ("What is PMI?," 2012).

Historical Perspective

In 1951, Dr. Ludwig von Bertalanffy, a theoretical biologist, described **general systems theory** using the human body as a metaphor. The body's subsystems, according to von Bertalanffy—including the body's circulation, skeleton, and muscles—work together for the overall system's survival. Von Bertalanffy proposed general systems theory as a process of collecting data and feedback, leading to self-organization and survival, subject to natural laws or constraints ("Ludwig von Bertalanffy," 2012).

Applied to business, systems theory suggests that management of complex activities requires data, a carefully planned process of managing resources, and the orchestration of sub-activities. PM is based solidly on systems theory. When a business employs PM techniques, the practice cuts across all departments and functions, while utilizing available resources to achieve project success and management goals.

Applying PM

According to author Harold Kerzner (2006), PM as a process becomes necessary when an enterprise realizes any or all of these parameters:

- The project to be undertaken is complex.
- The project will occur in a dynamic environment.
- The project is subject to tight constraints.
- The project will be achieved through several discrete activities.
- The project will only be achieved if functional boundaries are crossed successfully.

In terms of a substantial meeting or event, all of these parameters are likely to be met, and application of PM principles would be prudent. However, PM is a tool for achieving management goals; it is not a replacement for meeting planning skills, techniques, or strategies. In other words, the meeting/event must be planned. Since a complex meeting/event will require several discrete activities, across functional boundaries, and those activities are subject to tight constraints within a dynamic environment, PM techniques would help the enterprise realize a successful meeting/event.

Understanding the role of the project manager, in comparison to the role of an event professional, is critical to project success. A project manager is like the conductor of a symphony. The conductor is not playing an instrument, but is directing all of the musicians to play the same piece, at the same time, in the same place, for the enjoyment of all. The conductor typically does not write the music, choose the venue, tune the instruments, or select the clothes the musicians will wear during the concert. Qualified personnel handle these details, while the conductor concentrates on getting the best performance possible from the musicians.

The event professional, though, manages the logistics of the meeting/event, such as transportation arrangements, hotel accommodations, catering, and many other aspects to develop an effective meeting/event. The event professional could fulfill the project manager's role, of course. However, keeping these functions separate may be useful to large associations and corporations, where one department may handle transportation issues, another handles facility arrangements, and yet another handles exhibitors.

PM Life cycle

The management process has a **project life cycle**, according to Dow and Taylor (2008), authors of *Project Management Communications Bible*. This life cycle is predictable and follows the typical life cycle described for meetings and events (see Figure 1):

1. initiating
2. planning

FIGURE 1 Project Lifecycle Phases.

This table shows the various project lifecycle phases and their relationships, with key deliverables, phase type, and roles that are activated during each phase

	Project Lifecycles	Activate Roles	Phase Type	Key Deliverables
	Initiating Phase	Executive committee	Discrete	Establish purpose
		Project manager		Identify key stakeholders
				Analyze historical data
				Conduct cost/benefit analysis
				Determine goals
				Complete project charter
				Define project scope
				Identify enterprise policies and procedures, including approval process
				Prepare RFPs
Controlling Phase	Planning Phase	Executive committee	Concurrent with executing phase at some point; concurrent with controlling phase	Compile project plan
		Project manager		Develop work breakdown structure
		Meeting manager and other functional area managers		Develop milestones and quality standards
				Prepare evaluation procedures
				Research stakeholder profiles
				Review proposals and select vendors
				Negotiate contracts
				Collect current data
	Executing Phase	Executive committee	Concurrent with planning phase at some point; concurrent with controlling phase	Monitor contracts' implementation
		Project manager		Manage on-site operations
		Meeting manager?		Provide evaluation instrumentation
		Volunteers?		Collect current data
		Paid staff		
		Other attendees		
	Closing Phase	Executive committee	Discrete	Close contracts, pay for services rendered
		Project manager		Analyze collected data
		Meeting manager?		Conduct evaluations, analyze
		Volunteers?		Compile closing report and circulate to key stakeholders
		Paid staff?		Send thank-you notes

3. executing
4. controlling
5. closing

Two life cycle phases (initiating and closing) are discrete, where one begins and ends before the next one begins and ends. The other phases (planning, executing, and controlling) overlap throughout the project. The event professional may become involved in the project during the initiating phase, or, when this role is outsourced, may begin during the planning phase. Several stakeholders (see chapter 5) may help in the planning phase, but may not be needed during the executing, controlling, and closing phase. Dow and Taylor suggest that the controlling phase is more of a process that holds all of the other phases together, and this would be a function for the project manager. Another perspective, though, suggests the controlling phase is critical only during the planning and executing phases, where vendors are selected, contracts are signed, and numerous activities are set into motion. Key stakeholders comprise a **project team** or executive committee, where each member of the team is critical in one or more phases of the project life cycle. The project manager collects information from the members of the project team and disseminates that information appropriately throughout the enterprise. When the meeting or event is held, either the project manager or the event professional should attend, but both may not be needed.

Initiating phase   During the initiating phase, the enterprise is busy determining the purpose of the meeting/event, identifying stakeholders, setting goals and objectives, and establishing the project team. The purpose of the meeting/event must align with the organization's mission, meet the needs of meeting stakeholders, and serve as a directing force for many of the activities that occur in the next phase of the project's life cycle. During this initiating phase, the project manager or the executive committee should conduct a cost-benefit analysis to determine how much the event might cost and what, supported by quantifiable and qualitative data, the enterprise might realize as a result of this meeting/event. Historical information, if available, is collected during this phase. Historical data is considered primary information; it is directly related to the meeting/event under consideration. This information helps to guide the development of goals and objectives. When historical information is not available, the project manager may use comparison data. This data would be collected on other meetings/ events within the enterprise, or from external, yet similar, meetings/events. In this case, though, the information is considered **secondary data**; it is useful, but not directly related to the meeting/event under consideration. **Primary data** is generally more valid than secondary data.

The goals are broad statements that suggest intent, but provide little detail. Objectives, on the other hand, are based on those broad statements, get to specific information, and guide the evaluation process in later phases of the project life cycle. Effective objectives are "SMART"

- **M**easurable and stated in terms of a quantity;
- **A**ttainable, yet challenging;
- **R**elevant to targeted stakeholders;
- **T**ime constrained; there is a deadline by which they should be accomplished.

In other words, a goal for the symphony conductor might be to lead a flawless performance before an appreciative audience. Several objectives could be written for this goal, such as:

1. On October 29, host no fewer than 50 percent of the symphony's season ticket-holders at a performance of music by Beethoven at the annual concert.
2. At the annual concert featuring music by Beethoven on October 29, fill at least 90 percent of available seats.
3. At the concert on October 29, sell at least 10 percent more CDs produced by the symphony than were sold at last year's concert.

Each of these objectives reflect the time or deadline (October 29), provide a specific outcome (ticket or CD sales), target a group of stakeholders (season ticket-holders or attendees in general), are measurable (tickets or CDs can be counted), specify a quantity (50%, 90%, and 10% more), and can be assumed to be attainable, yet challenging (the historical or secondary data puts this aspect of the objectives in perspective).

Objectives that have no deadline are less effective because stakeholders might disagree on when the objective should be measured or met. Without a target audience, the quantity of the objective could be achieved, but the intended outcome missed entirely. For example, the objective of filling 90 percent of the seats could be met, but if only 10 percent of the season ticket-holders are present, another objective has not been fulfilled. Is the concert a success? Yes and no. Getting 50 percent of the season ticket-holders to the most important concert of the year could be a very important goal for the conductor!

Even when an objective is stated in terms of quantity to be achieved, the objective may not be measurable. For instance, without counting tickets, how would the conductor know if 90 percent of the seats were sold? This is a common problem with events that do not sell tickets (they may have no method for measuring outcomes). When objectives fail to be attainable, the effort to achieve them could be sabotaged. If failure is unavoidable, what is the incentive for achievement? However, a less than challenging outcome might also decrease motivation. When the employee believes an outcome is easily met, what is the incentive for maximum effort?

Additionally, as implied above, some objectives may be more important to the successful outcome of a meeting or event than other objectives. When this is the case, the project manager is responsible for identifying priorities and making sure enterprise resources are allocated appropriately to the objectives. Key stakeholders will be useful when prioritizing objectives and making decisions about the allocation of resources.

A **project charter** is developed during this phase and is often the critical piece to decide whether the meeting will be held. If approval to proceed is granted, a **request for proposals (RFPs)** may be sent out during the initiating phase to determine some of the project team members (for instance, the event professional could be an **independent planner** who is selected through the RFP process). The Convention Industry Council (CIC), which brings together international industry leaders, has developed numerous templates and standards for the industry. Two of their free resources are a request for proposals template and the RFP Workbook.

The following is a link for the CIC RFP Standards:
http://www.conventionindustry.org/StandardsPractices/APEX/RequestsforProposals.aspx
The following is a link to the new RFP Workbook:
http://www.conventionindustry.org/StandardsPractices/APEX/RFPWorkbook.aspx

Planning phase   If not part of the initiating phase, the event professional is a critical part of the team during the planning phase, to manage logistics, complete the event specifications guide, and secure contracts from meeting/event suppliers. The CIC has a free event specifications guide template on their website. During the planning phase, the project manager will develop profiles of the meeting stakeholders, the PM plan, and a work breakdown structure (described later in this chapter). **Milestones** and quality standards will be developed in this phase. Evaluation procedures, based on the goals and objectives described in the project charter and the PM plan will also be developed at this point. The milestones and quality standards will suggest the types of evaluation instruments needed. Since the RFP process typically starts during the initiating phase and continues through the planning phase, a review of proposals will also occur at this time. The executive committee, the project manager, and the event professional will review proposals. Selections are made following policies and procedures established by the enterprise. As selections are made, negotiations begin, and contracts are developed during the planning phase. Throughout this phase, the project manager is collecting current data (this data makes up a significant part of the PM plan).

The following is a link for the CIC Event Specifications Guide:
www.conventionindustry.org/StandardsPractices/APEX/EventSpecificationsGuide.aspx
The following is a link for the CIC Contracts Standards:
http://www.conventionindustry.org/StandardsPractices/APEX/Contracts.aspx

Executing phase   The executing phase is characterized by the fulfillment of contracts. Many contracted services are executed well in advance of a meeting/event (promotion, decoration, and some transportation, for instance), while other services occur during or after the meeting or event (shipping, financial management, and some transportation, for instance). On-site operations must be managed (either by the event professional or project manager). Data is collected during this phase and evaluation instruments are launched.

Controlling phase   Controlling is necessary during the meeting or event; however, controlling could also be necessary as contracted services unfold, well before the meeting or during the planning stage. An example would be a company that realizes tight budget controls must be instigated, and a new policy requires that out-of-region travel have supervisory approval or employee travel costs will not be reimbursed. This action would be considered controlling travel spending. During on-site operations, controlling measures might include monitoring as decorations are set up by the contracted event decorator and making changes to decorations that pose a hazard to traffic flow within the meeting facility (e.g., a registration area balloon display that extends into the hallway outside meeting rooms could be a problem). Controlling, then, occurs primarily during the planning and executing phases. It may also occur during the initiating and closing phases.

The project manager orchestrates all activities during all life cycle phases. While the project manager may not attend the meeting, he or she is responsible for the collection of all appropriate data connected to this meeting or event throughout all of the life cycle phases and communicating appropriate information to key stakeholders. This data is the foundation for control; without the data, control measures could be too lax or too stringent and could cause project failure. Through data collection and analysis, the project manager formulates control measures. If the project manager does not attend the meeting, he or she must know who will fulfill the controlling function during the meeting/event. This could be the meeting planner, which would be a logical choice if the planner was responsible for contract negotiations with suppliers during the planning phase.

Closing phase   The project close phase is a critical element in project success and may determine whether the company will attempt similar projects in the future. It begins immediately following the meeting/event and ends when all matters related to the event are complete. To guide this process, CIC offers the **post-event report or PER**. The closing phase includes paying all bills and completing all contract relationships. The key deliverable from the closing phase is the project close report, which includes all evaluation data and analysis. Recommendations for future events may also be included. The project manager will circulate this close report to key stakeholders, including the executive committee, the event professional, and enterprise management. Another activity common in the closing phase is sending thank-you notes to all volunteers and staff to recognize excellence in performance. The project close report is one of the historical documents that will be utilized when a similar project is initiated by the enterprise.

The following is a link for the CIC Post-Event Report: http://www.conventionindustry.org/StandardsPractices/APEX/PostEventReporting.aspx

PM Techniques and Processes

Just as CIC has organized templates, standards, and best practices for the MEEC industry, PMI has organized a body of knowledge (called **PMBOK**) and numerous seminars and conferences to guide project managers worldwide (PMI Global Standard, 2008). While the tips, tricks, and strategies become more sophisticated and intricate as project management matures, basic techniques for the practice have remained fairly constant. These include the development of a project charter and a PM plan, the definition of project scope, and the creation of a work breakdown structure.

Many other tools and techniques exist, of course, but these four components are critical to effective meeting management.

Project charter   Just as the RFP guides the person or company developing a proposal to provide a service or product, the project charter guides the project manager through all phases of the project's life cycle. The project charter contains these inputs at a minimum:

- scope (defines the project, provides the project's description, key deliverables, boundaries, constraints, assumptions, and acceptance criteria);
- business case (sets up the return-on-investment evaluation process and includes purpose and justification);
- measurable project objectives and success criteria (also used for the evaluation process);
- contract, if applicable (used to guide the project's execution phase);
- enterprise environmental factors that relate directly to the project (used to guide contract development and selection);
- description of project's assets and resources, including project governance (also used for contract development and selection);
- summary of financial management information (rough estimates);
- stakeholder identification (identifies project manager, assigns responsibilities, and defines the PM's authority level; may also do the same for the meeting planner);
- required signatures to indicate approval for the project (Dow and Taylor, 2008; PMI Global Standard, 2008).

Project scope   As the initiating phase often begins with identifying the purpose, goals, and a justification for the project, developing the project scope naturally evolves during this phase. That is a significant achievement, since the **project scope** not only tells the key stakeholders what the project *is*, the scope statement also tells them what the project *is not*. As the other phases in the project life cycle occur, the scope statement guides management and other stakeholders so the decisions made support the project's purpose and goals and helps the project participants meet milestones throughout the life cycle phases. Adding to the scope during the planning or execution phases is a serious threat to success, and this threat has earned the negative title of "scope creep." The scope might enlarge incrementally, with such sophistication and insidiousness that the meeting planner and other stakeholders simply do not recognize the additions.

The project's scope statement, to press the analogy of a symphony conductor even further, is like the sheet music in front of the conductor. It keeps the conductor on the musical piece selected for the symphony's performance, rather than playing other tunes in the symphony's repertoire.

Project management plan   The **project management plan** is a collection of all the functional area (such as risk management or communication) plans that are necessary to identify, track, utilize, control, and close the various sub-activities that comprise the project (PMI Global Standard, 2008). Many documents could be part of the project management plan, but this collection typically begins with these critical elements:

- work breakdown structure (WBS);
- **risk management plan** (for duration of project activities);
  - what the potential risks are
  - where these risks are in terms of functional areas in the project
  - what the projected probability is for each risk identified

- ◦ what the potential impact might be on the enterprise and stakeholders
- ◦ what the response strategy(ies) is(are)
- ◦ who is responsible for the strategy(ies)
- **communications plan**
  - ◦ what should be communicated
  - ◦ why this information should be communicated
  - ◦ when this information should be communicated
  - ◦ where this information should be sent/delivered
  - ◦ how this information should be communicated
  - ◦ who is responsible for this communication
- schedule, from project initiation through project close;
- procurement plan;
- cost management plan; and
- project close plan (Dow and Taylor, 2008).

Event management would add, at a minimum, the event specifications guide and the post-event report to this list of plans. Additionally, the PM plan should contain a 000A9; of all contracts, such as those for catering, transportation, and entertainment. All of these project management plan components are critical to success. The project management plan is primarily developed during the initiating phase.

The following is a link for the CIC Post-Event Report: http://www.conventionindustry.org/StandardsPractices/APEX/PostEventReporting.aspx

Work breakdown structure   Just as the **event specifications guide** records all of the logistical plans made for a meeting/event and is utilized by key stakeholders to control contract execution, the **work breakdown structure (WBS)** guides the project manager and the project team. According to Liliana Buchtik (2010), the WBS contains two essential components: discrete activities and level of effort. Discrete activities are defined as **deliverables** or tangible results. These results can be measured. The level of effort is made up of categories, each requiring various activities to achieve success, such as risk management, but the category itself is not measured (just its deliverables are). For each category, the discrete activities that must occur within the category are defined. The WBS then assigns resources, personnel, due dates, and other specific information to each discrete activity. The project manager monitors these "level of effort" categories and the activities throughout the project's life cycle. The project manager often identifies the level of effort categories during the initiating phase. During the planning phase, the various discrete activities are identified. So, the WBS is primarily developed during the planning stage.

The meeting itself may not be considered a deliverable from a PM perspective. Instead, project managers may look at meetings as a communications vehicle for a specific project or program (a collection of related projects) (Ware, 2011). An example might be training all members of an association in a new government-regulated process, where a website, a conference, and a hotline to answer questions are all implemented to achieve the project goals. From a meeting management perspective, though, PM may be considered a tool for managing a complex meeting with multiple stakeholder groups, numerous level-of-effort categories, and several discrete activities. So, during the initiating phase, the executive committee must decide what the meeting or event is—a discrete activity for a project or a program.

The WBS is developed through a technique called "**decomposition.**" Through decomposition, the project manager identifies specific required outcomes. Each outcome is separated into discrete activities that, when combined, achieve the desired outcome. For instance, if the meeting is defined as "a volunteer recognition celebration,"

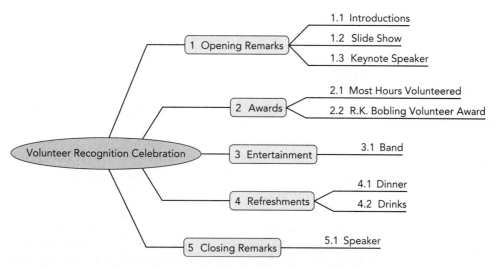

FIGURE 2 Decomposition Process.
This chart decomposes the project of hosting a volunteer recognition celebration by specifying discrete sub-activities. This chart was generated using NovaMind software, which is compatible across PC and Macintosh platforms.

the WBS will identify each component of that celebration (Figure 2). The decomposition diagram of this celebration might look like this (a mind map):

Decomposition could take a considerable amount of time. The project manager should answer the following questions to determine when to stop the decomposition technique:

- Given the lowest level of decomposition, am I able to assign this activity to a specific person?
- Can the cost, duration, and due dates be determined for this discrete activity?
- Can milestones and success criteria be determined for this discrete activity?
- Can I monitor and control the activity? (Buchtik, 2010).

If all of these questions are answered with a positive response, the decomposition technique provides the map, and that map is added to the WBS. The decomposition process helps identify the scope of the project, the discrete activities that fit within that scope, and utilizes mostly nouns and adjectives to describe the activities. Typically, the project manager, working with key stakeholders, develops the WBS. Then, the project manager develops the schedule of tasks and benchmarks, often working with the meeting planner or event professional and other functional areas within the enterprise (Buchtik, 2010).

Project schedules and charts   For a **time management plan**, the project manager creates a Gantt chart that looks much like an electronic calendar file, with dates and times indicated and discrete activities identified (see Figure 4). In this case, the focus is on how and when activities will be accomplished, utilizing verbs to describe the necessary tasks. This is the project schedule.

The schedule is linked to the WBS to be sure *all* identified activities and *only* identified activities are scheduled; this step helps prevent scope creep (Buchtik, 2010).

An example of **scope creep** might be the role of an event professional for a state association required to plan an annual convention. The event professional in this case plays the role of project manager and brings the key stakeholders together for periodic planning meetings. The association is politically active and decides to host a public forum for candidates running for governor. The event professional could be given the task of planning that event in addition to the original project's scope (planning the annual conference), and this becomes an added burden on resources. While the public forum may be a good idea, the project is subject to pressures that could jeopardize quality due to scope creep (the same people who would have been devoted to planning just the annual convention are now given extra duties planning the public forum for candidates).

To start the development of a project schedule, the project manager for a meeting or event will likely use three techniques known as **critical chain method (CCM), critical path method (CPM),** and the **program evaluation and review technique (PERT)**.

The critical chain technique recognizes that the successful organization completes projects as quickly as possible without adding resources (Kerzner, 2006). Critical chain methodology considers the project schedule and what enterprise resources will be required to complete that schedule, with attention to critical constraints to resources. In other words, if the meeting or event relies on supplier contracts that require substantial deposits at the beginning of the contract period (well before the meeting/event is held) and enterprise cash flow would limit what is available at a given point in the project schedule, critical chain methodology would help the project manager effectively schedule a contract payment date when resources are available.

According to Tobis and Tobis (2002), the critical path is the sequence of consecutive activities that represent the longest path through a multi-threaded project. Once the WBS is created and the activities determined for the schedule, the connections between tasks may be analyzed, including an estimate for how long each task will take. From there, whether using a computer program, spreadsheet, or diagram, the project manager can determine the longest path between connected tasks. Note that more than one critical path can exist in a complex project. The value of this method is that it lets the project manager (and team) make appropriate quick changes to the project schedule for activities on the critical path, when data is received about activities that impact other activities. Additionally, the CPM assists with putting tasks in their proper order.

If the meeting or event requires a keynote speaker, additional speakers for workshops will be determined based on how well they complement or add to the keynote speaker's presentation. The critical path would indicate a keynote speaker must be selected first. However, the organization may choose to find a sponsor to cover the keynote speaker's fee; since this will determine how much the organization can spend, a sponsor would have to be identified first.

The CPM isn't a schedule per se, it is an analysis method that shows all critical activities and the order in which they must occur. According to Kerzner (2006), CPM is predicated on a single time estimate and is deterministic in nature. If the project requires having the keynote speaker selected before the official event program is made public and the event program must be ready when marketing efforts begin, then the keynote speaker must be selected before the program piece is completed. CPM is utilized to determine a linear relationship between activities and is particularly useful when a project relies on one step being completed before the next step can begin. Of course, all of the logistics that must be planned before a meeting is held do not happen in a clear, step-by-step fashion.

Another process for project schedule development useful in meeting management is PERT. With this method, project managers make three estimates to determine an expected time for a specific activity to occur: the optimistic, most likely, and pessimistic scenarios. Tobis and Tobis (2002) explain PERT as being necessary for planning, scheduling, and coordinating multifaceted projects. The goal of PERT is to offer systematic plans on how to proceed and ongoing estimates of whether a project is on schedule and on budget. Dependencies between aspects of the project are carefully mapped out and valuable resources are allocated for specific time windows. Today, project managers often use complex software to support this effort.

For instance, say the event professional has been charged with waiting to select the keynote speaker until the director of development for this organization has secured a sponsor. An optimistic estimate could be that a sponsor is found within one week (the first sponsor asked agrees to cover costs); a pessimistic estimate is in one year. However, the most likely scenario is that the director of development needs four months to gain sponsor approval.

The PERT diagram (see Figure 3) shows more than a linear progression through project activities, and it is based on the answers to three questions:

- What activity (D) must precede this activity (E) in the WBS?
- What activity (F) must follow this activity (E) in the WBS?
- What activities (A, B, C, and E) can occur concurrently? (Kerzner, 2006)

To expand the example, once a facility has been selected, transportation can be arranged (activity A), food and beverage service can be determined (activity B), and a decorator can be chosen (activity C), all before the keynote sponsor is located. However, the keynote sponsor must be identified (activity D) before the keynote speaker is contracted (activity E), and that must occur before the workshop speakers are approached (activity F).

In planning meetings and events, the need for a schedule in the WBS is intuitive, especially when complex meetings require a long planning phase. Associations, for instance, with their tendency for a planning phase that is up to ten years long, would benefit from a detailed WBS and carefully constructed schedule, utilizing all of the techniques listed. When a corporate meeting is planned just months or weeks in advance, the schedule is less detailed, and the CPM system might work best. Selecting the technique that fits the meeting or event best is based on personal preference, organization culture, and meeting or event history. An experienced project manager and event professional and a detailed event history make the process of schedule development more accurate and less costly in terms of resource usage.

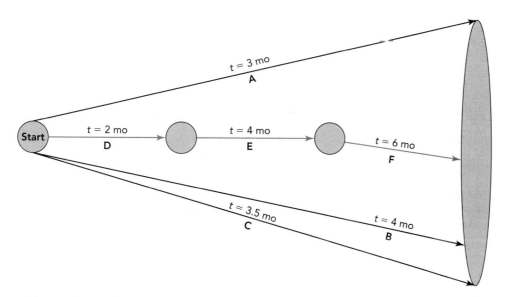

FIGURE 3   PERT Chart.
This chart reflects analysis for a sample project with four milestones as seen in the middle of the graphic. The critical (longest) path is in the middle: 2mo + 4mo + 6mo = 12 months total. Note that the critical path is not always the one with the most nodes. The critical path is based on time.

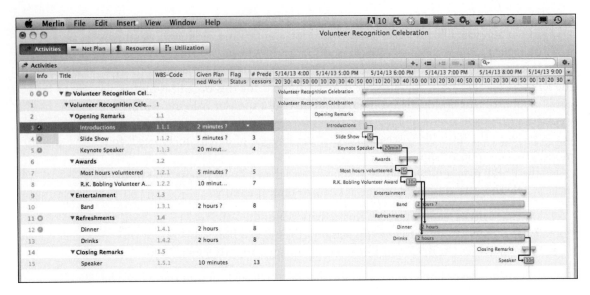

FIGURE 4   Gantt Chart.

This chart for a fictional meeting was created using Merlin (project management software for the Macintosh platform). Gantt Chart Created Using Merlin" from MERLIN SERVER. Used by permission of Frank Blome, Projectwizards GmbH.

To display project schedules, project managers often use a Gantt chart, named for mechanical engineer Henry Gantt, who first introduced the chart style in the second decade of the 1900s. A simple Google application for creating a Gantt chart is available, and project managers can purchase a variety of software packages for developing these charts and other visual displays. The value of using a Gantt chart is particularly obvious when communicating with busy executives who need a brief presentation on project status throughout initiating, planning, executing, and controlling life cycle phases. Presenting complex information in a simple visual format helps communicate quickly and, depending on the chart's style, dramatically. When a project is ahead of schedule or a task is running behind, the bars on a Gantt chart (see Figure 4) draw attention quickly to task status.

SUMMARY

Complex meetings and events are typically planned by a team of personnel working for or on behalf of the host organization. This team is comprised of key stakeholders, and each has a distinct role in the success of the meeting. Because meetings and events are part of a dynamic and constantly changing environment, within certain constraints across the enterprise's functional areas, the team may have need of a project manager. This person's role may be seen as complementary to the role of the meeting planner or event professional, but some situations may dictate blending these roles. Ideally, the project manager is responsible for the project charter and the project management plan, including a work breakdown structure and schedule, among other documents, all of which record what has been arranged for this meeting or event and what the status is on those arrangements at any point in time. The event professional, in this ideal situation, handles many activities and level of effort categories that occur primarily during the planning phase of the project's life cycle.

Depending on complexity, environment, and potential constraints, the work breakdown structure will identify who is responsible for the execution and controlling phases of the project's life cycle, as well as the project close phase. The schedule often contains a Gantt chart displaying the tasks assigned and their status along a time line for the project. As the life cycle phases unfold, the Gantt chart shows progress. A CPM analysis would highlight the project's critical activities, while a PERT chart would display relationships for concurrent activities, as well as consecutive activities. PERT charts are also often used in the project close report.

Through all of the life cycle phases, the project manager serves as a conductor, leading the symphony in a successful performance and conclusion. The project manager may also serve as an event professional or may be the lead person on a meeting planning (the project) team. In either case, the techniques and standards established by PMI (PMI Global Standard, 2008) and the CMP international standards (Convention Industry Council, 2012) should guide successful management of the meeting project.

Now that you have completed this chapter you should be competent in the following Meeting and Business Event Competency Standards:

MBECS—Skill 1: Plan Meetings or Event Project

Sub skills		Skills (standards)
B 4.01	Historical perspective of project management as a business process	
B 4.02	Description of project management	
B 4.03	Comparison of project manager and meeting planner roles	
B 4.04	Definition of the project charter	
B 4.05	Definition of the project plan	
B 4.06	Description of the project scope and work breakdown structure	
B 4.07	Additional plans and documents that comprise the collection of data throughout the project's life cycle	

KEY WORDS AND TERMS

Project Management
General Systems Theory (GST)
Project Life Cycle
Project Team
Secondary Data
Primary Data
Project Charter
Request for Proposal (RFP)
Independent Planner
Milestones

Post-Event Report (PER)
Project Management Body of Knowledge (PMBOK)
Project Scope
Project Management Plan
Risk management Plan
Communications Plan
Event Specifications Guide (ESG)
Work breakdown Structure (WBS)

Deliverable(s)
Decomposition
Time Management Plan
Scope Creep
Critical Chain Method (CCM)
Critical Path Method (CPM)
Project Evaluation and Review Technique (PERT)

REVIEW AND DISCUSSION QUESTIONS

1. The organization that is responsible for developing the project management body of knowledge is called what?
2. What is the mission of the Project Management Institute's local chapter?
3. How is systems theory related to project management and meeting planning?
4. Differentiate the role of the project manager from that of the meeting planner.

REFERENCES

Buchtik, L. (2010). *Secrets to mastering the WBS in real-world projects*. Newtown Square, PA: Project Management Institute.

Convention Industry Council. *CMP international standards* (2012). Retrieved March 10, 2012 from: http://www.conventionindustry.org/CMP/CMPIS.aspx.

Dow, W., and B. Taylor (2008). *Project management communications bible*. Indianapolis: Wiley.

Kerzner, H. (2006). *Project management: A systems approach to planning, scheduling, and controlling* (6th ed.) Hoboken, NJ: John Wiley & Sons.

KIDASA Software. (2012). *About Gantt charts*. Retrieved April 15, 2012 from http://www.ganttchart.com/history.html.

"Ludwig von Bertalanffy (1901–1972)" (2012). International Society for the Systems Sciences. Retrieved from http://www.isss.org/lumLVB.htm.

PMI Global Standard. (2008). *A guide to the project management body of knowledge (PMBOK Guide)* (4th ed.). Newtown Square, PA: Project Management Institute. Smartsheet. (2012). *Gantt chart template*. Google. Retrieved April 15, 2012 from https://www.smartsheet.com/gantt-chart-template?s=2&c=25&m=414&a=017gt&gclid=CJ23_t_lya8CFSQCQAodB2yccQ.

Tobis, I., and M. Tobis (2002). *Managing multiple projects.* New York: McGraw-Hill.

Ware, R. (July 5, 2011). "Meeting planning from a project management perspective." *Business Monthly.*

April 22, 2012. Retrieved April 3, 2012 fromhttp://www.bizmonthly.com/meeting-planning-from-a-project-management-perspective/.

"What is PMI?" (2012). Project Management Institute, Inc. Retrieved February 22, 2012 from http://www.pmi.org/en/About-Us/About-Us-What-is-PMI.aspx.

ABOUT THE CHAPTER CONTRIBUTORS

B. J. Reed, EdD, is a professor of Media Studies and the director of the Teaching and Learning Center at the University of Wisconsin–Platteville. Dr. Reed has been teaching courses in meetings and public relations for more than twenty years. After completing a master's degree in communications and serving the nonprofit sector for about fifteen years, she went back to college to complete a doctoral degree in higher education. She has been teaching full time since then. Her first adventure with meeting planning came as an extension of her role as magazine editor for a nonprofit organization. That eventually led to her interest in professional development and training as a niche in the MEEC industry. Just for fun, Dr. Reed is currently working toward certification as a registered parliamentarian.

Lynn Reed is a project manager at Iowa State University. She has been active in the meetings and events industry since the moment she could serve as a volunteer (about age ten). That led her to years working in the meetings and events industry, first as a volunteer, then as staff, and finally as a freelance meeting and event planner for a nonprofit special interest group. Returning to college, she earned a master's degree in project management from the University of Wisconsin–Platteville. That degree opened opportunities within the grants management industry. Currently she is the project manager for the installation of the Kuali Coeus research administration system at Iowa State University. In her free time, Ms. Reed is working towards certification as a FileMaker Pro database designer.

LINKS

Convention Industry Council
http://www.conventionindustry.org/index.aspx.

APEX Initiative: Contracts
http://www.conventionindustry.org/StandardsPractices/APEX/Contracts.aspx.

APEX Initiative: Event Specifications Guide
http://www.conventionindustry.org/StandardsPractices/APEX/EventSpecificationsGuide.aspx.

APEX Initiative: Post-Event Report
http://www.conventionindustry.org/StandardsPractices/APEX/PostEventReporting.aspx.

APEX Initiative: Request for Proposals
http://www.conventionindustry.org/StandardsPractices/APEX/RequestsforProposals.aspx

APEX Initiative: RFP Workbook
http://www.conventionindustry.org/StandardsPractices/APEX/RFPWorkbook.aspx.

Gantt chart shareware
https://www.smartsheet.com/gantt-chart-template?s=2&c=25&m=414&a=017gt&gclid=CJ23_t_lya8CFSQCQAodB2yccQ.

Risk Management for Meetings, Expositions, Events, and Conventions

CHAPTER 4

Risk planners must address flooding. © Coleman Yuen, Pearson Education Asia Ltd

Chapter Objectives

Upon completion of this chapter, the reader should be able to:

- Describe risk management as it applies to planning or hosting a meeting or business event
- Analyze risks associated with the specific characteristics of a particular meeting or business event
- Develop a risk plan that addresses mitigation measures and contingency plans for identified and analyzed risks
- Identify the relationship between liability and risk management

Chapter Outline

Risk Management Defined

Risk Planning

Creating a Risk Team
    Risk Team

Risk Assessment
    Identifying Possible
        Risks
    Risk Analysis—Which Risks Must
        We Plan For?

Developing a Risk Management
    Plan

Risk Mitigation
    Contingency Plans
    Insurance and Contacts

Security

Implementing the Risk Plan

Summary

Key Words and Terms

Review and Discussion Questions

References

About the Chapter Contributor

RISK MANAGEMENT DEFINED

Risk management can have different meanings depending on who is using the term. Insurance providers think of risk management as insuring against a risk. Accountants may think of it as managing financial risk. Lawyers may consider only legal risk.

For this chapter, the Convention Industry Council (2010) Accepted Practices Exchange (APEX) Glossary definition of risk management is used.

TABLE 1 Definitions and Terms

Term	Definition	Example
Risk	The possibility that a crisis, emergency, or disaster may occur.	Note: *Risk* is not the crisis, emergency, or disaster itself. Only the possibility that it may occur.
Business continuity	The process whereby an entity keeps on delivering products and services for its clients and stakeholders and perpetuates its viability before, during, and after a disaster or crisis.	Four people die in a freak tent collapse at an event, and several lawsuits for negligence and wrongful death ensue. A company with sufficient resources and planning can survive the financial, legal, and reputational damage and continue in business.
Crisis	An event characterized by having a small chance of occurring but when it does, carries significant risk that threatens the existence of an entity. Decisions regarding dealing with the crisis must be made quickly.	A tornado strikes the hotel where ABC Group is holding a meeting of 500 people. There are several serious injuries, power is out, and traditional communication channels are temporarily disabled.
Disaster	An event that has high impact, occurs abruptly, is unforeseen and usually results in significant loss or damage.	The roof of a convention center in which an exhibition is being held collapses, killing 100 people attending and participating in the exhibition.
Emergency	An event that is unforeseen and has significant impact such as mortal injury, property damage, and will result in the suspension of the activities of an entity.	A case of food poisoning strikes a corporate group following a dinner for 300 people. Many cases are serious enough to require hospitalization.

It states: *"recognizing the possibility of injury, damage or loss, and having a means to prevent it or provide insurance."* As this definition suggests, risk management for meetings and events must consider financial, legal, physical, and intangible risks (such as damage to reputation). It is not just one of those aspects, but all.

There are other related risk management terms that are important for any meeting and business event professional to be aware of. Some of these are listed in Table 1. A good resource for definitions for risk management is the online Disaster Recovery Journal. The link to the glossary is at the end of this chapter. You will find that professionals from each of the separate fields: **emergency** management, **crisis** management, **disaster** recovery, and **business continuity** professionals consider themselves unique. In few places do you get a comprehensive overview of all of the issues and how to deal with them, yet meeting professionals must take this comprehensive approach.

RISK PLANNING

Many meeting and event professionals think that writing the risk plan is the first step to implementing a crisis preparedness program. In fact, there are several crucial steps that must be undertaken first. This is why there are no "off the shelf" risk management plans for meetings and events. Each plan is (or should be) different, depending on the nature of the meeting organizer and the meeting. The steps to actually create a risk management program are listed in the left margin.

CREATING A RISK TEAM

Before a risk plan can be developed, a risk team has to be assigned to develop it. The very first step in becoming crisis prepared is for the risk team to determine which risks to plan for. Sometimes a single person develops a risk plan, but this is not as desirable as having a team develop it. A single person has a single perspective, and multiple

Steps to Create a Risk Management Program

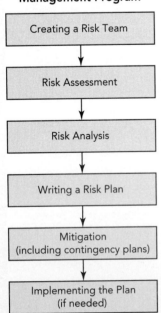

Creating a Risk Team

↓

Risk Assessment

↓

Risk Analysis

↓

Writing a Risk Plan

↓

Mitigation (including contingency plans)

↓

Implementing the Plan (if needed)

CASE STUDY

Hurricane Katrina, New Orleans

At 8:00 A.M. on August 29, 2005, Hurricane Katrina hit the Gulf Coast of the United States, including New Orleans, LA. Although many people had been evacuated, not all had the time or the means to evacuate before the hurricane. And in some cases, people refused to evacuate. With winds that exceeded 125 mph and storm surges of water that broke through retaining walls, the hurricane pounded the city of New Orleans, destroying 275,000 homes, killing many people, and leaving devastation in its wake. The hospitality industry was by no means untouched. As just one example, the Hyatt Regency Hotel in New Orleans was badly damaged and stayed closed for several years following the hurricane. Meetings expecting to use New Orleans as a destination during hurricane dates and for more than a year afterward either had to find another location or make a tough decision about whether to go through with using New Orleans in the hotels that were back in business, despite the clean-up going on around the city (Capello, n.d.).

- What if you had a meeting planned in New Orleans on August 29, 2005? Would you cancel it? Go through with it and hope for the best?
- Where would you find the information to monitor to help you make a decision about what to do with your meeting?
- Would you go through with holding a meeting in New Orleans six months after the hurricane, despite the clean-up going on around the city? What are the pros and cons?

Debris around convention center as New Orleans is evacuated after Hurricane Katrina. FEMA

people will bring different points of view and experiences to it, making the plan more robust and complete.

Risk Team

Risk management is not just the job of security personnel or the venue or the insurance company. In fact, the meeting professional has a legal and ethical obligation to take an active role in risk management. Risk management for meetings and business events requires involvement from everyone related to the meeting and everyone related to risks for the meeting organizer, including but not limited to:

- Meeting planner
- Event professional
- Venue representative
- Destination representative
- Lawyer
- Insurance company representative
- Accountant
- Security (both venue in-house security and separate security personnel, if hired)
- Emergency services

It is not coincidental, then, that people in these positions are involved on the **risk team**, the team of people who conduct the **risk assessment** and **risk analysis**, discussed below. In fact, the members of the risk team will vary depending on the nature of the meeting organizer, the meeting or business event itself, the venue, and so on. Consider for example the differences between who might do the risk planning in each of the following scenarios:

Scenario 1. A corporate client hires an independent meeting planner to plan an executive-level retreat for its top-level executives and the board of directors at a remote resort.

Scenario 2. In-house association meeting planners are planning the annual convention, to be held in a major U.S. city in the late spring. Attendees will be flying in from all over the country.

In the first scenario, if risk management planning is left up to the independent planner, she may not have the time and resources that the corporation itself has or may not have built risk management elements (such as insurance and security) into her proposal in order to keep it competitive.

In the second scenario, the association planners can use their own accounting department, lawyer (if they have one in-house), and insurance company to help address risks. However, they may become complacent and fail to plan if no crises or emergencies have occurred at prior annual meetings. One study found that although 65.6 percent of meeting planners found it important to have a crisis plan, only 41.5 percent actually had a plan in place (Kline and Smith, 2006). Additionally, association

CASE STUDY
Dozens Sickened

An antismoking conference was held in Kansas City, MO. As the convention ended, over fifty people came down with gastrointestinal distress. It was diagnosed as a food-borne illness. Whether the food was consumed at the hotel at which the event was hosted, one of the off-site events, or whether all fifty people independently ate at a restaurant in town was the first order of business during the Kansas City Health Department's investigation (CNN Health, 2002).

- While the health department is researching the cause, what should the meeting organizer's risk team be doing? What should the hotel be doing?
- What should be done to minimize the risk of this occurring?
- What might be the repercussions of this outbreak on the meeting organizer? The hotel? Does it matter if they are ultimately found not to blame?

planners often say they are unable to engage in many risk management activities due to a lack of budget, staff, or time (Hilliard, Scott-Halsell, and Palakurthi, 2011).

RISK ASSESSMENT

Identifying Possible Risks

Once the risk team has been assembled, the first task is to brainstorm a comprehensive list of risks—unexpected things that could happen that would affect the meeting, the meeting organizer, or the meeting participants. This phase is called **risk assessment**.

Risk Categories   Before risk planning can start, it is essential to consider all of the types of things that can be at risk as well as all of the people or entities that may be affected by risk. There are two ways to categorize risks:

1. By what *causes* the crisis, emergency, or disaster
2. By what *is affected by* the crisis, emergency, or disaster

The risk categories in Table 2 are those suggested by the National Fire Protection Association (NFPA) (2007) in its document NFPA 1600: Standard on Disaster/Emergency Management and Business Continuity Programs. They indicate what type of occurrence caused the crisis, disaster, or emergency. Table 2 below offers some examples and ideas of what/who is affected. This is by no means an exhaustive list.

Depending on the cause and nature of the crisis, disaster, or emergency, these things may affect the meeting organizer, one or more attendees, the meeting facility, vendors, or others.

Risk Analysis—Which Risks Must We Plan For?

Brainstorming all of the possible risks associated with a meeting or business event (or facility, or vendor services, or any other aspect of the industry) can yield a daunting list of possibilities ranging from minor (breakout session speaker no-show) to catastrophic

TABLE 2 Risk categories, examples, and effects

Categories	Examples
Natural	<ul><li>Hurricane</li><li>Tornado</li><li>Earthquake</li><li>Brushfire</li><li>Mudslide</li><li>Snow</li><li>Rain</li><li>Heat</li></ul>
Human-caused	<ul><li>Assault</li><li>Presenter no-show</li><li>Slander/libel/defamation</li><li>Copyright infringement</li><li>Theft</li><li>Entertainer cancellation</li></ul>
Technological	<ul><li>Power outage</li><li>Computer crash</li><li>Data loss or misuse</li><li>Communication loss</li><li>Audiovisual problems</li></ul>

(NFPA, 2007)

Exercise 1 – Risk Assessment

Suppose you are the meeting planner for ABC Association's 10th Annual Convention. You are responsible for planning the convention which draws 5,000 people in Washington, DC. The dates are the first week of February of next year. The venue is the Washington, DC Convention Center for the convention. The housing block includes four different hotels, each of which is a short Metro (subway) or taxi ride away (there is a Metro stop at the Convention Center itself). The mayor of the city will be giving the opening keynote session and someone from the White House (president, vice president, secretary of state) has committed to try to attend the closing keynote session. There are several on- and off-site special events included in the program including receptions, parties, and tours. The program includes both professional and volunteer speakers. The professional speakers are paid, the volunteer speakers are not. Session size varies from 25 attendees to 150 attendees. The keynotes are expected to draw 4,500.

- Conduct a risk assessment using the categories in Table 2.
- Make up additional details as needed to flesh out risks.

(a life-threatening earthquake). If an event professional tried to plan for all of the possible risks, she would have no time to plan the meeting or business event! So an important step in risk management is determining which risks to accept, which risks to avoid, and which risks need to be mitigated or managed through a risk management plan, insurance, contracts, security, or contingency plans.

To determine which risks to plan for, a **probability-consequences analysis** should be used. That is, the event professional needs to ask themselves two questions:

- How probable (or likely) is the risk to occur?
- How serious are the consequences if the risk does occur?

It may be helpful to plot each risk on a grid like the one in Table 3. To determine the probability of each risk, meeting professionals should look at the characteristics associated with:

- The type of meeting or business event
  - Program
  - Speakers and entertainment
  - Attendees
  - Duration
- The destination
- The facility
- Vendor services

Where is the meeting vulnerable to risk? For example, is the keynote speaker extremely high profile (e.g., Queen of England)? Is the meeting or event being held in a country with a lower standard of healthcare or emergency services? Is the facility located on a remote tropical island with limited transportation options? Are pyrotechnics

---

TABLE 3 Probability-Consequences Analysis

Probability		
	High Probability, Low Consequence ACCEPT or MANAGE	High Probability, High Consequence AVOID or MANAGE
	Low Probability, Low Consequence ACCEPT	Low Probability, High Consequence MANAGE
	Consequences	

Hot air ballooning is an activity with heightened risk. If your meeting or business event program utilizes hot air balloon rides, even as an optional activity, you may need extra risk mitigation measures.
Tony Souter, Dorling Kindersley

(fireworks) or elaborate stage sets being used that increase the likelihood of injury to staff or attendees?

Remember that some risks can't be avoided. For example, a meeting professional does not have the power to prevent an accidental fire breaking out in a hotel. However, if the risk is a hurricane and the meeting or event is being held during hurricane season, the event professional may choose to avoid the risk by not holding the meeting on a cruise ship in the Caribbean but instead holding it on land, away from the coast. In the years after Hurricane Katrina, the Gulf Coast of the United States has seen a significant decline in convention bookings during the season for hurricanes that runs from June through November.

It is important that the risk team not only explore its vulnerabilities, but also its strengths or capabilities. Some examples of capabilities that may need to be factored in are:

- Emergency equipment like automated external defibrillators (AEDs) on-site at the facility
- Several staff certified in CPR, AED, and First Aid
- Multiple languages spoken by staff members
- Security company has worked with this show numerous times and is highly aware of the risks associated with the meeting
- Facility staff are fully prepared for evacuation and are able to communicate procedures to meeting professionals in advance

Exercise 2 – Risk Assessment

Using the scenario provided in Exercise 1 for the 10th Annual ABC Association Annual Convention, do a probability-consequences analysis using a grid like the one above.

- Which risks will you accept? Why?
- Which risks will you (can you) avoid? Why?

DEVELOPING A RISK MANAGEMENT PLAN

Once the event professional has determined the team that will write the plan (and the event professional may have a separate team that will be responsible for implementing the plan on-site if something happens), he/she is finally ready to write the plan itself. Although the contents of risk management plans vary widely, the following is a sample table of contents of a typical risk management plan for a meeting:

A. **Summary and description of the meeting.** This section will need to change with each major meeting. Intangibles such as the meeting goals and objectives and a description of attendees of the meeting should be included here as well as the dates, duration, schedule of events, and so on. Keep this section brief. Create a form that can easily be filled out for each meeting so that no meeting details are missed.

B. **Risk Team (the staff who create and modify the Risk Plan) and Response Team** (the on-site staff who will monitor and implement the Risk Plan if needed) names and contact information (including mobile phones and emergency contacts). This section should include contact information and the role each will take in the event of an actual crisis. Sample roles might include:
   - Monitoring the news on the pending crisis/disaster/emergency
   - Communication with media, with staff, with venue/destination/vendor representatives, with emergency response services
   - Incident commander
   - Managing appropriate response: evacuation, shelter in place.

Other roles may be needed depending on the nature of the crisis.

C. **Emergency Response Procedures** categorized either by cause or response. For example, the responses can be categorized according to cause (human-caused, technological, natural disaster) or response (evacuation, shelter in place, first aid). Emergency response procedures should be written in simple, easy-to-follow steps. For example, if sirens are heard, the first step should either be "evacuate immediately" or "stay where you are until an announcement is made over the public address system." It's important that the risk response team members know which is the first step and that it be communicated properly to attendees and other staff.

D. **Facility information.** This section will also have to be changed and customized for each meeting or business event facility. There may be multiple facilities for a single event. This will include contact information for key facility representatives (including mobile and home phone numbers), floor plans, evacuation routes, emergency exits, location of emergency equipment.

E. **Communication list** to include staff of both the event professional and the facility, emergency services, attendees', and their emergency contacts. This section should include an up-to-date phone tree so that each person called calls two more people until everyone has been contacted. Some should be assigned to communicate internally with staff, board members, and the destination and venue representatives. Others will communicate externally with the news media, family of staff and attendees, emergency services, and so on.

F. **Forms and Appendices.** This section should include at a minimum an incident report form to be used if anyone is injured, lists of nearby emergency services (e.g., 24-hour medical and dental clinics), as well as other forms or information that may be needed by the meeting organizer, the facility, or the vendors in case of a crisis.

The risk plan should be reviewed and revised as needed at least once a year and ideally, twice a year. For a meeting or business event risk plan, parts of the plan will be customized for each major meeting or event (e.g., information about the closest emergency facilities to the facility or emergency services in the destination). In order to be able to implement the plan when it is needed, not only should the plan be reviewed, but drills or tabletop exercises should be done regularly. Drills may include evacuation drills or shelter in place drills (e.g., if you hear tornado sirens, the last thing you want to do is evacuate!). Tabletop exercises allow a group to walk through a mock disaster, making decisions at each stage.

RISK MITIGATION (OR MANAGEMENT)

Contingency Plans

For those risks that need to be managed, contingency plans need to be developed. These contingency plans will go into the risk plan and may include:

- Reserving an alternate venue in case inclement weather prevents an outdoor location for an event from being used.
- Having a backup speaker or session in case a major speaker doesn't arrive on time or gets sick. Some examples of these might include:
  - Asking one of your speakers to be prepared to do a second session elaborating on the topic he or she initially presented.
  - Asking the CEO to be prepared with a "State of the Organization" address or a "Trends in…" presentation.
  - Being prepared to do a roundtable or other interactive exercise with board members or others facilitating each roundtable topic.
- Being prepared to cancel an event if, for example, the entertainment does not show up or refuses to go on. Alternatively, you might research in advance local entertainment options that might be able to show up at the last minute.
- For very severe crises, a contingency plan might be as extreme as having an alternate city and venues chosen and negotiated with in case the entire meeting or business event needs to be moved due to weather, strikes, or other reasons.

Insurance and Contracts

There are other ways to manage some risks besides contingency planning. One is to shift the risks to others. Two of the most popular ways to shift risk are purchasing insurance and signing contracts.

Exercise 3 – Risk Mitigation

Using the scenario provided in Exercise 1 for the 10th Annual ABC Association Annual Convention, which mitigation measures will you put into place to help reduce the probability of a crisis/disaster/emergency from occurring or limit the consequences if it does occur? Take each of the risks that you said needed to be "managed" and specify one or more mitigation measures that you will use.

- For which risks will you:
  - Create a contingency (or backup) plan? What will it be?
  - Take out insurance? What kind?
  - Negotiate a particular contract provision? Which one?
  - Hire security? What kind?

CASE STUDY
The Silver Lining

Just as we learn from our mistakes, we learn from crises, disasters, and emergencies that we have had to live through. For example, on July 27, 2005, four suicide bombers killed fifty-two commuters in London when they set off bombs in the London Underground (subway system) and on a bus. A tragedy, to be sure. But what emergency experts learned from that attack, however, was used to plan and implement the security measures for the 2012 London Olympics. Lessons learned from the 2005 attack resulted in the implementation of new and improved emergency services and equipment. Nothing can bring the fifty-two people killed back. But perhaps the lessons learned from that attack saved lives during the 2012 summer Olympics (ESPN Olympic Sports, 2012).

- What lessons can be learned from some of the other case studies in this chapter or crises, disasters, or emergencies that you have heard about elsewhere?

Insurance   Buying insurance is a way of shifting the financial risk of loss, injury, or damage to the insurance company. In exchange for the payment of a premium, the insurance company agrees to accept the risk that property may be damaged or lost, for example. The higher the probability or likelihood of damage or loss, the higher the cost of the insurance premium.

Insurance can't be purchased for every risk. However, some of the popular types of insurance purchased for meetings and business events include:

- **Commercial General Liability (CGL):** A CGL policy is much like a homeowner's insurance policy. This insurance covers business premises and property. For example, if a pipe burst in the ceiling of the office overnight and damaged several computers, the carpet, and the walls, a claim may be filed to have the CGL policy pay for the damage and replace the computers. Event professionals want to be sure that their CGL policy covers the business while "temporarily off-premise" (such as at a meeting).
- **Event Cancellation Insurance:** Contrary to popular belief, event cancellation insurance does not cover financial losses if the meeting organizer decides to cancel a meeting for no reason. However, it may pay financial losses in the case of a force majeure event: a natural disaster prevents the group from holding the meeting. Force majeure is defined as an overpowering event that is completely unexpected and is not controllable. The term is of French origin and was first used in the late 1800s. It may also pay for measures to prevent the meeting from having to be canceled.

Contracts   A contract is an agreement between two or more persons or parties; especially one that has been written and is legally enforceable; for example, it could be an arrangement between two parties concerning the delivery of goods or services at a fixed price. Much of the language in a contract involves shifting risk and responsibility or putting an upper limit on the financial risk a meeting organizer is taking with regard to a specific meeting. This is true whether the contract is between a meeting organizer and a hotel, a vendor, a speaker, or an entertainer. Some of the key contract clauses that deal with risk are the performance clauses (cancellation, attrition) and the **indemnification clause** (often closely tied to an insurance clause).

- **Cancellation:** Any contract runs the risk of being canceled…by either party. However, cancellation of a contract is either a breach of that contract or an exercise of a **cancellation clause** that is included in the contract. Either way, the law basically requires the canceling party to make the other party "whole" or it puts them in the position they would have been in had the contract been fully performed. In this way, the risk of cancellation is somewhat shifted from the meeting organizer or mitigation by a hotel, vendor, speaker, or other entity may cancel the contract.

- **Attrition:** In the context of meetings and events, attrition is a reduction in numbers. Unique to facility contracts, the **attrition clause** shifts the risk the hotel or other facility takes that the event professional may not fill its contracted room block. It requires the event professional to pay contract damages (money) if a certain number of sleeping rooms remained empty. At the end of the meeting or event, the hotel will add up the actual total room-nights and compare this to the "reserved" or guaranteed block; if the event professional miscalculated the number of room-nights when there is an "attrition clause," then their company or client is liable for the room-nights not used. Attrition also applies to other services that the event professional "guarantees to use," such as the number of people attending a banquet: if fewer people show up, the event professional still pays for the higher number.

- **Indemnification** (sometimes called *indemnification and hold harmless*): This clause is one that tries to place responsibility for risk on the party that has control over whatever caused the loss or damage. For example, if a light fixture falls from the ceiling of a hotel ballroom, the event professional has no control over this (provided no one was swinging from it at the time!). The indemnification clause puts the responsibility where it belongs—on the hotel. In response, the hotel may try to shift the risk onto the electrician who hung the light fixture or the company that produced the light fixture or so on. This is a very important contract clause and yet one that many meeting planners do not spend enough time negotiating.

Reading, negotiating, and signing contracts is an important part of risk management. Although contracts can't prevent someone from getting hurt or property from getting damaged, they can shift the financial risk for loss to others. Financial risk is a very real risk and can sometimes mean the difference between whether an event professional can stay in business post-crisis or not.

SECURITY

Before hiring security for an event, several things should be considered including what kind of security personnel are already on-site. For example, if a meeting or business event is being held in a hotel, the hotel will already have security staff. It is important to find out how many security personnel are on-site during each shift, how they are trained, what equipment they have, and consider what other events are going on at the same time to get an idea of how busy those security personnel might be during the meeting. Only after that analysis can an event professional determine their security personnel needs.

In addition to determining what security personnel are already going to be on-site, the event professional needs to evaluate security needs by considering the following issues.

TABLE 4 Factors to Determine Security Needs

Factors to Determine Security Personnel Needs	Examples
Type of meeting or business event	• Outdoor festival • Meeting held in a hotel • Concert • Political event
Hours of operation	• Hours of meeting or business event, including setup and break down • Hours of venue or facility • Whether meeting materials and equipment will be left unattended overnight
Type of venue	• Hotel • Convention center • Fairground • City street
Types of activities	• Alcohol • Food • VIP presentation (e.g., political or celebrity figures) • Exercise or active team-building activity (e.g., ropes course, scavenger hunt)
Attendees	• Number of attendees • Age • Multicultural • High-profile celebrity or political figure • Religion • Dietary issues
Flow	• Number and type of entrances and exits • Places where groups may bottleneck
Insurance and contract requirements	• Security personnel requirements in insurance policy or contract • Security personnel requirements by facility

(Canadian Tourism Human Resources Council, 2011)

There are several different types of security that can be used. Which one(s) and how many vary depending on the nature of the meeting or business event and many of the factors listed above. Some of the types of security personnel that might be considered are:

Licensed unarmed security guards: This type of security personnel can be used for general patrolling, emergency response or evacuation, alcohol policy enforcement, door monitoring, or similar "routine" security issues. This type of security personnel can be useful for meetings or tradeshows.

Off-duty police officers: This type of security personnel may engage in some of the same services as the licensed unarmed guards, but may also be tasked with law and ordinance enforcement and executive protection. This type of security personnel should be the only ones armed with weapons, although they may also be unarmed. This type of security personnel can be used when the risks of loss or breaking the law is higher, such as a jewelry show or an outdoor block party where alcohol is served.

Crowd safety stewards: This type of security personnel is trained specifically to monitor and manage crowds. They are specially trained for tasks like traffic, parking management, and pedestrian route management, but may also perform tasks such as registration and ticket distribution and serve as greeters or ushers.

This type of security personnel can be used for ticketed events like concerts or sports events.

SOURCE: Event Safety & Security Services, LLC, 2012

IMPLEMENTING THE RISK PLAN

The risk plan can only be useful if it is easily accessible and if people are familiar with its contents. The time a crisis occurs is *not* the time to find out what is actually in the risk plan. The risk plan should also not be too unwieldy. Key people, both at the meeting and back at the office, should have copies of the risk plan in a 1- to 1.5-inch red binder, or an electronic equivalent, kept close to them or where they can easily access it. If something happens, the binder can be consulted and the appropriate actions taken.

One of the most important aspects of responding to a crisis is determining who is in charge. In risk management, this person may be called the "incident commander." This is the person who is responsible for making sure everyone plays their assigned role during a crisis or emergency. The CEO or president of the organization is generally not the incident commander because he or she may have other responsibilities including meetings, talking to the media, conferring with legal, and so on. The incident commander should be someone who can command authority and keep their head in a crisis or emergency. The incident commander assigns other roles for the response team members.

The incident commander (or designee) is the person who will confer with local emergency authorities in the case of a crisis or emergency. One of the other key roles that has to be assigned is that of communications. The media will be looking for a spokesperson and, if they don't find one, they will ask anyone and everyone for the story until they get one—accurate or not. Social media makes information available instantly and 24/7. Someone must be responsible for managing the message.

Workers bringing emergency equipment into the French Quarter to begin renovations on a hotel after Hurricane Katrina. FEMA

CASE STUDY
Left on the Mountain

Securian Financial Corporation was holding a conference for over one thousand people at the JW Marriott Desert Springs Resort in Palm Desert, CA. The corporation hired a destination management company (DMC), West Coast Transportation and Events, to provide optional tours and activities for attendees. One such tour was a tram ride up the San Jacinto Mountains. The DMC went up the mountain with forty-three participants and came down with only forty-one. They assumed that the other two found their own way down. Although the information about the two missing guests was communicated to the DMC representative's supervisor, it was not communicated to the meeting planner. With so many attendees, the two attendees were not missed until two days later, when they should have been back at work—but weren't. Only then was a search-and-rescue mission launched. Fortunately the two were found. They had survived by using materials found in a dead hiker's backpack.

- If a lawsuit was filed, who would likely be found liable? Why?
- What could Securian do better to ensure that nothing like this ever happens again?
- What should Securian's risk plan include to deal with this or a similar situation in the future?

(Bassett, 2006)

SUMMARY

Meeting and event professionals often think they don't have time for risk management because they are so busy planning and managing the meetings and business events for which they are responsible. The flaw in this mind-set is that risk management is not another thing to do. It is just part of the everyday job of being an event professional. Risk management should be kept in mind during each stage in the process of planning and managing a meeting, including (but not limited to):

- Choosing a destination and venue
- Planning the program (flow and traffic patterns, especially)
- Selecting speakers and entertainers
- Conducting the site inspection
- Negotiating contracts
- Purchasing insurance

Done properly, risk management becomes second nature. It becomes part of how meetings and business events are planned. A site inspection checklist, for example, may ask about square footage of meeting space, lighting, and other issues, but it should also be reviewed for emergency exits and nearby fire extinguishers and automated external defibrillators (AEDs).

Just like purchasing insurance, meeting and event professionals hope that they will never need to implement the measures in the risk plan. That would be a good thing because it means there was no crisis or emergency! But just like insurance, it takes only one crisis, disaster, or emergency to make the meeting professional glad to have incorporated risk management into their meeting planning and management process.

Now that you have completed this chapter you should be competent in the following Meetings and Business Events Competency Standards:

MBECS—Skill 6: Manage Risk Management Plan

Sub skills	Skills (standards)
C 6.01	Identify risks
C 6.02	Analyze risks
C 6.03	Develop management and implementation plan
C 6.04 C 6.05	Develop and implement emergency response Plan and arrange security

KEY WORDS AND TERMS

Risk Management
Emergency
Crisis
Disaster
Business Continuity
Risk Team

Risk Assessment
Risk Analysis
Probability-consequences
   Analysis
Commercial General liability
   Insurance (CGL)

Event Cancellation Insurance
Indemnification Clause
Cancellation Clause
Attrition Clause

REVIEW AND DISCUSSION QUESTIONS

1. Identify a recent crisis, disaster, or emergency (whether related to meetings or not) that you have seen in the news? What makes it a crisis or disaster or emergency?

2. Would you want to be a member of the Risk Team, the Response Team, or both? What skills or abilities do you have that you think would (or would not) make you a good fit for one of these teams?

3. Using a real meeting or business event in the city in which you live, conduct a risk assessment that identifies all of the risks that need to be considered. Circle the two you think are the most likely to occur and the two you think would have the most serious consequences (they may or may not be the same two).

4. If an alarm went off in your classroom, do you know what the emergency procedures are (stay where you are or evacuate)? If you evacuate and the building blows up, how would your instructor know whether you got out or not? Can you think of (or research) an emergency procedure that would ensure that he or she would know immediately who in the class got out?

5. Suppose the risk you are dealing with is the risk of food poisoning at a 2000-person conference. What risk mitigation measures would you put into place to minimize the risk of this occurring at a catered event? If it did happen, how would you respond?

6. How security personnel should be dressed (uniform, security t-shirt, plain clothes, etc.) and equipped (weapon, handcuffs, radio) is a big part of the decision in finding the right security for your meeting or business event. Discuss some different types of meetings and business events that might require different types of security.

REFERENCES

Bassett, M. (July 2006). A Planner's Cautionary Tale. Retrieved on July 29, 2012, from http://meetingsnet.com/news/securion_attendees/.

Canadian Tourism Human Resources Council. (2011). Meeting and Business Event Competency Standards, p. 22. Ottawa, Ontario, Canada.

Capello, J. (n.d.). Hurricane Katrina: An Overview. *EnviroMentor*. Retrieved on July 29, 2012, from http://www.asse.org/practicespecialties/environmental/docs/KatrinaSpecialNewsletter.pdf.

CNN Health. (2002, July 13). Dozens Sickened at Kansas City Conference. *CNN*. Retrieved on July 29, 2012, from http://articles.cnn.com/2002-07-13/health/kansascity.illness_1_hotel-guests-food-borne-illness-outbreak?_s=PM:HEALTH.

Convention Industry Council. (2010). APEX Industry Glossary—2011 edition. Retrieved on July 2, 2012, from http://www.conventionindustry.org/StandardsPractices/APEX/glossary.aspx.

Disaster Recovery Journal. (2008). Business Continuity Glossary. Retrieved on March 15, 2008, from http://www.drj.com/glossary/drjglossary.html.

Disaster Recovery Journal. (2012). Business Continuity Glossary by DRJ. Retrieved on July 2, 2012, from http://www.drj.com/tools/tools/glossary-2.html.

ESPN Olympic Sports. (2012, February 22). Security Test Staged in London Subway. *ESPN Olympic Sports*. Retrieved on July 26, 2012, from http://espn.go.com/olympics/story/_/id/7601164/uk-emergency-services-hold-big-olympics-test.

Event Safety & Security Services, LLC. (2012). Staffing Services. Retrieved on July 27, 2012, from http://eventsafetyservices.com/staffing_services.htm.

Hilliard, T. W., Scott-Halsell, S., and Palakurthi, R. (2011). Elements That Influence the Implementation of Crisis Preparedness Measures by Meeting Planners. *Journal of Contingencies and Crisis Management*, doi: 10.1111/j.1468-5973.2011.00644.x.

Kline, S., and Smith, S. (2006). *Crisis Planning for the Meeting, Planning and Convention Industry* (Report). Chicago, IL: Professional Convention Management Association.

National Fire Protection Association. (2007). *Standard on Disaster/Emergency Management and Business*

Continuity Programs (Report No. 1600). Quincy, MA: National Fire Protection Association.

Pearson, C. M., and Clair, J. A. (1998). Reframing Crisis Management. *Academy of Management, 23*(1), 59–76.

ABOUT THE CHAPTER CONTRIBUTOR

Tyra W. Hilliard, PhD, JD, CMP is an associate professor of Restaurant, Hospitality, and Meeting Management at the University of Alabama. She is also active in the meetings industry as a trainer and consultant. Early in her career, Tyra worked in the meetings industry as a meeting planner, a catering manager, a convention and visitors bureau representative and an association executive. Her combination of education and experience give her a unique perspective on the legal and risk management aspects of meeting and event management.

Stakeholder Management

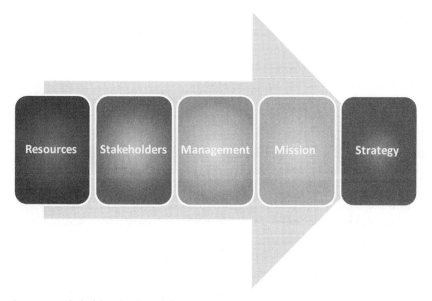

CHAPTER 5

Strategy stakeholders business diagram. © Kheng Guan Toh/Fotolia

Chapter Objectives

Upon completion of this chapter, the reader should be able to:

- Identify your stakeholders
- Determine potential impacts of stakeholders on meetings or events and vice versa
- Determine stakeholders' relationships in terms of power, influence, and interest
- Plan stakeholder programs and activities
- Manage stakeholder relationships

Chapter Outline

IDENTIFYING YOUR STAKEHOLDERS

What Is a Stakeholder?

A **stakeholder** is "any group or individual who can affect or is affected by the achievement of the organization's objectives" (Freeman, 1984: 46). This is certainly one of the most popular definitions of "stakeholder" in the literature. In contrast, Clarkson defined stakeholders as voluntary or involuntary risk-bearers: "Voluntary stakeholders bear some form of risk as a result of having invested some form of capital, human or financial, something of value, in a firm. Involuntary stakeholders are placed at risk as a result of a firm's activities. But, without the element of risk there is no stake" (Clarkson, 1994: 5). A risk or stake, in this sense, is either something or an opportunity that can be lost. In addition to the above definitions, it is very important to know that some stakeholders have a legal or moral stake in an organization, while other stakeholders may have an ability to influence an organization's behavior, direction, process, or outcome.

According to Savage, Nix, Whitehead, and Blair (1991), two attributes are necessary to identify a stakeholder: (1) a claim and (2) the ability to influence a firm. However, a rational analysis of these attributes pose these attributes as components of the definition of those with a stake in the organization (Brenner, 1993; Starik, 1994). These attributes can also be associated with stakeholders who have a legal stake (claim) in an organization. In contrast, there are also stakeholders who have a moral (ethical) stake in an organization. These stakeholders are mostly associated with corporate social responsibility (CSR) issues. Their main stake in an organization is to ensure that each organization is socially responsible within their environment.

Internal and External Stakeholders

Stakeholders can also be identified as either internal or external stakeholders. **Internal stakeholders** are groups or individuals that are directly working within an organization. Some of them might have a legal and/or moral stake in the organization, but the unique similarity between internal stakeholders is that they operate within the organization. Some examples of internal stakeholders include business owners, managers, and employees. In contrast, **external stakeholders** are groups or individuals who are not directly working within an organization, but are affected in one way or the other by the decisions or activities of the organization. Examples of external stakeholders include government officials, clients, sponsors, vendors, suppliers, community, special interest groups, participants, and the press/media. Based on the above description of internal and external stakeholders, it is not unusual for some external stakeholders to be both external and internal stakeholders at the same time if they are directly working within the organization.

Stakeholders' Interest in Event Planning

The concept of stakeholder is not limited to shareholders or owners of big companies alone. It includes managers, employees, clients, sponsors, vendors, suppliers, special interest groups, participants, the press/media, the local community, and the government who are directly or indirectly associated with event planning. Each stakeholder has at least one interest in the organization or a specific event. For instance, the sponsors of an event will be concerned with the return on their investment and/or the impact that sponsorship will have on their image. Similarly, clients will be concerned about the quality of the products and services provided by the event organizers. Exhibit 1 displays various stakeholders and some of their specific interests in regard to event planning.

EXHIBIT 1 Stakeholders and Their Interest in Event Planning

Stakeholders	Interests
Event Managers (planners or coordinators)	Income Salary Safety and security Successful event
Employees	Wage/Salary Safety and security Successful event Fair treatment
Sponsors	Return on investment (ROI) Sales and promotion opportunities Image building opportunities Awareness opportunities
Vendors	Return on investment (ROI) Sales and promotion opportunities
Shareholders/Creditors	Return on investment (ROI) Risk (stake) Cash flow Financial performance
Clients	Relative value of the event for the cost Quality of the event Safety and security Successful event
Suppliers	Prompt payment Repeat business Safety and security
Press/Media	Image building opportunities Awareness opportunities Safety and security
Participants	Safety and security Successful event
Local Community/Government	Lack of negative externalities Economic impact (employment, taxes, etc.) Lawful operations Safety and security Successful event

Opportunities and Challenges Stakeholders Present

Obviously, stakeholders are a great asset to event planning. They also bear some form of risk as a result of their having invested some form of capital, human resources, financial resources, and/or something of value, into either the event or the city in which the event is taking place. Hence, there are challenges that event professionals should be aware of and be ready to deal with in order to enjoy the benefits of having stakeholders. During meeting/event planning, an event professional must identify all stakeholders' concerns and develop the means to address these concerns. Some of these concerns are based on the claims promised to the stakeholders prior to the stakeholder's investment in the event, whereas other concerns are unpredictable issues that could arise because of the events or some activities related to the events.

Challenges are almost inevitable. The more the stakeholders are associated with an event, the more the challenges they present. This is simply because the interests of all the diverse stakeholders are not necessarily the same. This increases the possibility of divergent interests between the event professional and some of the stakeholders. An event professional's judgments can be affected by the divergent interests of the stakeholders. In order to mitigate the challenges of the stakeholders and enhance the opportunities they present, event professionals need to consider the following:

- Which stakeholders' interests are most important for the event and the future of the organization planning the event?
- Which stakeholders' interests are most likely to positively or negatively affect the image of the organization planning the event or the perception of the event?
- What is the level of each stakeholder's influence on the event and/or organization planning the event?

The solutions to these concerns are very critical to the survival of many organizations and to the events' production. Event professionals should take the above concerns seriously because the wrong solutions to the above concerns could negatively affect the **event production** and/or the organization planning the event. For example, if some sponsors provided funding for an event production that entitles the sponsors to some specified claims and the event professionals failed to deliver on the claims as agreed, the sponsors could stop funding the event in the future. As far as the sponsors are concerned, their claims should be given the highest priority regardless of other challenges the event professionals might be facing. Similarly, other stakeholders may have interests and priorities that could pose further challenges to the event professionals, thereby requiring rational and proactive solutions.

Just as stakeholders present some challenges to event professionals or organizations, they also present numerous opportunities for the event professionals by which to achieve their event or organization's objectives. In order for the opportunities to be fully realized, event professionals must be proactive in their endeavor to overcome the challenges the stakeholders might present.

Some of the best ways to overcome challenges and realize the potential opportunities is to include the following: effective collaboration between the event professionals and stakeholders, effective planning, keep promises (claims to stakeholders), have an awareness of the impact of the event in the community, and maintain excellent communication between the event professionals and all the concerned stakeholders. If event professionals are proactive about resolving the stakeholders' challenges, this will lead to opportunities for a successful and prosperous event. Exhibit 2 below outlines some challenges that each stakeholder might present and some potential solutions for event professionals.

EXHIBIT 2 Stakeholders' Challenges and Potential Solutions

Stakeholders	Challenges	Potential Solutions
1. Participants 2. Clients 3. Employees 4. Event Managers (planners or coordinators)	Safety and security	Plan for adequate security and safety prior to the event
	Successful event	Effective planning, effective collaboration between the event professionals and stakeholders, and excellent communication between the event professionals and all the concerned stakeholders
5. Sponsors	Return on investment (ROI)	Keep promises to sponsors (e.g., sponsors' literature distribution, complimentary registration, complimentary invitation to special receptions, and providing other opportunities to promote their products and/or services)
	Providing awareness and recognition	Recognize sponsors on website, programs, flyers, media/press, acknowledgment during sessions, and so on
6. Vendors	Sales and promotion opportunities	Provide vendors the opportunities to sell and promote their products and/or services, and encourage attendees to check out the vendors products
7. Shareholders/Creditors	Profit maximization	Effective planning and clear understanding of financial management
8. Suppliers	Prompt payment	Pay suppliers on time and as promised

EXHIBIT 2 (Continued)

Stakeholders	Challenges	Potential Solutions
9. Press/Media	Press questions on the community's critical matters	Rationally acknowledge the press/media as needed
	Response to safety and security concerns	Provide adequate security and safety for the event
10. Local Community/ Government	Lack of negative externalities	Prior communication about the impact of the event on the community
	Economic impact (employment and tax)	As much as possible keep the economic impact of the event within the community and encourage the payment of vendors' taxes
	Safety and security	Provide adequate security and safety for the event
	Successful event	Effective planning, effective collaboration between the event professionals and stakeholders, and excellent communication between the event professionals and all the concerned stakeholders

DETERMINING POTENTIAL IMPACTS OF STAKEHOLDERS

It is obvious that each stakeholder poses one challenge or another for event professionals. As a result, stakeholders will tend to take advantage of their legitimacy, power, and urgency in achieving their own interests. It is very critical for event professionals to manage their relationship with stakeholders with even greater legitimacy, power, and urgency without jeopardizing the relationship with others. In order to accomplish this objective, event professionals must determine the potential impact of their stakeholders on the event or the organization planning the event and vice versa. However, before describing the potential impact of stakeholders on the event or the organization planning the event and vice versa, it will be clearer if legitimacy, power, and urgency are concisely described in regard to the stakeholders' management.

Legitimacy

Suchman defines **legitimacy** as "a generalized perception or assumption that the actions of an entity are desirable, proper, or appropriate within some socially constructed system of norms, values, beliefs, and definitions" (Suchman, 1995: 574). This definition could be further simplified and defined as the notion that the action of a stakeholder is proper within some socially accepted value system. A careful and rational analysis of these definitions implies that legitimacy may mean different things at varying levels of social organization, as well as having a different meaning to people with different socially accepted value systems. Bearing the above in mind, this is explicitly why event professionals must learn to manage their relationships with stakeholders with more legitimacy in regard to the event professional's activity or organization, without jeopardizing the relationship with others.

Power

One of the common definitions of power derived from the Weberian idea of **power** is "the ability of one actor within a social relationship to carry out his own will despite resistance" (Weber, 1947). According to Pfeffer, power is "a relationship among social actors in which one social actor, A, can get another social actor, B, to do something that B would not otherwise have done" (Pfeffer, 1981: 3). Therefore, a stakeholder in a relationship may have enough power, based on their stake in an event or the organization planning the event, to impose their will on the relationship. Since this sort of power is not permanent, it can be lost based on the context of the relationship. The issue of this sort of stakeholders' power is a major challenge for event professionals, who are trying to maximize their benefits from the most powerful stakeholders without jeopardizing the relationship with other stakeholders. Regardless of the challenge, event professionals must be rational in their decision-making process not to overlook the impact of other stakeholders' power in their attempt to satisfy the claims of their most powerful stakeholders.

Urgency   According to Mitchell, Agle, and Wood (1997), **urgency**, in regard to stakeholder management, can be defined as the intensity to which stakeholders' claims call for immediate attention. Urgency is very paramount when a relationship or claim is highly time-sensitive and when that relationship or claim is very important to the claimants. Some examples of why a stakeholder would view its relationship with an event or the organization planning the event as being very important include the following:

- The stakeholder's ownership of event-specific assets, or those assets tied to an event that cannot be used in a different way without loss to the event professionals or the organization planning the event.
- The stakeholder's expectation that the event professionals will continue to satisfy their interest because of their stake in the event or the organization planning the event.

Bearing the above in mind, it is obvious that some stakeholders have more influence over an event than the others. Thus, event professionals must not hesitate to adopt all the necessary means to avoid promoting the benefit of one stakeholder at the expense of others.

Stakeholder Roles, Desired Support, and Resulting Obligations

Event professionals are increasingly soliciting support when executing events. One of the most popular groups that event professionals explore for support is their stakeholders. The role of their stakeholders in this regard falls within the interest of any of the following: sponsors, vendors, and/or attendees. Whatever the role and interest of each stakeholder is (sponsor, vendor, and/or attendee), each of them will support the event professionals either via financial means or by gifts in-kind.

Sponsors

Sponsors are stakeholders that contribute to the support of an event via financial means or by "in-kind" donations of products or services that reduce the cost of producing the event. Event professionals should ensure that "sponsorships in-kind" is useful toward the production of the event and actually reduces the cost of producing the event. If sponsorship in-kind is not useful toward the production of the specific event, the desired support from the sponsors' concerned will not be attained, and the event professionals will be providing claims to the sponsors in exchange for what is not useful toward the event production. For example, a sponsor that provides marketing and publicity that usually costs $30,000 or more, at no cost in exchange for access to the event attendees, is a splendid way for the event professionals to reduce $30,000 or more in the cost of producing the event. Sponsorship spending in North America and in the global arena is a big business. In 2011, over $18 billion was spent on sponsorship in North America alone, and about $48.7 billion was spent on sponsorship worldwide (IEG, Inc., 2011).

Based on the cost of sponsorships, it is not inconceivable for the sponsors to expect certain obligation(s) from the event professionals as a result of their sponsorship.

Event professionals should emphasize how the sponsorship of their event would do one or more of the following:

- Help the potential sponsors' sales and enhance their visibility in society.
- Create or enhance the image of the potential sponsors as well as their product(s) and/or service(s), especially if they are supporting a not-for-profit community event.
- Create awareness not only about potential sponsors' generosity, but also about the sponsor's involvement in the community, which will ultimately set the sponsor apart from the rest of their competitors.

Due to the different level of sponsorship possibilities, the event professional should develop a benefits package outlining the desired support and the resulting obligation to sponsors. Exhibit 3 and 4 display different examples of sponsorship benefit grids. Exhibit 3 is applicable to big or multiple-day events with a high volume of attendees (target market) which appeal to the sponsors. Exhibit 4 is applicable to small or one-day events with a low volume of attendees (target market) which appeal to the sponsors. In addition, Exhibit 5 displays a different example of sponsorship benefit that is mostly applicable at expositions or trade shows.

Event professionals seeking sponsorships should explain to potential sponsors, prior to the conclusion of the sponsorship contract or agreement, the importance of effective planning in order to maximize the benefits received from their sponsorship. In addition, it is very important for the event professionals to collaborate effectively with the sponsors, develop good communication with them, and, to top it all off, deliver on their resulting obligations or claims to sponsors.

EXHIBIT 3 Sponsorship Benefit Grid

BENEFITS	DIAMOND $100,000 plus	PLATINUM $75,000 -$99,999	GOLD $50,000 -$74,999	SILVER $25,000 -$49,999	BRONZE $10,000 -$24,999
Online attendee registration confirmation ad	*				
Event professional website banner ad	*	*			
Attendee newsletter banner ad	*	*			
Registration bag insert ad	*	*	*		
Opportunity to use the pre- and post-conference registration list with certain guidelines	*	*	*		
Acknowledgment during one or more of the general sessions	Verbal and Visual (Logo)	Visual (Logo)	Scrolling Listing	Scrolling Listing	Scrolling Listing
Recognition in the conference preliminary program	Brief Description + Logo	Brief Description + Logo	Logo	Listing	Listing
Recognition in the conference final program	Logo	Logo	Logo	Listing	Listing
Recognition in the organization or a media partner's magazine following the annual conference	Logo	Logo	Logo	Listing	Listing
Conference lobby banner ad	Logo	Logo	Logo	Listing	Listing
Signage recognizing the sponsor at the annual conference	Logo	Logo	Logo	Listing	Listing
Complimentary conference registration	5	4	3	2	1
Invitation to the chair's reception	5	4	3	2	1
Invitation to the president's VIP reception	5	4	3	2	1

EXHIBIT 4 Sponsorship Benefit Grid

		Verbal and Visual Recognition During the Event	On-Site Promotion and Sales	Media Recognition (TV, Radio, and/or Newspaper)	Personal Poster for Your Business	Poster and/or Flyer Ads	Featured on the Event Website
Diamond	$1000 and above	*	*	*	*	*	Logo
Platinum	$750 to $999		*	*	*	*	Logo
Gold	$500 to $749		*	*	*	*	Logo
Silver	$250 to $499			*	*	*	Listing
Bronze	$100 to $249				*	*	Listing

EXHIBIT 5 Sponsorship Marketing Contract

	Value of Desired Support*	Resulting Obligation
Pre-Event Sponsorship Opportunities	$1,000/month (Exclusive opportunity)	Attendee Newsletter Banner Ad
	$1,500/month (Exclusive opportunity)	Event Professional Website Banner Ad
	$2,500 (Exclusive opportunity)	Online Attendee Registration Confirmation Ad
	$3,000 (Exclusive opportunity)	Preliminary Program Ad
On-site Sponsorship Opportunities	$1,500 each (Multiple opportunities)	Network Lounge Ad
	$1,500 each (Multiple opportunities)	Registration Counter Ad
	$3,000 each (Multiple opportunities)	Standing Sign Boards Ad
	$5,000 each (Multiple opportunities)	Attendee Lunch Ad
	$5,000 each (Multiple opportunities)	Event/Expo Hall Banner Ad
	$5,000 each (Multiple opportunities)	Lobby Banner Ad
	$6,000 each (Multiple opportunities)	Conference Pen Ad
	$6,000 (Exclusive opportunity)	Registration Bag Insert Ad
	$10,000 (Exclusive opportunity)	Hotel Room Key Card Ad
	$15,000 (Exclusive opportunity)	Registration Bag Ad
Final Program Sponsorship Opportunities	$3,000 each (Multiple opportunities)	Final Program – Full Page Ad
	$4,000 (Exclusive opportunity)	Final Program – Inside Front Cover Ad
	$4,000 (Exclusive opportunity)	Final Program – Inside Back Cover Ad
	$7,000 (Exclusive opportunity)	Final Program – Front Cover Ad
	$6,000 (Exclusive opportunity)	Final Program – Back Cover Ad

*The value of each desired support varies depending on the need of the event professionals and the target market (attendees) that will be exposed to the resulting obligation (the ads).

Vendors

Vendors are stakeholders who, in the form of a merchant, pay a specified fee to sell their products at an event venue. The vendor fee is another source of financial support for event professionals. Thus, event professionals must take time to plan for vendor management and promotions. Some of the critical questions they should answer include the following:

- Why should a vendor be associated with their event?
- What are the vendors' limitations in terms of products and/or services?
- What should be the vendors' rate?
- Should there be different rates for different vendors or for different square feet of space?

- How should vendors handle the income tax issues?
- Who is going to be the vendor coordinator?
- How many vendors are needed, and how many could sell the same products/services?
- Should we use exclusive vendors for each product/service?
- What are the rules and regulations for vendors, and how does it apply to the community?
- What is the impact of each vendor on the community?
- How should the vendor be promoted?

It is very important for event professionals to understand the need for vendors in their events. Vendors actually add more value to events because they provide various products, including foods and beverages, that are appealing to attendees. In fact, it is not uncommon for event professionals to partner with vendors to promote their events while promoting the vendor at the same time. Regardless of the level of planning for vendor management and promotions, event professionals should endeavor to point out the vendor benefits if they participate in their event. Potential benefits event professionals should point out include the following:

- The use of the event professional's website to promote vendors through a link or a logo/link (if provided).
- The pre-event and during-event promotion of vendors to all attendees.
- The promotion of vendors in the event program.
- The vendors' website links for vendors in good standing will remain on the event professional's website until edits are due for the next event.
- The promotion of vendors via the event professional's social media.

Just as it is important for event professionals to emphasize vendors' benefits, they should also stress vendors' limitations in terms of products and/or services as well as the rules and policies all vendors must obey. Event professionals are highly encouraged to take a comprehensive approach to plan for vendor management and promotions in order to maximize the benefits of vendor partnership.

Attendees

Attendees include any of the stakeholders in Exhibit 1. In most events, including association meetings, attendees are the major source of financial resources for the event professionals. In fact, without attendees there is no event. The importance of attendees to each event cannot be overemphasized. Hence, just as event professionals should develop a strategic plan to attract sponsors and vendors to their event, they must also plan to attract a lot of attendees to the event. Without attendees, the sponsors and vendors will not benefit from the event. Following the example described above, a sponsor who provides marketing and publicity, which usually costs $30,000 or more, at no cost, in exchange for access to the event attendees, will certainly not be happy without attendees or enough attendees to justify the value of the investment. Hence, event professionals must offer appealing and benefiting programs to attract attendees to their events.

It is obvious that event professionals need the support of the attendees at the event to make the sponsors, vendors, and many other stakeholders happy. Thus, the event professionals' obligation to the attendees is to ensure that the programs and entertainment planned for the event are good enough to keep the attendees coming to their events. In addition, event professionals must plan a great marketing campaign that appeals to the target markets. For the marketing campaign to appeal to many attendees, the event professionals should consider including advance information about the following in their campaign:

- Date and location of the event
- Key attractions in the event destination
- Benefits and opportunities of the event to attendees
- Planned content and entertainment for the event
- Event keynote speakers and other special speakers
- Things to do in the event destination
- Accommodation and transportation at the event destination
- Potential scholarship or financial support for the event
- Job opportunities, career networking, coaching opportunities, and so on
- Availability of internet accessibility and Wi-Fi lounges with recharging stations at meeting venues (if available)

Most importantly, the event professionals should make sure that all that was promoted via the marketing campaign are readily available for the attendees as promised. They should also take advantage of various marketing channels and communications mix in order to reach most of their target market and/or attendees.

Developing Plans for Alliances

In order to maximize the revenue and other benefits from stakeholders, event professionals have to take a better assessment of their assets and develop plans for alliances before approaching the stakeholders. In order for the plans to be more attractive, event professionals might consider the following when developing the plans:

Strategy: The plan should be strategic enough to attract any of the stakeholders (such as sponsors or vendors) to build a long-term relationship that will provide them with the desired value over the duration of the relationship.

Economy: What is the economic importance of the plan to the stakeholders and the event planners? A good plan for alliances should not only provide economic benefit to the stakeholders, but should also be economically profitable for the event professional.

Politics: The government is a major stakeholder with interests that need to be satisfied. A good plan should consider the interest of the government with a clear outline of how the government interest (such as tax, safety, and security) will be attained.

Local: It is very essential for the event professional to develop local alliances in the community where the event will take place. Promoting the benefits of the event to the local community should be a big component of the plan.

Regional: Similar to local plans, event professionals should develop regional alliances with the communities where the event will take place. Promoting the benefits of the event to the region should be a big component of the event professional's plans for alliance.

National: Most events are not restricted to one local community or region. Hence, an event professional who is involved with nationally recognized events should develop alliance with various regions of the nation where the event could take place. In addition, the event professionals or the organizations planning such events need to maintain a good public image across the nation.

International: Similar to national plans for alliance, an event professional should develop international plans for alliances with other nations where the event could take place. Promoting the benefits of the event to these nations should be a big component of the event professional's plans for alliance.

Each of these plans should be developed to highlight stakeholders' roles, desired support, and the obligation of the event professionals to satisfy the stakeholders' interests. The sponsors benefit grid and marketing contract (Exhibits 3, 4, and 5) are good examples of well-developed plans for alliance with sponsors.

STAKEHOLDERS' RELATIONSHIPS

It is obvious that the event professionals and stakeholders have a relationship. However, what is the nature of that relationship in terms of power, influence, and interests? The nature of the relationship could affect the extent of the stakeholders' dependency on the event professionals for upholding their rights and achieving their interest and vice versa. Event professionals should be aware of the implications of overdependence on a stakeholder.

Power

If an event professional is overdependent on a stakeholder, the stakeholder will have power over the event or the event professional's ability to satisfy other interests without the stakeholder's approval. The stakeholder's influencing power over the event professional can disrupt the event so severely that other stakeholders' interests cannot be met. This could lead to a situation whereby the event would cease to occur, and the organization planning the event may not survive without the support of the stakeholder. Event professionals are urged to solicit similar support from multiple stakeholders in order to prevent overdependency on one dominant stakeholder.

Influence

A stakeholder could exert undue influence on an event professional that is overdependence on the stakeholder. In order not to disrupt the interest of the event professional and other stakeholders, the event professional needs to maintain a mutually dependent relationship with the stakeholder, a relationship in which the stakeholder cannot overpower or over-influence the event professional. The event professional must also develop a reasonably good relationship with other stakeholders in order to prevent the influential stakeholder from negatively influencing other stakeholders. As a result, the influential stakeholder will have a legitimate claim on the event or the organization planning the event because of its investment (resources), without implicating the interest of other stakeholders and the event professional.

Interest

Another common **stakeholder relationship** with an event professional or the organization planning the event is the stakeholder's legitimate interest in the event. This interest could sometimes be challenging to event professionals if the stakeholders tend to overpower or over-influence the event professionals with their legitimate interest on the event. Event professionals should be aware of this possibility and strive to satisfy the interest of such stakeholders without jeopardizing the interest of other stakeholders.

PLANNING STAKEHOLDERS PROGRAMS AND ACTIVITIES

The importance of making stakeholders happy cannot be overemphasized. In most event planning organizations, stakeholders are important to event professionals because of what they provide to make events successful, such as funds, materials, or services that will help reduce the cost of producing the event. In addition, some stakeholders can impact the success or failure of an event through their action or inaction. Hence, event professionals must do everything they can to make their stakeholders happy. Planning stakeholders' programs and activities is a great approach to making stakeholders happy. When planning programs and activities for stakeholders, event professionals should be mindful of the following factors:

- Be aware of varied interests and goals of stakeholders
- Plan activities that meet the needs of stakeholders
- Develop plans for dealing with stakeholders
- Establish protocols
- Plan sequence and flow of stakeholder activities
- Interact with stakeholders

Be Aware of Varied Interests and Goals of Stakeholders

As displayed in Exhibit 1, event professionals have various stakeholders with different interests. It is very essential for event professionals to plan programs and activities that will make each of the stakeholders happy. It is not unusual for some stakeholders to be more satisfied than the others based on their stakes or investment in the event or the organization planning the event. However, it is very critical for event professionals to consider the following questions when planning programs and activities for stakeholders with varied interests and goals:

1. What is the importance of each stakeholder to our event?
2. What is the stake or investment of each stakeholder in our event or organization?
3. What is the interest of each stakeholder in our event or organization?
4. What opportunities and challenges does each stakeholder present?
5. What kind of programs or activities will satisfy each stakeholder?

Solutions to the above questions will help event professionals plan programs and activities for stakeholders with varied interests and goals. Obviously, planning programs and activities for stakeholders with varied interests and goals might not be easy. In fact, some stakeholders might be happier or benefit more from the events than the others. However, what the event professionals should be concerned about is their ability to involve each of the concerned stakeholders in one or more programs and activities that will satisfy its interest. For example, Exhibit 3 displays different benefits for different levels of sponsorship. In regard to the sponsors' invitation to the chair's reception and an invitation to the president's VIP reception (the last two benefits in the Sponsorship Benefit Grid), you will notice that even though all the sponsors were included in those activities, some sponsors were given more opportunities to attend than the others.

Plan Activities that Meet the Needs of Stakeholders

What is the benefit to your stakeholders if you plan programs and activities that do not meet their needs? Event professionals must do everything possible to consider the interests of each stakeholder when planning programs and activities for the stakeholders. Some of the programs and activities event professionals should consider when planning activities to meet the needs of their stakeholders include the following:

1. Invitation to committee meetings
2. Invitation to site tours
3. Recognition of stakeholders at pre-event programs

4. Verbal and visual recognition at programs and activities
5. Awarding sponsors during appreciation activities

Develop Plans for Dealing with Stakeholder' Concerns

No matter how great the programs and activities event professionals planned for stakeholders are, they should also plan for potential stakeholders' concerns that may arise during the programs and activities. Some of these concerns may be due to unintentional or intentional exclusion of some stakeholders in the planning and/or production of the programs and activities set aside for stakeholders. Event professionals should have contingency plans in place to take care of such concerns, even if it means giving the concerned stakeholders more recognition than they deserve. For example, in an event in which each individual on the entire board of directors was supposed to be honored at the board meeting, two members of the board of directors were left out by mistake. A splendid contingency plan undertaken by the organization was that the two board members were both honored at the organization's reception dinner in the presence of hundreds of other stakeholders. A mistake that would have cost the organization a lot of negativity was turned to a memorable award and recognition for the stakeholders.

Protocols

When planning programs and activities for stakeholders, event professionals are urged to develop protocols that can be followed. It is very essential for the protocol to be developed into a manual and enhanced as necessary. The protocol should contain all kinds of special programs and activities that could be planned for stakeholders from time to time. Some of the special programs and activities that event professionals should consider including in the protocol are as follows:

1. Stakeholders' award and recognition gala
2. Chair's reception gala
3. President's VIP gala
4. VIP treatment
5. Dress codes for various different events as necessary

Plan Sequence and Flow of Stakeholder Activities

Event professionals could satisfy various stakeholders' interest by planning stakeholders' programs and activities that follow an organized sequence and flow. Organized stakeholders' programs and activities with a planned sequence and flow could prevent event professionals from unintentionally excluding some stakeholders in the programs and activities set aside for stakeholders. When planning stakeholders' programs and activities that follow an organized sequence and flow, event professionals should consider including the following in the plans:

1. The interest of each stakeholder
2. The programs or activities that could satisfy each stakeholder
3. An organized schedule that provides stakeholders the opportunity to be involved
4. Avoid conflicting scheduling of activities that are of interest to a stakeholder
5. Develop an itinerary for each stakeholder, highlighting some of the activities that might be of interest to them

Interaction with Stakeholders

One of the best ways to overcome stakeholders' challenges and realize the potential opportunities they present is to maintain excellent communication with them. Similarly, when planning stakeholders' programs and activities, event professionals must endeavor to interact with stakeholders and keep them informed about the activities that are specially planned for them. The system of interaction must be as effective as possible, and the information should be the correct amount without overcommunicating or under-communicating. Event professionals should also be mindful of the different channels of communication and the best channels for each stakeholder. When in doubt, event professionals should use all the possible channels of communication to interact with their stakeholders in order to increase the chances of getting the information to as many stakeholders as possible. When interacting with stakeholders, event professionals should consider starting with high-power, high-influence, and high-interest stakeholders in a sequence that will allow all the necessary stakeholders to be contacted including stakeholders with low-power, low-influence, and low-interest.

MANAGING STAKEHOLDERS' RELATIONSHIPS

Event professionals that are good at managing stakeholders' relationships will increase their chances of planning successful and profitable events. Stakeholders are obviously different interest groups, each with the capability to influence an event's outcome negatively or positively. Event professionals should know their stakeholders' interests, challenges, level of power, level of influence, and other necessary characteristics that will aid them in managing the stakeholders' relationships. The amount of time event professionals should allocate to stakeholder management depends on the impact of the stakeholders on the event, the available time for communication, and the resources needed to ensure a successful event or the desired outcome. Event professionals should consider the following factors when managing stakeholders' relationships:

- Identification of the stakeholders
- Stakeholders' interests and challenges
- Legitimacy, power, and urgency of stakeholders
- Effective communication with stakeholders
- Plan programs and activities that would ensure stakeholders' claims or benefits

Event professionals must be aware that communication is very critical in the management of stakeholders' relationships. The factors offered above should be coupled with strategic communication plans, the missions, goals, and objectives of the event professionals and the impact of the event on the stakeholders in order to successfully manage stakeholders' relationships.

SUMMARY

A stakeholder is "any group or individual who can affect or is affected by the achievement of the organization's objectives" (Freeman, 1984: 46). This is certainly one of the most popular definitions of stakeholder in the literature.

Voluntary stakeholders are stakeholders that bear some form of stake or risk because of their investment in an organization.

Involuntary stakeholders are stakeholders that are placed at risk as a result of an organization's activities in the society.

A stake or risk in this sense is either something or an opportunity that can be lost.

Internal stakeholders are groups or individuals that are directly working within an organization. Some of them might have a legal and/or moral stake in the organization, but the unique similarity between internal stakeholders is that they operate within the organization.

External stakeholders are groups or individuals who are not directly working within an organization, but are affected in one way or the other by the decisions or activities of the organization.

Some of the challenges stakeholders present are concerns based on the claims promised to the stakeholders prior to the stakeholder's investment in the event, whereas other concerns are unpredictable issues that could arise because of the events or some activities related to the events.

Some stakeholders will tend to take advantage of their legitimacy, power, and urgency in achieving their selfish interests. Hence, it is very important for event professionals to critically manage their relationships with stakeholders with a higher level of legitimacy, power, and urgency in order not to jeopardize the relationship with other stakeholders.

Event professionals should ensure that sponsors and other high-power and high-interest stakeholders expected claims are met as much as possible. It is better for event professionals to over deliver on the claims of sponsors and other high-power and high-interest stakeholders than to under deliver. The interest of these stakeholders should take priority because of the importance of their investment toward the production of the event and the reduction in the cost of producing the event.

Now that you have completed this chapter, you should be competent in the following Meetings and Business Events Competency Standards:

MBECS—Skill 15: Manage Stakeholder Relationships

Sub skills	Skills (standards)
G 15.01	Identify stakeholders
G 15.02	Assess stakeholders
G 15.03	Classify stakeholders
G 15.04	Manage stakeholder activities

KEY WORDS AND TERMS

Stakeholder	Event Production	Sponsors
Internal Stakeholder	Legitimacy	Vendors
External Stakeholder	Power	Attendee(s)
Stakeholder's Interest	Urgency	Stakeholder's Relationship

REVIEW QUESTIONS

1. What is a stakeholder?
2. Why is it important to manage stakeholders while planning events?
3. What is the difference between a voluntary or involuntary stakeholder? Give two examples of each.
4. What is the difference between internal and external stakeholder? Give two examples of each.
5. Why do you need a stakeholder for an event?
6. List three event production stakeholders, describe the stakeholders' roles and desired support, and the event professional's obligations?
7. What are the issues that event planners need to address when managing stakeholders' relationships?

REFERENCES

Brenner, S. N. 1993. The Stakeholder Theory of the Firm and Organizational Decision Making: Some Propositions and a Model. In J. Pasquero and D. Collins (Eds.), *Proceedings of the Fourth Annual Meeting of the International Association for Business and Society*, 205–210. San Diego.

Clarkson, M. 1994. *A Risk Based Model of Stakeholder Theory*. Proceedings of the Second Toronto Conference on Stakeholder Theory. Toronto: Centre for Corporate Social Performance & Ethics, University of Toronto.

Freeman, R. E. 1984. Strategic Management: A Stakeholder Approach. Boston, MA: Pitman.IEG. Inc. (2011). Sponsorship Spending: 2010 Proves Better Than Expected; Bigger Gains Set for 2011. Retrieved November 19, 2012 from http://www.sponsorship.com/IEG/files/fc/fcbe683b-d2a8-4f0b-9b35-121a86ab3a2b.pdf.

Mitchell, R. K., Agle, B. R., and Wood, D. J. (1997). Toward a Theory of Stakeholder Identification and Salience: Defining the Principle of Who and What Really Counts. *Academy of Management Review*, 22 (4), 853–886.

Pfeffer, J. 1981. *Power in Organizations*. Marshfield, MA: Pitman. Professional Convention Management Association, (2006). *Professional Meeting Management*, 5th ed. Kendall/Hunt Publishing Company, Dubuque, Iowa.

Savage, G. T., Nix, T. H., Whitehead, C. J., and Blair, J. D. 1991. Strategies for Assessing and Managing Organizational Stakeholders. *Academy of Management Executive*, 5: 61–75.

Starik, M. 1994. Essay by Mark Starik, pp. 89–95 of the Toronto Conference: Reflections on Stakeholder Theory. Business & Society, 33: 82–131.

Suchman, M. C. 1995. Managing Legitimacy: Strategic and Institutional Approaches. *Academy of Management Review*, 20: 571–610.

Weber, M. 1947. *The Theory of Social and Economic Organization*. New York: Free Press.

ABOUT THE CHAPTER CONTRIBUTOR

Godwin-Charles Ogbeide, PhD, MBA, is a faculty member in the department of Food, Human Nutrition, and Hospitality Management at the University of Arkansas Fayetteville. He is an active member of the Professional Convention Management Association (PCMA) and the International Council on Hotel, Restaurant, and Institutional Education (I-CHRIE). His teaching/research interests are in the areas of Meetings, Events, and Convention Management, and Strategic Management and Leadership Development in the Hospitality Industry. Dr. Ogbeide is an award-winning professor with over twenty-five years of experience in the hospitality industry, a member of I-CHRIE Strategic Committee, a board member of ICHRIE, and a member of PCMA Faculty Task Force.

Accounting and Financial Planning

CHAPTER 6

Good financial planning helps balance revenues and expenses in your meeting or event. James Graham, Dorling Kindersley

Chapter Objectives

Upon completion of this chapter, the reader should be able to:

- Undertake accounting responsibilities and evaluate the return on investment and the return on equity
- Define, determine, analyze, and construct a budget based on organizational goals and objectives
- Establish registration and other pricing for events
- Establish a budget review, cash control, and other financial procedures
- Manage cash and cash flow

Chapter Outline

INTRODUCTION TO ACCOUNTING AND FINANCE ESSENTIALS

Today's meeting and event planner (hereafter referred to as event professional) functions at a higher strategic level of thinking than ever before. Planning competencies include an understanding of accounting and finance fundamentals that afford the event professional the opportunity not only to contribute to the growth and financial success of the organization, but also to effectively demonstrate those contributions.

Essential Terminology

There is no expectation that event professionals possess the same financial knowledge as certified public accountants. However, event professionals must have enough knowledge of accounting and financial basics to be able to read and evaluate financial statements, create and adjust budgets, and understand the entire process of cash inflows and outflows. Such knowledge includes an understanding of accounting and finance terminology.

Accounting Methods   Accrual and cash are the two primary accounting methods. The accrual method of accounting records revenue and expenses at the time they are *committed*, while the cash method records revenue and expenses at the time they are *transacted*. To illustrate the difference, consider a fiscal year that runs from January through December. The event professional is responsible for planning a meeting in March of that fiscal year, but work began eighteen months prior to March, with transactions taking place within and outside the fiscal year. Using the cash method, the revenue received prior to the current fiscal year is reflected on the prior year's financial statements, while, using the accrual method, the revenue is shown on the prior year's financial statements as current liabilities. At the end of the prior year, journal entries are made in the accrual system to move the revenue from current liabilities to appropriate revenue categories.

Expenses are treated in the same manner. For example, contractual obligations to pay for meeting space are often paid in installments or deposits, with the deposit due in a prior accounting period. Using the cash method, any deposits are recorded and reflected in the prior period, while, using the accrual method, the deposit would be shown in the prior period as a current asset (usually classified as prepaid expenses), and, in the current fiscal year, moved to the appropriate expense category.

Assets and Liabilities   An asset is anything of value owned by or due to the organization, while a liability is anything that the organization owes.

Accounts Payable and Accounts Receivable   *Accounts payable* or liabilities are the amounts an organization owes for purchased goods or services on credit from a supplier or vendor. *Accounts receivable* or assets refer to amounts an organization can collect for sales of goods or services on credit to a customer.

Break-Even Analysis/Break-Even Point   Break-even analysis is a process when revenue and expense items are adjusted until a break-even point is reached—revenue equals expenses. Break-even analysis is based on two types of costs: fixed costs and variable costs. Fixed costs are overhead-type expenses that are constant and do not change as the level of output changes. Variable costs are not constant, change with the level of output, and are frequently stated on a per unit basis. A third type of cost, *indirect costs*, is used by some organizations to assess a portion of wages and other expenses to the meeting. Indirect costs are included in fixed costs.

The **chart of accounts** is a uniform system by the organization to define specific groups of items for both monies received (revenue) and spent (expense).

Many organizations use a **double-entry bookkeeping system**, which is a method by which every transaction is entered into at least two different accounts; one of the entries is a **credit** and the other a **debit**. Credits *increase* balances in liability, revenue, and capital accounts and *decrease* balances in asset and expense accounts. Debits *increase* balances in asset and expense accounts and *decrease* balances in liability, revenue, and capital accounts.

A **contribution margin** is the difference between total sales revenue and total variable costs. The term is applied to a product or product lines and generally is expressed as a percentage. For example, after subtracting total variable costs from sales, the annual contribution margin was calculated to be 42 percent. In other words, for each dollar (USD) of sales, 42 cents was left to contribute toward direct costs and profit.

Financial Statements   Several financial statements illustrate the financial health of the organization.

Balance sheet. The **balance sheet** (called a **statement of financial position** in not-for-profit organizations) is a picture of the organization at a given point in time and reflects the assets owned, liabilities owed, and residual net assets.

Income or profit and loss statement. The **income or profit and loss statement** (called a **statement of activities** in not-for-profit organizations) shows financial activity, reporting revenue generated, expenses incurred, and results in net profit/loss.

Statement of cash flows. A **statement of cash flows known as a cash flow statement** is a financial statement that shows changes in balance sheet accounts, income cash, and cash equivalents and breaks the analysis down to operating, investing, and financing activities. Essentially, the cash flow statement is concerned with the flow of cash in and out of the business. As an analytical tool, the statement of cash flows is useful in determining the short-term viability of an organization, particularly its ability to pay bills. Exhibitions realize a substantial amount of income far in advance of the actual event. Effective use of the statement of cash flows affords the organization the opportunity to make substantial revenue-producing short-term investments until the funds are needed to pay expenses.

Both the income and cash flow statements are important finance tools for the event professional. Financial software makes it easy to create income statements that compare budget to actual amounts, illustrating variances in actual amounts, percentage differences, or both and allows the event professional to quickly and accurately track the status of budgeted items. The income (profit and loss) statement is also useful to the event professional as it shows the status for a current month, for year-to-date, and for prior year comparison.

An analysis of Table 1 reveals that the current year's performance compared to the prior year is positive, with a substantial increase in net income over the prior year. However, a review of the expense items might raise questions as to why there was a significant decrease in marketing expenses. It may signal problems or may simply result from cost-effective marketing efforts. The event professional who understands how to read and analyze this type of statement can confidently discuss the variances and provide reasonable explanations for the decrease.

Most organizations either have an accounting or finance department that manages all matters of finance. Various brands of accounting software are used to track financial and reporting activities. However, the reports generated from financial software are often easily exportable to user-friendly spreadsheet software, where a "comments" section can be added to address issues and answers that arise in reviewing reports.

TABLE 1 Sample Income Statement – Prior Year Comparison

Income	This Month	Year-to-Date	Prior Year	Actual Change
Registration Fees	$10,000	$175,000	$165,000	$10,000
Sponsorship	$50,000	$125,000	$110,000	$15,000
Social Events	$15,000	$25,000	$15,000	$10,000
Total	$75,000	$325,000	$190,000	$35,000
Expenses	**This Month**	**Year-to-Date**	**Prior Year**	**Actual Change**
Facility Rental	$5,000	$35,000	$32,000	$3,000
Food and Beverage	$35,000	$75,000	$72,000	$3,000
Marketing and Promotion	$25,000	$40,000	$50,000	$<10,000>
Total	$65,000	$150,000	$154,000	$<4,000>
Net Income	$10,000	$250,000	$36,000	$39,000

The value to the event professional is that by tracking activities for the current event being planned and by entering comments and variances on the spreadsheet, the budgeting process, as discussed later in this chapter, becomes a more accurate process for the next event.

Undertake Financial Management

Determine Budget Philosophy   Prior to developing an event budget, it is necessary to clarify the organization's financial objectives and **budget philosophy**. There are three budget philosophies:

1. Make a profit, meaning revenue received exceeds expenses paid out
2. Break-even, meaning that revenue minus expenses equals zero
3. Lose money, meaning expenses paid out are in excess of revenues received.

Why would an organization intentionally decide to lose money? There may be several reasons for this. The event may be internal to the organization, such as sales meetings, when expenses are incurred but revenue is not generated. Another reason may be that the event is a *first time* event, and the organization is willing to take a loss in year one but expects the event to realize profitability in the next business cycles.

Determine Potential Sources of Revenue   The major sources for event revenue are sales, registration fees, exhibitor fees, advertising, sponsorships (including in-kind contributions), and grants.

Sales. An event may feature ancillary events for which tickets may be sold, such as a fun run, a golf tournament, or a concert. Products and souvenirs, such as event-branded merchandise (tee shirts, ball caps, key chains, and other event mementos), can produce additional revenue for the event, as can educational materials, such as CDs or other recordings of educational sessions made available post-event.

Attendee registration. This source of revenue is the amount charged the attendee to participate in the event. As discussed later in this chapter, setting early, advance, and on-site registration fees is one strategy to help in achieving budget goals for attendee registration.

Exhibit sales. Exhibit sales often constitute the largest portion of an event's revenue, assuming the event features an exhibition. Booth sales can be divided by type of booth/stand (island, peninsula, end cap, in-line), for which rates can be set based on the date the exhibit contract is processed (early, advance, and on-site). Exhibit sales may also promote additional revenue sources, such as advertising, promotions, and exhibitor badges (for booth staff beyond those allowed in the exhibit space contract).

Advertising. A well-thought-out advertising strategy produces additional revenue for the event. Web-based advertising for the event, in addition to pre- and on-site materials, such as a conference program, are other sources of potential revenue.

Sponsorships. Next to exhibit sales, sponsorships can be one of the largest sources of revenue for the event, if properly packaged and aligned to sponsor needs. Those who contribute to the event as sponsors do so for a variety of reasons, including that they wish to enhance the organization's image, promote sales, increase visibility, portray themselves as good corporate citizens, differentiate themselves from competitors, and enhance business relations.

Allocate Expenses for Meetings, Conventions, and Other Events

Defining Costs and Expenses   To prepare a budget for the meeting, convention, or other event, it is essential to identify all possible expenses. Organize expenses into categories and then classify them as either fixed or variable expenses. In some organizations, indirect costs are also included. As noted elsewhere, indirect costs are costs borne by the organization that are proportionately affixed to the event on a percentage basis. Staff wages, telecommunication expenses, rent, and similar expenses are considered indirect costs.

As the event professional begins to prepare to budget for the event, there is a temptation to begin the process by forecasting revenue. On the contrary, identifying expenses first is a more accurate way to budget. When revenue is eventually forecast, items such as registration fees can then be adjusted to cover the cost of the expense items. Factor into the equation the organization's desired profit and financial goals. It is not unusual to include a line-item expense for desired profit in the budget so that the targeted amount is always at the forefront. Also, consider including a contingency expense line item for factors such as possible attrition costs that adversely affect the budget, should contractual obligations not be met.

If the organization has environment initiatives it wishes to incorporate into the event, these initiatives must be known in advance of the budgeting process to ensure that appropriate line items and attendance costs are incorporated into the budget. For example, if offering locally grown food is desired, the cost of procuring that food must be identified and factored into the budget.

Event technology costs, including audiovisual charges, are fast becoming one of the more expensive line-item expenses in budgets. As attendees desire more virtual access to events and as they desire to use mobile devises and other technology advances during the event, costs to the organizers grow. Working with an event technology partner is advisable to ensure that the right questions are asked and the appropriate equipment ordered so that the event professional may stay on budget.

Typical Event Expenses   Expenses for events vary depending on the type of event being held.

Accommodation expenses are classified into various categories, depending on lodging to be paid by the organization. For some events, such as a sales meeting, all attendee rooms are paid for by the organization and a subcategory for attendee lodging would be created. Staff lodging would be another subcategory, and speaker lodging would be another. In some instances, organizations prefer to classify accommodation expenses with the purpose for which the accommodation is made (speaker lodging in speaker expenses, staff lodging expenses, and attendee lodging in its own category).

Event technology expenses cover a wide range of items including telecommunications, microphones, projection equipment, sound equipment, teleprompters, monitors, computers, laser pointers, technician and operator services, flip charts and markers, easels and specialty equipment, stage crews, and lighting for events such as concerts.

Exhibition expenses (assuming the event includes a trade show component) include exhibit hall rental (if separate from the event rental), material handling charges, power distribution, equipment, floor plan design, permits and licenses, and general service contractor costs (including pipe and drape, signage, and labor costs).

Facility and other fees include facility rental, parking, permits and licenses, janitorial costs, and waste removal.

Food and beverage fees include not only food items ordered (continental or full breakfast, refreshment breaks, lunch, receptions, dinner, or other banquet costs), but also serving station fees, bar service (hosted or cash), bartender fees, gratuities, service charges, and taxes. Gratuities are distinct from service charge fees in that gratuities are given to individuals for excellent service, while service charges and taxes are mandatory fees included in the event contract. Calculating the cost of food and beverage items without including the service charge and tax adversely affects the budget. Example: The organization's contract with the event facility states that the organization will secure food and beverage equivalent to $35,000, plus service charge and tax fee. For purposes of this example, assume that the service charge is 27 percent, taxes are 9.75 percent (state) and 1.85 percent (local). Were the budget to reflect only the $35,000, the line item would be understated by $13,510 ($9,450 service charge, $3,412.50 state tax, and $647.50 local tax).

General or administrative expenses include insurance (such as event cancellation insurance), credit card processing expenses, design and décor, awards and other recognitions, and website design and maintenance. Human resource costs are grouped either within these general expenses or broken out into their own category. Expenses to be included would be staff wages (proportionately allocated), temporary staffing, security and other law enforcement personnel as needed, emergency medical technicians (as may be required by local regulations), and volunteer expenses.

Marketing and promotion expenses include advertising and public relations costs (including an on-site media office), graphic design costs, photography and videography costs, printing and reproduction costs, and postage and delivery costs.

Programming expenses include speaker expenses (honorarium, speaker lodging, travel, and other contractually agreed upon expenses), reproduction expenses if speaker handouts are to be provided, technology expenses for any speaker management software, and other printed materials such as proceedings from scientific conferences.

Registration costs include registration supplies (badges, ribbons, lanyards, and tickets), equipment rental, registration unit, web-based on-site registration kiosks, and, if not included in the general staffing budget, temporary staffing costs.

Transportation expenses include airport transfers, shuttles from hotels to event facilities, and other transportation-related expenses for ancillary events held in conjunction with the main event (for example, transportation to off-site laboratory/testing facilities for a scientific conference, or transportation to a special event held at another facility).

Green Initiative Options: Budgeting for the Greatest Green Impacts Incorporating green initiatives into an event does not always mean spending more. Budgeting tips include:

- Select hotels and suppliers with green policies
- Host all multi-session meetings at a central location to limit transportation needs
- Minimize paper with web-based invitations, online event registration, and electronic follow-up
- Use double-sided printing for all collateral and meeting-related materials
- Give recycled materials precedence when making meeting supply purchases
- Choose a venue with an in-house recycling program and encourage recycling
- Decrease the usage of paper and plastic by using real china for all food and beverage
- Select buffet-style menus and donate leftovers to eliminate waste
- Coordinate with venues to use bulk dispensers for all food and beverage
- Encourage speakers to use electronic means of presentation
- Recycle conference bags
- Green practices and long-term sustainability goals should never take a backseat to the bottom line
- Incorporating green and corporate social responsibility practices can be beneficial both for establishing the company as a good corporate citizen and for saving money
- The current economy is a "great tool" for leveraging green efforts
- Beware of greenwashing (the practice of companies spinning their products and policies as environmentally friendly, such as by presenting cost cuts as reductions in use of resources—aka green whitewash).

The Convention Industry Council's website (www.conventionindustry.org) contains additional information on the APEX/ASTM Environmentally Sustainable Meeting Standards.

DEVELOPING THE BUDGET: WHAT TO INCLUDE

The event professional gathers all available historical information and documents from prior events that contain financial information essential to preparing the current budget. If the event is a first-time event, the event professional should research other events to assist in structuring the budget to maximize profit.

The event professional begins to construct the budget by defining categories for both revenue and expense items that are consistent with or match the line items in the organization's chart of accounts. When necessary, the event professional should prepare a list of items and subcategories and discuss the budget line items with the organization's finance department to ensure consistency with the chart of accounts. For expense line items, the event professional also gathers information from the event's contract and other vendor contracts and estimates the costs of other items with the help of potential vendors. If any prior history summaries are available, those should be made available, as should meeting agendas, speaker agreements, promotional costs, facility menus, event technology pricing, and pricing for extras such as tours, entertainment, and transportation.

For those planning international meetings, other factors must also be weighed. For instance, in the United States, visa barrier issues historically have had a negative financial impact on exhibitions estimated to account for $2.4 billion from incremental attendance of international exhibitions and attendees. Accurate prediction of these areas and attendant expenses must be estimated so the total expense figure can provide the basis for more accurate calculation of revenue.

Further, if a meeting is held in a country other than the organizer's origin, *value-added tax* (VAT) must be included, preferable as its own line item. VAT amounts differ, depending on the country where the event is held and what tax rates and exemptions may exist. VAT rates range from a low of 5 percent to a high of 16 percent, but, depending on the country, VAT may be waived for international conferences and other events. If the event professional is unfamiliar with all aspects of VAT, it is advisable to consult with experts to ensure compliance with regulations and to realize VAT refunds, where applicable.

Factors Affecting Budgets

Both internal and external factors can affect budgets. Internal factors include higher organizational expenses, inadequate collections, inferior accounts receivable practices, and aggressive revenue projections in the budgeting process. External factors include economic downturn, unanticipated competition that results in lowered sales, market conditions (inflation rate, stock market condition), and unanticipated legislative changes such as a change in taxation rates.

Projecting Revenue

Once all expenses have been forecast, the minimum amount of revenue to break-even is also known.

Setting Registration and Exhibit Fees

Many factors are involved in the decision as to what to charge for registration and exhibit fees. The organization's budget philosophy, the projected expenses compiled for the budget, and what the market will bear (or at what point will a fee decrease the likelihood of attendance). The event professional conducts research on similar events held by competing organizations, comparing those fee structures and contrasting them when different or fewer items are included in the fees.

If the event is a multiday event, create a single day registration fee. If the organization is membership-based, develop member and nonmember prices. If there are students aligned with the organization, develop a separate rate for them. In developing a one-day registration, the event professional also develops a policy and procedure to ensure that the attendee participates only on the day for which the attendee is registered. A single-day registrant who participates fully in the event negatively affects the budget.

For attendee registrations, also consider early, advanced, and on-site registration rates for each of the types of attendees created (e.g., member, nonmember, student). Doing so has a multi-prong effect. First, people tend to register earlier to avoid higher rates, and second, earlier registration helps the organization's cash flow.

Also, consider offering a discount fee structure for multiple registrations from the same company. A standard offering is for a full fee for the first registration and discount fees for the other registrants.

Complimentary registrations do not generate revenue for the organization but they do generate expense. Determine who will be afforded complimentary registrations (speakers, media, VIPs). Establish whether these individuals will receive complimentary access to ancillary events or whether those must be purchased separately. Calculate the total cost of one complimentary registration by calculating the cost of all expense items directly related to the attendee (food and beverage, printing, marketing, to name just a few) and then divide that total number by the anticipated number of attendees to arrive at a per attendee cost. Add an expense item to the budget for complimentary registrations, ensuring it is *at cost* and not at the listed revenue for registration fees. For example, if the *cost* of an attendee registration is $350 and ten complimentary registrations are extended, the line-item entry would be $3,500.

Calculating the Attendee Registration Fee

First, construct the attendee registration fee to a break-event point, using one of two methods: (1) when the number of attendees is known or projected but the fee is not known, and (2) when the fee is known or projected but the number of attendees is not.

The steps for calculating a registration fee when the number of attendees (for this example, we estimate 1,000 attendees) is known or forecast but the fee is not known are as follows:

STEP ONE. Identify expenses as fixed, variable, or indirect. Fixed costs do not change depending on the number of attendees, while variable costs do. Indirect costs can be either fixed or variable, but are not part of the attendee registration fee calculation. For example, if the event professional orders LCD equipment for each of the rooms in which speakers will make their presentations, the equipment will be ordered based on the size of the room, not the number of attendees, and is therefore a fixed cost. Food and beverage, on the other hand, is a variable cost. For example, if lunch on day one of the event costs $55.00 per person inclusive, then that number is multiplied by the number of anticipated attendees for that day to arrive at the total variable cost for that expense line item. Here, the cost varies with the number of attendees.

STEP TWO. Calculate fixed costs. Identify and total all fixed costs, such as event signage, marketing expenses, website development and maintenance, and event technology. For this example, total fixed costs equal $100,000.00.

STEP THREE. Calculate variable costs. Identify and total all variable costs such as food and beverage, speaker and VIP lodging, and the production of on-site attendee programs. For this example, total variable costs equal $145,000.00.

STEP FOUR. Add fixed costs and variable costs. Add the total fixed costs and total variable costs together. For this example, the total is $245,000.00.

STEP FIVE. Divide the total costs ($245,000.00) by the number of attendees (1,000) to equal the per person cost ($245.00).

The steps for calculating a registration fee when the registration fee is known but the number of attendees is not are as follows:

STEP ONE. Using the same calculations used in the prior example, we know that the registration fee break-even point is $245.00 per person, fixed costs are $100,000.00, and variable costs are $245.00.

STEP TWO. Subtract the per person variable costs from the registration fee to arrive at the contribution margin. In this example, $245.00 minus $145.00 equals $100.00.

STEP THREE. Divide the total fixed costs by the contribution margin to arrive at the number of attendees. In this example, $100,000.00 divided by $100.00 equals 1,000 attendees.

While the examples used above equal whole dollars, some calculations will end with cents, for example, a contribution margin could be $103.73. Keep in mind that the registration fee *break-even point* is just that: a break-even point and not the lowest registration amount to be charged.

Calculating Exhibit Space Fees

Deciding exhibit space fees involves more than simple financial calculations. Incorporate into the decision what the financial objectives of the exhibition are and what the desired profit from this event (or component of a larger event) is. Identify who and how many potential exhibitors, sponsors (including in-kind sponsors), and attendees will partici-pate in the event. Then research what similar or competitive exhibitions establish as their fee structures. Compare and contrast the offerings between the event being orga-nized and competitor events. If the event being organized includes food and beverage events and the competitor event does not, fees for this event will most likely be higher than the competing event. Also, the event professional should research economic and other trends that will affect the number of exhibit spaces likely to be sold.

Use the same types of formulas for calculating exhibit space fees as for calculat-ing registration fees (Examples 1 and 2 above). For exhibitions, fixed costs will in-clude items such as security and exhibit space rental. Variable costs will include such items as the cost of pipe and drape and lead retrieval equipment (if included in booth rental fee). For additional exhibitor badge fees (fees for exhibit staff above the allotted per booth number), use the per attendee cost figure to determine the minimum that should be charged for additional exhibitor badges. Just as early, advance, and on-site fees are recommended for attendee registration fees, so are they recommended for ex-hibit space fees. Table 2 illustrates how using a single registration fee (and not achiev-ing the desired number of exhibit spaces sold) can negatively affect the budget.

The event professional then conducts a "what if" analysis on the anticipated fees to determine actual exhibit space fees. The purpose of this exercise is to determine what would happen if the projected number of exhibit spaces was less than actual experience and what impact that would have on the budget.

In Table 3, and using similar data to the single rate exhibit space above, for example, only 275 of 300 exhibit spaces sold, note that by using tiered exhibit space fees, the desired budget amount is not only achieved, but also exceeded by $12,500.00.

The event professional may also elect to offer varying exhibit space rates for different types of exhibit space (islands, peninsula, end caps, and corner booths) and for location on the exhibit floor. Doing so can generate additional revenue for the event. If this op-tion is chosen, the event professional must take caution to ensure that the rates offered are competitive with other events, or risk not selling the projected number of exhibit spaces.

Establishing Sponsorship, Advertising, and Promotional Fees

Determining sponsorship fees is not an easy task. The event professional conducts research into what competitors offer their sponsors (and for what benefits), the role sponsorship dollars play in achieving the event's financial goals, and how to pair the needs of potential sponsors with the event's financial goals. Susan A. Friedmann, in

TABLE 2 "What If" Analysis of Booth Space Fees (Single Fee)

Booth Fee	# of Exhibit Spaces	Income	Actual Income	Variance
$1,000.00	300	$300,000.00	$300,000.00	$.00
$1,000.00	275	$300,000.00	$275,000.00	$<25,000.00>
$1,000.00	250	$300,000.00	$250,000.00	$<50,000.00>

TABLE 3 "What If" Analysis – Tiered Booth Fees

Registration Fees	# of Exhibit Spaces	Exhibit Fee	Actual Income
Early	200	$1,000.00	$200,000.00
Advance	75	$1,500.00	$112,500.00
On-site	0	$1,750.00	$.00
Totals:	300		$312,500.00

Is Sponsorship Right for My Company?, describes sponsorship as a "financial or in-kind support of an activity, used primarily to reach specified business goals." When setting fees for sponsorships, also determine how the sponsors' return on investment (ROI) is to be calculated. The ability to demonstrate ROI may be the tipping point as to whether a sponsorship is obtained. Consider also the sponsor's reputation and whether that sponsor is a good fit for the event.

In *Is Sponsorship Right for My Company?*, Friedmann delineates six measurable sponsor goals.

1. Image enhancement
2. Driving sales
3. Increased visibility with positive publicity
4. Good corporate citizen role
5. Differentiate from competitors
6. Enhance business, consumer, and VIP relations

Understanding these six points helps the event professional to establish appropriate levels and fees for sponsorships and to establish sponsor benefits that match the sponsor's own financial and marketing objectives. Typical sponsor benefits include such things as sponsor acknowledgment, exclusive networking events, opportunities to meet key individuals at VIP receptions, and sponsor visibility in event marketing materials.

Standard Formula for Setting Sponsorship Fees: Multiply the cost of delivering sponsor benefits plus the cost of sale plus any cost for servicing by a factor of 3, 2, or 1.5. Be consistent in using the same factor for various sponsor options.

To maximize sponsorship revenue, test your proposed sponsorship fees to see if they are what the market will bear. Reach out to sponsors early in order to give them sufficient time to maximize their sponsor experience. Understand who else is competing for those same sponsor dollars and plan a campaign that creates a unique value proposition for the sponsor. Sponsor opportunities can be highly competitive. If few opportunities are available, ensure that sponsors understand this so they may take action quickly. Offer high-level sponsors the opportunity to create their own benefits list and then test the feasibility for budget sensitivity.

Setting advertising and promotional fees rely on the same factors and research as for setting sponsorship fees. Research rates charged by competing events and offer similar rates, taking into account any variances for number of attendees, size of the event, and related factors. Formulas exist for assessing the value of advertising rates based on the number of readers, frequency of advertising, and other factors, but those formulas do not work with a one-time publication. The event professional should determine advertising rates that are consistent with competitive analysis and other internal and external factors. Advertising rates can be tiered based on the position in the program (e.g., inside front cover, outside back cover, inside back cover, first five pages of the program, with right page positioning, and run of press), although sponsors may insist on the highest profile pages as part of their sponsor package. Promotional fees should also be assessed against competition. The event professional assesses whether the value of the promotional is significant when weighed with the total cost to the exhibitor for participating in the event.

TYPES OF BUDGETS

There are various types of budgets that can be created, each serving a different purpose.

Zero-based. This is budgeting that emphasizes what will happen in the future and aligns with goals and objectives. The "downside" is that, because it is built almost entirely from scratch, it is time-consuming. On the positive side, it does eliminate the "we've always done it this way" mentality.

Incremental. This budget is prepared using a previous period's budget or actual performance as a basis and then makes incremental changes for the new budget period. While much quicker to prepare than the zero-based budget, it fails to make adjustments for other external factors because it only looks at prior performance. For example, an incremental budget process might review prior period postage and delivery expenses and determine that a 5 percent increase in postage and delivery expense is warranted while the zero-based process looks to other external factors, such as potential fuel surcharges on deliveries because of higher fuel costs.

Line Item. This type of budget is commonly prepared and can be either zero-based or incremental. Each category of activity that is included aligns with an item in the chart of accounts. Ease of preparation and as a means of comparing performance from one fiscal period to another are the most evident advantages of this type of budget.

Performance/Function. This budget focuses primarily on what functions are performed and is useful in developing unit costs. The primary disadvantage of this type of budget is that it emphasizes the quantity, not quality, of the activity being monitored.

The budget is a vital financial tool for the event professional. It provides estimates of expected revenues and expenses in producing the event. Financial software makes it easy to create income statements that compare budget to actual amounts, illustrating variances in actual amounts, percentage differences, or both.

A sample event budget is shown in Table 4 (Budget vs. Actual), Table 5 (Revenue), and Table 6 (Expenses), based on 1,000 attendees, 75 VIPs and speakers, 275 booths, 10 sponsors, and 50 additional exhibitor badges. No group discounts, special or ancillary events are factored into this budget. The sample is not representative of all revenue and expense items one might expect to find in a typical event budget.

Table details the calculations used to arrive at budget figures and allows space for notes when modifications are made. Table 6 categorizes expenses into fixed, variable, and indirect costs. By subtracting the total expenses from Table 6 from the total revenue in Table 5, at first glance it would appear that the event is projected to receive a net profit of $68,750. A closer look, however, reveals that the expenses include line items for desired profit of $300,000 and contingency expense of $40,000. Assuming the desired profit level is achieved and no untoward expenses occur that would deplete the contingency expense, the event could realize an additional $340,000 in net profit.

BUDGET APPROVAL PROCESS

The budget approval process varies with the organization and organizational structure. For some, the approval process is submitted to one level of decision makers, while in other organizations, there may be two, three, or more levels of management that the

TABLE 4 Budget versus Actual

Expense	Budgeted Amount	Actual Amount	Variance	Notes
Food and Beverage	$60,000	$67,000	$7,000	Catering guarantees increased due to higher than anticipated number of participants
Printing and Reproduction	$6,000	$5,000	$<1,000>	Decision made to provide exhibiting companies with one on-site program only and not one per exhibit staff person

TABLE 5 Sample Event Budget—Revenue

Exhibition Income					
Standard, In-line Booths	100	@	$1,100.00	=	$110,000.00
Corner/Peninsula Booths	100	@	$1,700.00	=	$170,000.00
Island Booths	50	@	$2,000.00	=	$100,000.00
Additional Exhibitor Badges	25	@	$150.00	=	$3,750.00
Sponsorship Income	10			=	$150,000.00
Total Exhibition Income					$533,750.00
Conference Income					
Attendee Registration					
Early Registration	500	@	$350.00	=	$175,000.00
Advance Registration	400	@	$450.00	=	$180,000.00
On-site Registration	100	@	$525.00	=	$52,500.00
Total Attendee Registration Income					$407,500.00
Total Revenue					$941,250.00

TABLE 6 Sample Event Budget—Expenses

Fixed Costs					
Desired Profit					$300,000.00
Contingency Expense					$40,000.00
Exhibition Space Rental					$67,000.00
Marketing					$50,000.00
Security					$15,000.00
Audiovisual Equipment					$35,700.00
Event Website Development					$25,000.00
Event Signage					$11,300.00
Total, Fixed Costs					$544,000.00
Variable Costs					
Food and Beverage					$98,000.00
On-site Attendee Program					$15,000.00
Speaker/VIP Lodging (75 VIPs/3 nights each)	225 nights	@	$200.00/night		$45,000.00
Exhibit Hall Pipe and Drape	250 booths	@	$70.00/each		$17,500.00
Lead Retrieval Equipment	250 units	@	$200.00/each		$50,000.00
On-site Registration Staff					$9,000.00
Total, Variable Costs					$234,500.00
Indirect Costs					
Staff Wages	45%	of	$200,000.00	=	$90,000.00
Telecommunication Charges				=	$4,000.00
Total, Indirect Costs					$94,000.00
Total Expenses					$872,500.00

proposed budget passes through. A well-constructed budget, which includes easy to understand calculations, notes where there is no clarity, and comments where appropriate, has a high chance of quick approval, assuming the individual presenting the budget is well-versed in how the budget is constructed. If the event professional is not the person presenting the budget, it is imperative to review the budgeting process with the person making the presentation so the individual has a clear understanding of the budget and its assumptions.

Monitoring the Budget

The event professional works closely with the finance department to monitor the budget performance, preferably on a monthly basis. The financial statement necessary for this monitoring is the one that shows budget versus actual performance for year-to-date. This review helps when decisions to modify the budget need to be made. These adjustments are tracked in a narrative field on the budget (sometimes called a budget diary) with comments as to why the modification is being made. Such commentary assists in more accurately forecasting future budgets.

The event professional reviews the current statement to determine performance levels. Table 7 reflects information on revenue and expenses as they exist three months prior to the event.

Exhibit space sales for islands and peninsulas are at 100 percent of capacity but standard booths are lagging by 10 percent. Increased sales efforts are indicated. For sponsorship income, the window for selling sponsorships is nearly closed, and selling sponsorships this close to the event becomes increasingly difficult. Additional exhibitor badge sales are just above 50 percent but do not pose great concern because most additional exhibitor badges are purchased within the last two months prior to the event. Conference income is less than 50 percent of budget but causes little concern because the advance registration rate just opened, and on-site registration rates are not yet open. The event professional will monitor these items two months' out to evaluate performance.

On the expense side, exhibition expenses are low and reflective of deposits being made as contractually required. Conference expenses are likewise low and expenses for lodging, staffing, and printing/production have not yet occurred. However, the marketing expense line item could be problematic in that it is only at 34 percent of budget, with about 2.5 months remaining to market the event. Possible reasons include delayed receipt of billings from vendors, innovative and more cost-effective methods of marketing, and free social media marketing have lessened marketing costs. The event professional should investigate why this number is low and have answers ready at hand when asked for explanations.

EVALUATION

Once an event has concluded, post-event analysis and reporting are conducted in order to wrap up details of the event and to make informed assumptions for future events based on current performance. The budget diary, if correctly maintained, provides valuable information, as does reconciliation of the master account discussed elsewhere. Once these evaluations are complete, reports, including the post-event report, are prepared and include successes, recommendations for improvements, and even enhanced policies and procedures.

Return on Investment

Return on investment (ROI) is defined as a financial ratio indicating the degree of profitability. The basic calculation is net profit divided by net worth. For the event,

TABLE 7 Budget versus Actual – Three Months' Prior to Event

Income	Actual – Apr.—Oct., 20__	Budget	% of Budget
Exhibition Income			
Booth Sales			
Islands and Peninsulas	370,000.00	370,000.00	100.00%
Standard Booths	99,000.00	110,000.00	90.00%
Add'l Exhibitor Badges	2,000.00	3,750.00	53.33%
Total, Booth Sales	471,050.00	483,750.00	97.37%
Sponsorship	124,500.00	150,000.00	83.00%
Total, Exhibition Income	595,500.00	633,750.00	93.96%
Conference Income			
Attendee Registration			
Early Registration	178,500	175,000.00	102.00%
Advance Registration	18,000	180,000.00	10.00%
Onsite Registration	.00	52,500.00	.00
Total Attendee Registration Income	196,500.00	407,500.00	48.22%
Total Income	792,000.00	1,041,250.00	76.06%
Exhibition Expenses			
Pipe and Drape	5000.00	17,500.00	28.57%
Facility Rental	33,500.00	67,000.00	50.00%
Security	7,500.00	15,000.00	50.00%
Exhibit Hall Food & Beverage	24,500.00	98,000.00	25.00%
Total Exhibition Expenses	70,500.00	197,500.00	35.70%
Conference Expenses			
Marketing	17,000.00	50,000.00	34.00%
Speaker/VIP Lodging	.00	45,000.00	.00%
On-site Reg. Staff	.00	9,000.00	.00%
On-site Program	.00	15,000.00	0.00%
Total, Conference Expenses	17,000.00	119,000.00	14.29%
Total Expenses	87,500.00	316,500.00	27.65%
Net Income over Expenses	704,500.00	724,750.00	97.21%

that calculation works. For sponsors and exhibitors (if there is a trade show component to the event), they will want a better way to identify, explain, and justify their ROI for participating in the event. Attendees and other stakeholders will also want to measure their ROI. Sometimes ROI become **return on objectives (ROO)**, where the measurement is how well participating in the event met their overall objectives (nonfinancial).

For the event professional's understanding of sponsor and exhibitor (if any), ROI is critical. For sponsors and exhibitors, their focus is on their marketing activities, sales promotions, advertisements, and other expenses that drive sales. A simple calculation is gross sales resulting from sales leads divided by total expenses to complete this sales strategy, with the resulting figure expresses as a ratio. Since it is sometimes difficult to decide which sales leads from the event result in actual sales, the ROI calculation is an estimate. For example, if a company generates $1,500,000 in gross sales and spent $600,000, the result would be expressed as:

$$1,500,000 \div 400,000 = 3.75$$

Expressed as a ratio, this would be 1:3.75, where for every one dollar the exhibitor or sponsor spent, it received three dollars and seventy-five cents in return.

Return on Equity

Return on equity (ROE) measures an organization's efficiency at generating profits from units of shareholder equity (net assets). The measurement, typically stated as a percentage, is the rate of return on ownership interest of shareholders. A 15 to 20 percent ROE is considered good. The formula for calculating ROE is net income divided by shareholder equity (net assets).

Net income	divided by	Net Assets	=	Return on Equity
$45,000	÷	$250,000	=	18%

POLICIES AND PROCEDURES

To ensure that budget and finance matters are clear to all involved, it is necessary to develop policies and procedures for those working with budgets and other financial matters. For the event professional in particular, this means the establishment of policies and procedures that directly affect the event. Policies include at least the following:

Establish and publish a written refund policy. Refund policies for both attendees and exhibitors are essential. Whether the organization allows a full refund until a specified date, deducts an administrative fee and refunds the balance, has a declining scale of refunds available by certain dates, or declines to refund after a specified date, policies should be clearly stated and visibly posted. Best practices dictate posting on the event website, on all registration materials, and at the on-site registration date. The policy should state that requests for refunds must be in writing and must be received by a specified date. Otherwise, individuals could claim that they canceled by phone or other method.

For exhibitors, the refund policy should include what percentage of exhibit space fees, badge costs, and other exhibitor charges are and are not refundable. Specify a date when refunds will no longer be honored.

THE MASTER ACCOUNT AND ESTABLISHING CREDIT

Master accounts are set up with vendors, especially facilities, well in advance of the event. The master account allows the organization to accrue charges, sometimes without prepayments, other times with incremental payments toward the master account.

Establishing credit benefits the organization and assists in managing its cash flow. Without credit, all payments to facilities must be made on an installment basis and all fees due paid prior to the date of the actual event. Economic downturns typically result in tighter credit policies, where even the most credit-worthy organization may be required to make incremental deposits to the vendor to improve the vendor's cash flow. The result is that the event professional's ability to maximize positive cash flow for the organization is diminished.

The event professional must ensure that policies and procedures for establishing, reviewing, and reconciling the master account are in place and that all parties involved understand how charges to the master account are to be handled and by whom. Policies should, at a minimum, cover the following areas:

1. Contain a list of eligible charges that can be posted to the master account
2. Specify who is authorized to charge to the master account
3. Require that daily review (while on-site) of the master account be conducted
4. Insist that detailed documentation in support of the master account be provided
5. Demand that extraordinary charges require a high level of approval before they can be posted to the master account.

Payment Reconciliations

Reconcile the master account when the final bill is received. If the final bill is large, create a spreadsheet and enter the information into appropriate categories such as food and beverage, event technology, and lodging. Include a column for the banquet order number. Calculate the total for each category and review the data to determine if discrepancies exist. Verify that all charges were authorized and that no charges were duplicated. Subtract room and other rebates from the total of the categories to see if the balance due agrees with the amount shown on the final bill. Consult the vendor immediately regarding discrepancies and resolve the issues. If necessary, request a revised final bill to reflect the changes.

Managing and Controlling Cash

No matter how successful the event, if the cash does not balance, the organizer will be displeased. Cash handling procedures may already be in place within an organization for other purposes and may be adaptable for the handling of cash before, during, and after the event. If not, it is essential to ensure responsible handling of all cash, checks, credit cards, and other methods of payment. Best practices dictate that anyone responsible for handling receipts should be bonded, particularly the person in charge of reconciling monies received on-site during the event. Best practices also prescribe that pre-numbered receipts be used, with a minimum of two copies, more if other departments within the organization require copies. Include in any written procedures for cash management that no pre-numbered receipts may be destroyed, including those that are voided. Whoever is charged with reconciling cash on-site should not be the individual who collected the cash.

When anticipated revenues are received dictates how cash and other funds are handled. If revenue is received early in a cycle, there may be an opportunity to transfer it to a higher yield account. This assumes that the revenue is significant and can be held for months at a time.

PAYMENT METHODS AND CURRENCY CONSIDERATIONS

It is not unusual to set up bank accounts in the place where the event will be held, whether that is in a different location but within one's own country or outside one's country. International meetings require decisions unnecessary if one is holding the event in one's own country. Questions that need to be answered in advance include how payables will be made and in what currency, what additional expenses will be incurred in addition to transaction fees and currency fluctuations, will the organization accept payments in multiple currencies, and will additional online processing fees be incurred if transacting in multiple currencies. If the event professional or other staff is not knowledgeable in foreign currencies, currency exchange experts should be consulted.

MANAGING CASH FLOW

After budget development and approval, preparation of a cash flow statement is advisable. The benefit of using a cash flow statement is that it charts the flow of cash into (inflows) and out of (outflows) bank accounts. Excel or other spreadsheet software is ideal for preparing this kind of statement. Determine when both inflows and outflows are expected and enter into the chart. Review the chart to determine when and if there are months when inflows exceed outflows and for how many subsequent months that condition exists. If the situation is favorable, transferring monies into higher yielding accounts creates additional revenue that, in strong economic times, can generate sizeable amounts of interest. Conversely, in months where outflows exceed inflows, reserving funds from prior months to cover that excess is advisable and, if necessary, money from higher yield accounts may need to be transferred.

SUMMARY

Event professional competencies have increased and expanded to include additional skill sets. With a shift from tactical to strategic responsibilities, the meeting planner's responsibilities increase the value of the event professional's position to the organization and enhance the event professional's profile in the marketplace. Effective budget and financial management skills increase the organization's ability to remain successful, to grow its business model, and to enhance its reputation as a solid business entity.

Now that you have completed this chapter you should be competent in the following Meetings and Business Events Competency Standards:

MBECS—Skill 8: Principles of Accounting and Finance

Sub skills		Skills (standards)
D 8.01	Develop budget	
D 8.02	Establish pricing	
D 8.03	Establish financial controls and procedures	
D 9.01	Establish cash handling procedures	
D 9.02	Monitor cash handling procedures	

The Need for Financial Planning

In October 2010, 300 Public Building Service/General Services Administration (GSA) employees attended a conference in Las Vegas, Nevada. Videos of the event were made and posted, evidencing the good time that was had by all. From all perspectives, the conference was a smashing success. Yet in the spring of 2011, rumblings of excessive spending and employee misconduct began to surface. By April 2012, the House Oversight Committee was calling GSA officials to testify, but instead of testifying, they invoked the Fifth Amendment.

Public outrage demanded action against those responsible, characterizing the spending of public funds for "over the top" excesses ($822,751) as tantamount to criminal activity. In short, the GSA had failed in its obligation to be a "responsible steward of the public's money." As the investigations continue, yet another GSA scandal emerges, this time to the tune of $268,732 for a one-day awards ceremony, including the purchase of $20,578 worth of drumsticks.

Policies and procedures, rules and regulations are in place for a purpose—to keep things on the straight and narrow. What was a huge triumph in 2010 is now a black mark on the credibility of government employees at GSA . . . all because they did not follow financial guidelines and regulations in planning their meetings.

SOURCE: http://www.gsaig.gov/?LinkServID=908FFF8C-B323-14AD-270C38936310AEBD&showMeta=0. Office of Inspector General, U.S. General Services Administration. 2010 Western Regions Conference Management Deficiency Report. April 2, 2012.

KEY WORDS AND TERMS

Accounting Methods
Assets and Liabilities
Accounts Payable
Accounts Receivable
Break-Even Analysis/Break-Even
   Point
Chart of Accounts
Double-entry Bookkeeping
   System
Credits
Debits
Contribution Margin
Financial Statements
Balance Sheet

Statement of Financial Position
Income or Profit and Loss
   Statement
Statement of Activities
Statement of Cash Flows/Cash
   Flow Statement
Budget Philosophy
Accommodation expenses
Event Technology
Exhibition Expenses
Facility and Other Fees
Food and Beverage Fees
General or Administrative
   Expenses

Marketing and Promotion
   Expenses
Programming Expenses
Registration Costs
Transportation Expenses
Green Initiative Options
Zero-based Budgets
Incremental Budgets
Line-Item Budgets
Performance/Function Budgets
Table
Return on Investment
Return on Objections
Return on Equity

REVIEW AND DISCUSSION QUESTIONS

1. Why do event professionals need to acquire and be well-versed in accounting and financial knowledge?
2. What are the different methods of accounting?
3. How does one complete a break-even analysis?
4. What are the potential sources of revenue for a MEEC event?
5. What is the chart of accounts?
6. What are the typical expenses for a MEEC event?
7. What are the factors that an event professional must consider while managing event budgets?
8. Why is managing cash flow crucial in event planning?
9. What is the difference between ROI and ROE?
10. Discuss payment methods and currency considerations.

REFERENCE

Friedmann, Susan A. *Is Sponsorship Right for My Company?* Web. 15 April 2012. http://www.businessknowhow.com.

ABOUT THE CHAPTER CONTRIBUTOR

MaryAnne P. Bobrow, CAE, CMP, CMM, CHE, is the principal in Bobrow & Associates

Bobrow & Associates. They provide project-based and full-service association management services, including financial management, database management, membership recruitment and retention programs, board and corporate meetings, strategic planning facilitation, convention management, and trade show coordination. MaryAnne received the prestigious MPI RISE Award for 2011.

ACTIVITIES: FINANCIAL PLANNING CHAPTER

1. Students determine an event they wish to organize
   a. Students prepare budget for the event, using the Sample Budget
      i Three variations of the budget should be prepared
         1. One showing a profit
         2. One showing break-even
         3. One showing a loss
   b. Using the figures from the budget, prepare financial statements (a balance sheet and a profit and loss statement)
      i Adjust the financial statements to show (1) a greater profit for the event than was budgeted and (2) a lesser profit than budgeted
      ii Students calculate ROI and ROE for event

c. Change the cost figures for calculating attendee registration fees using both formulas and have students calculate new registration fees.

d. Test student's knowledge of return on investment using the following formula:

Attendee Registration Fee—Break-Even Calculation When Number of Attendees Is Known

Determine fixed costs (include line items for desired profit and contingency expenses)
Determine variable costs
Variable costs = variable costs per person times the number of persons
Add the total fixed costs plus the total variable costs
Calculate the break-even point by dividing total costs by the number of attendees.

Exhibitor/Sponsor Return on Investment

Gross sales generated from sales leads $\times$ Total cost of execution $=$ Return on Investment

Attendee Registration Fee—Break-Even Calculation When Registration Fee Is Known

Subtract the per person variable costs from the known registration fee to arrive at the contribution margin.
Divide the total fixed costs by the contribution margin to arrive at the number of attendees required to reach the break-even point.

Event Program Planning

CHAPTER 7

Event program planning is like putting the pieces of a puzzle together.
© Marvelens/Shutterstock

Chapter Objectives

Upon completion of this chapter, the reader should be able to:

- Analyze previous programs
- Embrace adult education learning styles
- Ascertain attendee expectations
- Determine program components
- Consider legal and regulatory requirements
- Develop cost estimates
- Garner stakeholder support
- Determine requirements for each program component
- Develop program agenda/itinerary
- Develop personnel assignments

Chapter Outline

SECTION 1

PLAN PROGRAM COMPONENTS AND ELEMENTS

"Fail to prepare, prepare to fail." This everyday phrase has validity to many commercial environments but it is perhaps best suited to the world of international events management and to the international event planner and professional (hereafter referred to as event professional). In order to conceptualize, organize, and deliver a successful meeting, exposition, event, or convention (MEEC—hereafter referred to as event), effective advanced planning is a crucial necessity, without which many complex issues will arise. The best event professionals are able to foresee issues in advance through the use of such planning, incorporating a wide variety of techniques to ensure that the success of their event is maximized.

One of the key initial phases for this is to establish event content that, most importantly, is of interest and relevant to the target audience. Being able to accurately establish who is likely to attend the event and which type(s) of content they are interested in will provide a sound foundation to build upon. Such content can be incorporated from the strategic aims of the organization, association, or charity hosting the event. For example, this may include updating staff on recent company developments or discussing new fund-raising initiatives for a charity. Whichever content is established by the professional, it is paramount that its relevance to the attendees (also referred to as delegates) is considered fully.

A second important activity for the event professional is to initially undertake a thorough feasibility study into the planned event to ensure that it is capable of success. Such factors as other events taking place at the same time to a similar target audience, date, month, pricing, budget, and marketing methods will all be reviewed within the feasibility study to establish whether plans for the event should continue. For example, a company organizing an event for staff is unlikely to hold it in a period popular with taking annual vacation leave (e.g., August in much of Europe), or a ticketed event with a cost per head to attend would look to avoid similar events at the same time targeted at a similar target audience. For all different types of stakeholder groups, a decision taken at this point to cancel plans saves a great deal of time, money, and effort on a project that potentially would not succeed.

In conjunction with the feasibility study, the event professional also needs to consider the relevant choice of destination and the site and duration of the event in question. During the past twenty years, cities and countries have paid much greater attention to the role that events can have in providing a wide variety of significant benefits to their destination and therefore are much more interested in persuading event professionals to choose their destination.

Economic, social, environmental, and infrastructural benefits can all be achieved by the regular attraction of a wide variety of small and large events. For example, a common social benefit experienced by the local community, particularly around large-scale mega-events, is increased social pride from living in the city/region where such a large event is taking place and witnessing the international coverage that it brings. Economic impacts are often seen as a key priority for those attracting events to the destination, as delegates are prone to spend larger sums of money on their visit in comparison to leisure tourists. Thus, local bars, restaurants, hotels, and transportation providers may all see clear increases in revenue during this period.

In determining a location and venue choice, there has also been a real increase in recent years in the use of unusual venues within the MEEC industry. In a move away from the traditional hotel or conference center, the rise of venues such as sports stadiums, museums, castles, and theme parks now provides the event professional with a much wider selection of options from which to choose. A key benefit of using such venues is the atmosphere and "uniqueness" provided by the setting, something that is less likely to be found at more traditional venues.

In order to attract the maximum number of delegates, the event professional must also consider the duration of the event and how this fits with the anticipated target audience. Busy corporate employees are unlikely to be able to spare three or four days out of the office at key times of the year, whereas a more focused half-day or one-day event may attract their attention. Many professionals now promote the use of "Masterclasses" that take place over a half or full day and attempt to provide all necessary information on a topic area in a shorter, more condensed period of time.

Linked to the duration of the event is another important consideration. The event professional must understand the goals and objectives of those likely to attend and focus plans on achieving these goals and objectives through all of the above factors

All contracts should be viewed with a proverbial magnifying glass. © Lucian Milasan/Fotolia

including program content, location, and venue type. A younger corporate audience may prefer to be located in a city center venue offering many varied activities after the formal content has finished. On the other hand, an international association with important strategies to set and confidential matters to discuss may prefer to be in a countryside location, away from day-to-day disturbances. Being able to understand these goals and objectives and apply them to all aspects of event organization is the mark of a true professional in the field; only then will the success of the event be maximized.

Before further plans on the event are made, the event professional will also be required to face one of the trickiest, yet vital parts of their role: working with and understanding event contracts. Contracts provide the legal documentation between a company and a venue or a supplier and the event professional, for example, and are fundamental in ensuring that plans for events are properly made. Here, it is important that the event professional provides strong attention to detail to highlight any areas of concern between themselves and the service provider (whether a hotel, caterer, or band, for instance) in order that these may be resolved before the event takes place. Checking quantities of items, delivery times, set-up requirements, cancellation charges, and insurances are all issues that need to be covered through the use of accurate contracts. Many financial and operational mistakes can be avoided if time is spent at this point going over the fine details of the event. It may also be beneficial for the event professional to ask another colleague to review the contract before signing and returning it, just in case they might have missed something (that does happen!). Better yet, have a lawyer (US) or solicitor (UK) review the contract. (See chapter 11 in Fenich; *Meetings, Expositions, Events and Conventions: An Introduction to the Industry* for details on legal issues in MEEC.)

In conjunction with the use of contracts, it should also be highlighted that the event professional has a duty to be responsible for and look after everyone who is either attending or working on their event. This includes the use of volunteer staff, company staff, and, most importantly, event delegates (whether adult or child). Poor risk management at an event is likely to lead to physical and financial harm that does not benefit anyone involved. Therefore, in planning for events of any nature, the inclusion of effective risk management at all stages is as important, if not more important, than the overall attraction of the event itself. (See chapter 6 for more detail on risk management.)

Organizing a Fund-raising Charity Run. Just a Walk in the Park?

Sonia Morjaria

Marketing Coordinator, Courses and Conferences Producer

R3 Association of Business Recovery Professional

The preplanning stage of organizing an event is very important to ensure the event turns out the way the event professional expects. Having recently organized a 5K charity run, it was crucial that the perfect event plan was written with the goals and objectives set in mind to make the day go smoothly.

First, consideration was given to who my target audience would be and how the event would appeal to them. As this was a charity event, it was important to bear in mind that this group of people would be interested in fund-raising for the charity so enough funds were generated to cover the costs and make a significant amount for the charitable cause. The following factors were considered during the preplanning stages:

- Finding the ideal venue and location;
- Getting permission from local authority;
- Obtaining a license; and so forth.

As one of the event objectives was to generate a significant amount of charitable funds, it was important to produce a marketing plan to get the word out about the event. A few free/low-cost marketing tactics were used including putting the word out on Facebook (on the group wall and advertising), using Twitter, emailing those who were on the events database (people who had taken part in an event for the charity previously). Local newspapers were also contacted to request free advertising space and were sent an event advertisement along with a related press release.

People were also enticed into taking part in the event by introducing a competition. So top female/male fund-raisers receive a prize, fastest male/female runner wins a prize, and youngest runner also receives a prize. As this was all for charity, local businesses were contacted requesting donations of prizes to the cause. These organizations were made aware that they would gain awareness from the target audience, as their company name/logo would be inserted in our marketing materials such as newsletters, flyers, and so forth.

From experience, however, it is clear that no matter how much planning goes into an event, things can go wrong on the day, so preparations should always be made for the worst. Always stay calm and ensure you know everything about what is going on because when things go wrong, people will turn to the event manager, so the answers need to be at hand!

Excerpt from "ORGANIZING A FUNDRAISING CHARITY RUN. JUST A WALK IN THE PARK?" by Sonia Morjaria from THE PRE-PLANNING STAGE OF ORGANIZING AN EVENT. Used by permission of Sonia Morjaria

Pre-Event Research

One characteristic of events is that there is no second chance. Event failure has serious consequences. It is therefore crucial to plan the event in every detail to minimize risks, commercial or safety-related. During the planning stage, provided time and resources are available, the event professional should carry out research as part of the process. Pre-event research will give the professional invaluable information on:

- Client's Brand
- Event History (similar or otherwise)
- Event Risks

The client's brand forms the attributes all event activities will be based on. It is essential for the event professional to have a good knowledge of the brand attributes, what it stands for, and how it functions in the industry it represents. Brands tend to have a "Brand Police" to ensure that the brand has consistency of key messaging throughout. This information can be obtained during the briefing session with the client when the creative look and feel of the event and approval of event concepts can also be obtained. The brand will set the tone for the planning process. For instance, an annual conference for an energy drinks manufacturer will probably differ from that of a drug manufacturer.

When planning an event, one of the most important aspects to consider is whether the client has commissioned similar events in the past. Events may have a history and that history will tell you a lot about the task in hand, such as:

- Previous Event Themes, Locations, and Decor
- Past Events Objectives
- Post-Event Analysis

If previous event planners have had the time and resources to carry out a detailed event plan, they will have worked on the event's Key Performance Indicators (KPI), considered the risks involved with organizing the event, and produced a post-event analysis or report. A good starting point is to look at previous event reports. When clients produce similar events annually, examples from previous years will give the event professional who is doing the planning useful data on audience profile, likes and dislikes, choice of venues, locations, and so on. The information gathered will help the professional to decide on the next event's theme and avoid repetition, provide insight into what locations would be preferable or work best for the type of event being worked on, and how to create the desired atmosphere for the event. Understanding past events will also give the planner an insight into how previous professionals have dealt with risk management planning.

Corporate clients usually see the event as one of the tools at their disposal to achieve corporate and marketing objectives. The event itself, however, will have event-specific objectives such as the expected **footfall**, i.e., the number of people expected to attend, the successful delivery of event activities, and so on. Event objectives can and should be tied in with the client's corporate objectives. Apple works hard to maintain its image as the leading provider of computer technology. It organizes each of its product roll-out events with great care and secrecy in order to support the brand image.

Similarly to any business activity, events are subject to risks that should be managed based on a formalized process known as Risk Management Planning (RMP) (see chapter 4 for more detail]). Defined as the process of identifying, eliminating, and controlling hazards and risks, the process is a cyclical one and involves the identification of potential risks, planning on how to minimize or eliminate them, and to review the process once again for further adjustments.

As previously mentioned, the management of risk involves the establishment of KPIs. These derive from the event's strategic objectives (see chapter 2 for more information) and aim to provide a set criteria that the event may be evaluated under. The process involves consideration to what the event is trying to achieve, how this is to be done, and how it is going to be measured. Once clearly established, KPIs may also be used to create event return on investment objectives (ROI). (See chapter 6 for more detailed information on ROI.) The level of detail and complexity of KPIs depends on

The Party Where Nobody Came

A hospitality management program at a university was coming up on its twenty-fifth year of operations. Students spent almost a year preparing for a gala dinner celebration determining the date, venue, décor, menu, price, and so on. One month before the event was to take place, the "planners" came to the realization that no one had purchased tickets due to lack of marketing. The students thought people would "automatically come" to the event. Due to lack of footfall, the event had to be cancelled.

various factors such as time-scales, e.g., planning lead-time, resources, objectives, and so on. Regardless of the size or type of event, it is essential that KPIs be created. It is preferable to have a few simple KPIs than none at all. From KPIs, a set of risk factors may be arrived at. Generally, risk factors involve content, delegates' experience, attendance targets, and budgetary restraints. For each KPI, risks are identified and possible mitigation procedures set in place.

Safety is a major issue for events, can impact negatively on events, and may, in some cases, result in serious damage, lawsuits, and criminal charges. An important part of the planning process is the identification of health and safety risks that may occur in the pre-, during, and post-event stages. To achieve this, event planners must produce an event safety plan. Best practice recommends the creation of a 7-Point Event Safety Plan that should include the following:

1. Venue Assessment
2. Site Safety
3. Crowd Management Plan
4. Emergency Plan
5. Traffic Management Plan
6. Risk Assessment
7. First Aid/Medical Plan

Other considerations must be made as far as health and safety policies are concerned. In the United Kingdom, for instance, business organizations with more than five employees are required by law to produce a health and safety policy. Pre-event research must include an investigation on the legal requirements for event businesses and event activities in the city, state, or country where the event is to be held.

Content risks can impact on the event in two ways. It may generate a negative first impression that will prevent delegates from being interested in the event in the first place. This will result in poor registration numbers and a shortfall in attendance numbers. To avoid this, event planners must ensure the theme-ing and content stage explore all viable possibilities to create the most exciting content possible within the given circumstances—the WOW factor! Post-event reports provide an insight into what worked, what did not, and what delegates thought of the event as a whole, but it is only useful when planning future events. Goldblatt (2008) suggests the "5 Ws" as important questions when conceptualizing an event. They may be interpreted and adapted as below and should help planners minimize risks when planning the event content. The answer to these and many other questions relating to the event concept will be collected during the briefing session with the client.

- What is the purpose of the event?
- What is the event's main audience?
- What are the best times and place for the event?
- What is the most effective order for the event content?
- What is the relevance, interest, and usefulness of the event content?

Corporate events, such as conferences, seminars, workshops, and training sessions, all have learning as a common feature, and this should be considered carefully. Delegates must feel a sense of achievement, development, and progress after an event, seeing that outcomes will greatly impact on the delegates' impressions on whether the event has been successful or not. Recently, the use of technology has greatly contributed to the content and learning environment of events, in particular to corporate events. Pre-event activities may include drawing from the audience, whenever feasible, suggestions on content, running order, and many other aspects of the event. This provides the delegates with a sense of ownership of the event and helps generate interest, motivates delegates to attend, and, as a result, contributes to the target footfall. A balanced event content, with a combination of hands-on activities, workshops, and lectures, interspersed throughout the day will also help motivate participants. The factors that influence learning are vast and include conference space layout and location, interaction among speakers and delegates, and many others. Creating the right learning environment is one of the challenges of event professionals. The IMEX Power of 10 Research, conducted by Fast Future Research, points out the need to rethink the event experience and promote more engaging and satisfying learning opportunities.

Innovating Events

The inclusion of strategic and appropriate content within an event has been highlighted as a key consideration for the international event professional. Many different methods may be adopted by the professional to help decide which content is most appropriate to those planning to attend the event. For example, existing surveys and research may be reviewed to establish the nature of the content and activities appropriate to the age group and/or gender of delegates. It may be likely, for example, that a younger audience would appreciate shorter sessions with a greater percentage of outdoor activities during an event, whereas a more mature audience may prefer longer sessions within an indoor setting. Much has been reported in recent years of the specific event requirements of "Generation Y," those individuals born between 1977 and 1995, who are increasingly forming a higher percentage of event delegates. The Professional Convention Management Association Education Foundation just completed a major study entitled "What Millennials Want from Their Meetings and Conventions" (Fenich, Scott-Halsell, and Ogbeide, 2012). Therefore, it is important for the event professional to be able to match the requirements of the delegates and the proposed content of the event together.

Without having to reinvent the wheel every time, many event professionals are anxious to review the strategies employed by other organizations in the industry, especially if they proved to be successful! It may be decided that what worked well for one group of delegates at a similar event may also work well for another. This can also provide the event professional with the opportunity to perhaps fine-tune one or two parts of the event that were not so appreciated by the guests, based on their feedback to the event, and avoid making similar mistakes.

On similar lines, for large events, congresses, and conferences, often with thousands of delegates attending, research should be conducted with prospective individuals in advance to establish the nature and type of content that would be preferable. Establishing the needs, wants, and expectations of international delegates (often with many differing requirements) enables the event professional to carefully plan the length, location, and content of the event to maximum effect. Once such feedback has been collected, the marketing of the event to prospective delegates may be enhanced by incorporating the use of supporting statements by key individuals, either speaking at or attending the event. Once again, this information contributes to the decision-making process of the delegate, providing another positive reason for them to attend.

In developing new and innovative content used to entice delegates to attend an event, technology is increasingly playing a more important role, particularly for the younger generations. Recent commercial events have seen delegates provided with iPads on arrival to ensure that interactivity within the event's content is at a premium, something that resonates highly with this audience. Whether used for providing content, feedback, or social media interaction before, during, or after an event, technology has a powerful part to play in the modern-day international events industry.

As proof of how effective the use of technology can be within an event, the United Kingdom recently witnessed an example that is perhaps one of the first of its kind. Delegates attending a large medical conference in Liverpool, England, were offered the opportunity via videoconferencing technology and as part of the event to witness a live surgical procedure in an American hospital, with derived educational objectives. However, not only did delegates have the chance to witness the procedure and the latest advancements in the field, delegates in the United Kingdom were able to post questions to the American surgical team that could be answered in real time during the procedure. For such an audience, this provided a fundamental reason to attend the event and be part of a truly memorable experience. For the twenty-first-century event professional, creating and delivering such experiences is now part of the job description. (For more information on event technology, see chapter 12 in *Meetings, Expositions, Events and Conventions . . . by Fenich.)

Legal Aspects of Events

Event clients, suppliers, and delegates take for granted that legal requirements have been complied with and that all necessary licenses and/or permits have been taken care of by the event professionals. The legal obligations associated with events include contracts, the adherence to legal obligations; protection to property, intellectual and private; and, above all, that due diligence has been exercised to ensure everyone's safety.

In the pre-event stage, it is the event planner's responsibility to ensure that everything, within practical reason, has been done to comply with the legislation to promote safety and protect life. This is described in the literature as **duty of care** or **due diligence**. When failure to achieve this is due to negligence or omission, the event professional may become legally liable for losses and damages. As such, **liability** means legal responsibility for actions (or the omission of) that may lead to damage or loss, including financial obligations.

In order to ensure that all "reasonable" action has been carried out, the event planner must carry out research, record in writing the formal procedures that must and have been followed. If in doubt he or she must seek legal advice to avoid problems further down the line. This includes, but not exclusively, investigation of general and event-specific legislation in the following areas:

- Laws and Acts
- Contracts and Insurance
- Licenses and Permits
- Intellectual Property, Copyright, Music Licensing, and Privacy Laws
- Health and Safety
- Other Important Considerations

Laws and Acts   Every country has its own legislative framework and organizes legislation pertinent to events in its own way. Event professionals should research, be aware of, and ensure adherence to legal requirements through internal procedures. For instance, with regard to immigration law, the event professional must make reasonable provisions of advice and recommendations for delegates traveling overseas for a conference.

This would include visa requirements, health and safety advice, such as medical checks prior to travel, and other considerations. Another example is that in Brazil, for instance, no gambling or gaming is permitted. Therefore a Vegas or casino-themed event for a corporate event is not a viable option. Legislation pertinent to events will also include import/export laws, antidiscrimination, liquor laws, and zoning laws. For example, in the United States the laws governing alcohol sales and services are not national but rather local. What pertains in Salt Lake City, Utah (high Mormon population) will not apply in New Orleans (very laissez-faire and where alcoholic beverages can be carried and consumed on the street). Failure of compliance could result in fines, closure of the event, and even criminal prosecution.

Contracts and Insurance All event business activities must be recorded in writing, and contracts must be provided, be it for procurement, supply of goods and services, or the registration to attend an event. A **contract** is the legally binding agreement between two parties and includes disclaimers regarding the limit of liability undertaken by the event professionals. It is best practice to provide a confirmation letter or email prior to the drafting and signing of the final contract. For events, particular attention must be paid to force majeure, in other words, conditions or eventualities outside the control of either party. Those include floods, earthquakes, terrorism, epidemics, natural disasters, and disruption of public transports. For an event organization, contracts are required for (to and from) the following: sponsors, entertainers, venues, suppliers, broadcasters, and clients.

If contracts act as legal protection for both parties, i.e., the event professionals and the persons or organizations doing business with them, insurance policies act as a failsafe net in case something goes wrong. Insurance companies specializing in events can provide most, if not all, information needed and arrange insurance cover for events, including sample policies. Paul Cook, MD of Clarity Event Insurance, in his highly publicized website Planet Planit, gives insurance tips for people organizing events. Among those, the ones that stand out most are the fact that event professionals must make sure they understand the insurance language, the policy exclusions, and warranties that apply to their events and that event professionals fully describe *all* the activities that will take place at their event.

When obtaining advice and taking out insurance for events, event professionals must ensure that they only obtain advice from brokers authorized and regulated by the country's authorities. In the United Kingdom, event intermediaries are regulated by the Financial Services Authority, the independent watchdog that regulates financial services.

There are many regulations that event professionals must adhere to, including **licenses** and **permits**. Large, complex events will have similarly complex regulations to follow, and it is the event company's responsibility to find out what they are and to comply with them. They may be countrywide or local government specific and may include building, noise, and electrical installations regulations, fire precautions as well as health and safety ones. Events with catering elements must ensure that food safety regulations are adhered to and that food hygiene and Hazard Analysis and Critical Control Points (HACCP) are provided. In some countries, such as Scotland, a temporary public entertainment license is required. Many countries also require licenses for the commercialization of alcoholic beverages. In the United States, it is up to the local jurisdiction to issue either a permanent or temporary "liquor license." Smoking bans are also important points to consider when organizing events in different parts of the world.

Event professionals must be fully aware of their responsibility to ensure all aspects of licensing are adhered to. **Intellectual property** of concern to the event industry includes artistic work, conference proceedings, databases, films, plays, music and lyrics, software, websites, registration materials, recording and broadcasting, and so on.

WHY SHOULD EVENT PLANNERS INSURE EVENTS?

Sometimes it will be mandatory to insure an event or elements of an event so that it can actually take place. For example, the law of the land often is a key factor in helping event planners work out which insurance policies they absolutely must have. But, in addition to that, there will be other parties that may well insist on evidence of insurance. For example, the company that owns audiovisual equipment is highly unlikely to let a renter of the equipment take the equipment away if there is no insurance policy in place. Another example would be a venue that refuses entrance on the basis that the event planner has no public liability (third party/general commercial liability) in place.

As well as any contractual obligations, insuring an event brings two other key benefits for event planners. First, it provides "peace of mind," which is so crucial when the planner already has many other issues to deal with, and second, having an insurance policy means that there are known financial containments, i.e., the planner is aware that in the event of a claim the policy will pay up to the limit of indemnity/liability.

HOW A SPECIALIST EVENT INSURANCE BROKER CAN HELP

A specialist event insurance broker brings benefits in three main ways. The broker is able to arrange insurance coverage with specialist insurance companies who really understand the events business, the broker also has a deep understanding of common claims and can advise on risk prevention techniques, and last, the specialist broker often can negotiate strongly both when placing the insurance and also in dealing with any loss.

EVENT INSURANCE COSTS VERSUS BENEFITS

Insurance is a cost, and it is often looked on by many as just that, which is unfortunate as there are significant benefits that the possession of an insurance policy can provide. There is of course the peace of mind. If you don't have the insurance, do you really want to be worrying throughout your event as to whether something will go wrong, and, if it does, will you be able to fund it? Even for those planners that may have a poor claims history, the cost of insurance is usually pretty inexpensive in comparison to the overall financial exposure. And should there be a loss, then the insurance company will be there to deal with the legal defense issues.

EVENT INSURANCE AND FINANCIAL IMPACT

As a hypothetical example, an event costing £200,000 in all to put on, including the venue, catering, entertainment, speakers, kit hire, and so on, would have an insurance price, with a policy to cover the £200,000 in the event of a cancellation caused by some unforeseen circumstance, of £2,000.00. The decision is really whether to spend the £2,000 on the insurance policy or rely on funds from reserves (or some other avenue) up to £200,000 in the event of a loss.

EVENT INSURANCE IN THE UNITED KINGDOM

Over recent years the number of insurance products for events has been on the increase. Many products are sold via the web directly to the customer. This is acceptable as long as the customer understands precisely what is in the product they have purchased. In the United Kingdom the control of the sale of insurance products is heavily regulated, which in turn does affect the pricing that insurance companies charge as they have to factor in increased costs for making sure they adhere to the strict regulations. Lloyds of London still remains the worldwide center for underwriting risks of all sizes and descriptions.

Particular attention must be paid to **music licensing**. The event professional must always check with the local authorities to find out what the legal requirements are for the event being worked on. Even the smallest things must not be overlooked. For instance, it is not unusual to see presentation material produced by speakers that infringes **copyright laws**. Event planners can demonstrate due diligence by reminding speakers and delegates of copyright and **privacy laws**, along with obtaining written and signed disclaimer forms for the protection of intellectual property.

Another concern of the event professional when planning an event is the safety of everyone involved with the event. From a legal perspective, health and safety at work is compulsory in many countries. In the United Kingdom, for instance, business organizations with five or more employees are legally required to produce a health and safety policy, which is equally applicable to event companies in their duty of care to ensure the overall safety of the event, employees, attendees, and everyone else involved with the event. The event organization may consider creating an overarching **event safety policy** encompassing the event company's employees, suppliers, crews working on-site and the safety of anyone involved with or attending the event. This should include a health and safety policy statement, as well as information about the management and level of responsibility of those in charge of it.

There is, however, an overlap between the safety of employees, suppliers, crews, and attendees, due to the nature of the business. Thus, a distinction between an event safety policy and an event-specific **risk assessment** must be made. The event company must ensure the most comprehensive and detailed assessment of risks, including control measures, is prepared. Consultation, advice, licenses, and permits must be sought from local and regional governments, and the plan should ideally be worked on under the advice and inspection of local emergency services (the police, fire brigade, and ambulance services).

Other important considerations when planning events are accessibility, environmental protection, and ethical and privacy issues. Many countries in the world have accessibility laws or acts that must be complied with. (For more detailed information on accessibility, see chapter 11, "Legal Issues in the MEEC Industry" in, *Meetings, Expositions, Events and Conventions: An Introduction to the Industry,* Fenich [2012].) When planning an event, the professional must consider how accessible the venue is for people with physical or mental impairment. Staff must be trained to handle special requests, and information on accessibility must be provided through the event information channels. In the United States, such issues are covered under legislation called the Americans with Disabilities Act (ADA), whereas in Canada there is no such legislation. Environmental issues are topical concerns of modern life. Event professionals must ensure legislation pertaining to environmental protection is followed. Although initiatives such as paperless conferences, recycling, and environmentally friendly venues are laudable, modern-day event planners must investigate new and innovative ways of promoting sustainable practices both within their own organizations and at events. Other initiatives may include sourcing suppliers with ISO 14000 certification for environmentally sustainable activities, investigating suppliers' approaches to socially responsible employment practices, and similar initiatives. (For more detailed information see chapter 13, "Green Meetings and Social Responsibility" in, *Meetings, Expositions, Events and Conventions: An Introduction to the Industry,* Fenich [2012].) Responsible employment practices relates to ethical practices and includes transparent employment, and management and procurement practices. New legislation, for instance, the UK Bribery Act 2010, must be understood and followed to ensure compliance.

SECTION 2

EVENT PROGRAM

Events can and should be seen as **projects** that should be planned, managed, and evaluated. Projects have specific characteristics and are often one-time endeavors, limited by time and resources that aim at achieving specific goals and meeting specific needs.

An event project focuses not only on what happens during the event, but also on the process of creating the event in the first place. A formal process is created whereby the event can be described, analyzed, and improved. However, caution must be exercised for, unlike ongoing management processes, such as manufacturing, the product of an event project, the event itself, cannot be improved once it takes place. It is therefore crucial to get the event right the first time, and this is achieved through careful planning. Principles from theories of **project management** apply (see chapter 3 in this book on project management).

In the early stages of the planning process, the **event concept**, i.e., the event theme, sponsors, and media partners, is worked on. This stage of the planning process depends on how the need for the event came about, in other words, the generating source of the event. Events may come directly from corporate clients, marketing and advertising agencies, or event companies themselves. For instance, favored events among event management companies are corporate Christmas parties. The event company will create products much in the same way as a tour operator creates packages and will sell these to all types of businesses. Another aspect of the early planning process is the type of event being organized, i.e., whether the event is an ongoing existing concept, a new event, or whether the event is a bidding proposal for an existing event. An example of an existing concept may be an annual conference while a bidding proposal may be a government commission for the organization of an annual festival. Events may also be created by an organization, which then franchises or sells the rights to that event, i.e., jewelry shows.

The identification of a successful event concept requires a lot of creativity and research. The definition of purpose, theme, timing, audience, and venue can be a very strenuous and time-consuming process. Once the concept is created, a feasibility study is conducted to ascertain how viable the event is in its marketing, operational, and financial aspects. Stakeholders' involvement during the screening process is crucial (see chapter 5, "Stakeholder Management" for more details). In a nutshell, the early stages of the planning process will consider:

- Event concept
- Event breakdown
- Time line
- Budgeting (accommodation, meals, transport, entertainment)
- Sponsorship package
- Media plan

Once every aspect of the event concept is in place, the event professionals must decide on how to structure the **event program**. Again, this will vary according to the type of event being organized. For sporting events, this may be provided by the organizing committee or a sporting association, and there will be little scope for alterations. For new event concepts, a range of options will be available to the event planner, but these are invariably subject to the influence of event stakeholders. For instance, an educational conference will depend on a call for papers and submission of those by presenters willing to take part. The event professional will also come across difficulties regarding the availability of keynote speakers. This is when the event professional's network becomes evident. Attendance at networking events, gauging interest, and providing a strong pull factor that motivates people to take part and contribute to an event are important skills for the event professional.

When organizing the program, the event professional will need to consider the availability of space, the proposed range of activities, such as workshops, seminars, keynotes, site visits, and so on, and the facilities available. For instance, distributing the activities of a conference will depend on the availability of space, the time allocated for each activity, the provisions for coffee breaks, lunches, and dinners and must be organized in a way that is both relevant and engaging. The program should also consider arrival and departure travel times and eventualities that may impact on attendance figures.

Once the agenda is created, it should be made available to prospective attendees and delegates in various formats, i.e., as a printed or printable program (PDF), on the event's website, and regular updates should be sent to attendees using social media such as Facebook, Twitter, and Google+. Accessibility maps, itineraries, and other useful information must also be made available. These include accommodations in the area, travel advice, local transport maps, and so on.

Many events have concurrent or ancillary activities and programs with a range of options outside the main event for delegates. The event professional should try to learn about those events, such as an after-hours party organized by one of the exhibitors at a conference or fair, as those activities may impact on attendance the next day. Creating a "fringe" itinerary or agenda and establishing some sort of partnership with smaller side events may greatly improve the appeal of the event, add to the experience of delegates, and help improve registration numbers.

The event agenda must ensure that all considerations have been made. Itineraries must be carefully planned and have achievable time frames. If the conference includes site visits, time allocation must allow for small delays. The number and type of activities must be carefully considered so that there is a balanced range of choices for all delegates. Over-subscription to one or another popular activity is inevitable. It is the event professional's responsibility to ensure those are forecasted and strictly controlled.

In order to assist everyone producing and managing the event, **production schedules** (or **running orders**) and **call sheets** (also called **event specification guides**) are created. These are breakdowns of the event activities and serve as guides for the event professional, media crews, stage managers, and everyone involved with the event. Running orders include the time, duration, activity (action), and cue time. Call sheets are guides for managers and technical crews including standby lighting, sound and AV cues as well as those for the stage manager. Event professionals should be fully versed as far as **protocol** is concerned. This refers to the rules guiding the activities at events and particularly important in formal and diplomatic contexts. It relates to courtesy rules, which acknowledge hierarchical standing in chronological order, i.e., who sits where, who speaks first, and so on. In many countries, there are written protocol rules to be followed. It also refers to modern etiquette and civility. Templates are available at http://www.conventionindustry.org/Files/APEX/APEX_Event_Specifications_Guide.pdf

When planning the **registration process**, consideration must be given to the best method for registration or whether different methods will be available, how many people will be in charge of that, and how registration information will be collected. The information to be collected must include medical conditions, dress code, and other issues. The use of technology greatly facilitates the process, but thought must be given to what information is to be collected, for what purposes, and how this information will be handled and used in the future. One of the common mistakes made by conference professionals is that many potential attendees will fill out registration forms with the intention of attending the event, but will not inform the professionals if he or she decides not to attend. Regular checks between payments and registered attendance must be made to ensure consistent and accurate numbers that can help inform the marketing team of any possible additional promotional efforts, for instance.

Before advertising, those in charge of marketing should consider the best way to reach their target audience (e.g., posters, newsletters, website, changeable copy signs, schools, flyer drop-offs, social media, and so on). It is always useful to try a variety of approaches to ensure better reach. Once again, the look and feel of the venue will positively impact on participants' experiences at the event. A conference aimed at a specific group of professionals will be better promoted in industry-specific publications, through social media, and via direct mail. Databases of prospective attendees can be built, but this is time-consuming and hardly ever accurate as people change addresses, jobs, email addresses, and so on. Social media, such as Twitter, Facebook and LinkedIn, has great potential as a viral spread of the message will reach a wide audience (for more information on marketing, advertising, and promotions, see chapters 11 and 12.) It is usual, at the end of corporate events, to provide entertainment activities for delegates. This can vary in form, type, and location, but usually includes food, drinks, music or artistic performances, and other forms of entertainment. The event professional's role is to create the right atmosphere and opportunities for delegates to relax and enjoy each other's company. It is also important to provide similar opportunities for the event crew, suppliers, and volunteers. At the end of the event, the event professional can gather the team together for an informal wrap-up meeting, discuss the successful activities that have taken place, and thank everyone for contributing to the event. It is also a useful time to discuss improvement points for future events, but in a lighthearted way as a formal debriefing meeting should take place at a later date.

The **evaluation process** is equally important and must be planned at the early stages of the planning process. Discussions on how the event evaluation will be carried out, how information is to be collected, and how the information is to be used are a key aspect of event planning. The client may have requested information to calculate the event's ROI, to obtain event data for follow-up business activities, and to gauge the overall success of the event. How the information is to be presented is a very important aspect. For instance, in mega or hallmark events, such as the Commonwealth Games, the Olympic Games, and so on, a very comprehensive post-games report is produced. This includes information on all aspects of the event, from operational and commercial to ceremonies and sporting activities. For small corporate events, the report will not be so large, but it should be equally detailed in all aspects for evaluation agreed upon during the client briefing session (post-con) (see boxed text on next page). In either case, both hard and soft outcomes should be measured (hard might be how many people attended and soft might be how much was learned at a seminar). An executive summary is provided as a separate document, with key aspects of the event.

Contingency plan refers to the structured process of producing a backup plan for the event program. It consists of brainstorming a range of scenarios that may occur in case of failure of one or more aspects of the event. Among things to consider are the weather, unexpected poorer or higher attendance, catering availability, technical issues such as sound, IT, and other events. Some of these will be beyond the event professional's control. Although not everything can be avoided, their impact can be minimized. For instance, negotiating some leeway with caterers will ensure that a few additional guests will have something to eat and drink at the event. Backup power generators will also ensure the event can go on in case there is a power cut and the existing power generator does not work. Ensuring that enough volunteers turn up is another challenge for event professionals doing a charity dinner, for instance. Getting telephone and/or email confirmations a couple of days earlier will help. Additionally, when using students as volunteers, ensure one or two teachers are in charge of the group, oversee their work, and motivate students to show up to work.

The Client Brief

Adam Proto

Production/Creative Director of Terbell Ltd.

"What you put in is only what you can expect to get out"—a statement that sums up the importance of a good client brief or RFP (Request For Proposal) and most other things in life itself!

The purpose of a client brief is to cascade the correct information and create the blueprint a supplier needs to develop a project that is on brand, meets all the objectives, and delivers all the key messages. The event that lacks these key ingredients will have no DNA to hold it together; the result will be no clear direction other than that presumed by the agency or producer.

Collaboration at the very beginning of the process is often the best way to get the most out of each other's time and really understand what is possible given the budget, time, and boundaries. The starting points will always be:

- What do you want to say?
- Who is saying it (brand or not)?
- How do you want to say it?
- How much do you want to spend?
- When and where do you want to do it?
- How many do you want to see it?
- What do you want them to go home thinking?

The lack of a good brief is possibly the single biggest waste of time our industry has to deal with; ironically it is the lack of time that is often blamed for not producing a good brief in the first place!

Excerpt from "The Client Brief" by Adam Proto. Used by permission of Adam Proto.

INTEGRATION OF ADDITIONAL MARKETING ACTIVITIES WITHIN THE EVENT

With the use of events becoming a more popular tool within the marketing plan of many different organizations (whether profit or nonprofit), there are also wider possibilities to incorporate other marketing activities within an event itself. Being able to attract large numbers of people together, often with similar interests, provides an opportunity to derive greater commercial or financial gain. For example, a corporate dinner for employees may provide the opportunity to include an awards ceremony for high-performing staff or those who have shown the most potential during the year.

Many different charities use a wide variety of events to publicize and enhance their fund-raising activities, as the positive atmosphere generated at such gatherings often leads to increased generosity from those taking part. It is common to see events that run different types of auctions during their day/evening in order to benefit the organizing charity. For example, a charity may host an annual fund-raising event at which guests have the opportunity to bid on various items of sporting memorabilia or exotic holidays, with all funds raised going to the organization. With guests often in high spirits at such events (often linked to the intake of alcohol!), significant funds can be raised for the most worthy of causes.

On a slight variation to the standard event auction, guests may also be invited to take part in a "silent auction" on the night, where similar prizes are on offer but the bidding method is a little different. In this instance, guests are invited to put forward a bid of their own (above a set minimum or "reserve" price) and place it into a sealed envelope, which is then passed to the event professional or charity representative. At the designated moment of the event, the winner of the prize is announced and is the person who has bid the highest amount for the item, without having any prior indication of which other bids were also being placed for it. For the professional and the charity, a silent auction can have many positive outcomes, as guests offer significant sums, often way above the suggested value of the item in question.

In a commercial environment and for organizations with many different customers (existing or potential) or members, competitions may also be run in conjunction with events, so that winners may be announced at the event. For an international association bringing members to an event from many different parts of the world or for an established organization, competitions can increase the interest in an event and provide another reason for an individual to attend. Possible examples in this area may see the inclusion of an "Outstanding Employee" award to be presented at an international corporate or association event or retail organizations offering luxurious holidays or expensive household items in prize giveaways at large consumer-based events.

This contribution to the decision-making process of the attendee is an important consideration for the event professional. It is their responsibility to do everything possible to maximize the number of attendees present at the event and to understand why people are coming. As mentioned previously in the chapter, influences such as the event's location and venue may also provide an important reason to attend, along with the content or program of the event itself. Therefore, this should be linked to the correct pricing of the event (if payment is required), so that the cost of attending does not discourage a potential attendee.

Within the wider marketing sphere, events are also used by well-known companies and organizations to interact with their customers and provide an "experiential marketing" experience. Many brands take the opportunity to publicly show that they seek and value interaction with their customers and use events to achieve this in a number of ways. Competitions have already been highlighted as one of these methods, but having the chance to speak to customers, provide "value-added experiences," such as test drives, free concerts, tasting sessions, or personal appearances by well-known celebrities, increases the perception of the organization to the customer and theoretically makes them more likely to stay loyal to that company for a longer period of time.

This method is now commonly used by telecommunication companies, for example, with many millions of customers, running exclusive and attractive events for which tickets are won by new or existing customers in a variety of ways. Commercially, the organization may derive greater return on investment through these events, often costing less than wider advertising campaigns, for example, as the feel-good factor generated by them and the positive word-of-mouth it spreads exceeds the perceived benefits gained from other marketing activities.

Another increasingly popular inclusion within events over recent years has been team-building activities designed to increase the morale and team spirit of the staff or employees in attendance. Many different types of activity may be seen as appropriate, with an increasingly varied amount of companies now offering services in this area. Whether staff are taken rock climbing, white-water rafting over rapid waterways, led into the countryside to camp in the middle of the night, or asked to write and perform a song together, team-building exercises have taken on a new importance in recent times, as organizations seek to get the best out of their people and keep them for longer periods of time. During a recent Meeting Professionals International Congress held on the beach in Florida, a team-building activity was organized. Groups of participants were charged with building a sand castle using the props provided, and prizes were awarded. For the event professional, several issues arise around these activities, as there are many health and safety requirements present, and the selection of the most appropriate supplier is key. Here, relying on a recommendation from a fellow professional or a professional association may prove valuable, in order that confidence may be gained in the company delivering the experience.

SUMMARY

This chapter has described the importance of preplanning the event in its strategic and operational aspects. Understanding the event goals and objectives of both the event itself and that of delegates is of the utmost importance to increase the chances of success. Events are highly risky projects, both commercially and safety-related, but event risks can be minimized and sometimes completely avoided through detailed pre-event research and planning. When planning an event, professionals must consider the event's key performance indicators (KPIs) and use post-event evaluation tools to measure whether, and if possible how, the event objectives have been achieved. As far as commercial risks are concerned, careful consideration of suppliers, venue, and the event program is crucial and will determine the event's successful achievement of objectives. Marketing activities included in the event program should tie in with the overall event marketing objectives and can greatly im-

pact on a delegate's experiences and positive feedback of the event. As far as safety risks go, a detailed risk assessment must be carried out and contingency plans put in place whenever possible. All of these activities must be done in an innovative and creative way, and this is arguably the biggest challenge for event professionals.

Now that you have completed this chapter, you should be competent in the following Meetings and Business Events Competency Standards:

MBECS—Skill 16: Design Program

Sub skills		Skills (standards)
H 16.01	Determine program components	
H 16.02	Select program content	
H 16.03	Structure and sequence program components	

KEY WORDS AND TERMS

Footfall
Duty of Care
Due Diligence
Liability
Contracts
Licenses
Permits
Intellectual Property

Music Licensing
Copyright Laws
Privacy Laws
Event Safety Policy
Risk Assessment
Projects
Project Management
Event Concept

Event Program
Production Schedule
Running Orders
Event Specification Guides
Protocol
Registration Process
Evaluation Process
Contingency Plan

REVIEW AND DISCUSSION QUESTIONS

1. The statement "fail to prepare, prepare to fail" holds true for all event professionals. Do you agree?
2. How might an event be impacted if the event professional fails to fully read and understand its various contracts?
3. A Singapore-based event management company, with over 2,000 members in the Asia-Pacific region, is hosting a five-day conference-exhibition in Kuala Lumpur. What are the possible strategies that the event planners can use to maximize attendance?
4. What is the purpose of conducting pre-event research? How can event professionals use the information to make decisions?

5. Events can be divided into pre-, during and post-event stages. What aspects should be considered when planning each of the stages?

6. Legal aspects are of particular importance to events. How can the event professional ensure the event organization and the event itself comply with legal and regulatory requirements of a given destination?

7. The organization of events involves risks. Discuss the types of risks affecting event organizations and how these can be minimized or prevented.

REFERENCES AND ONLINE RESOURCES

Fenich, G.G. (2012). *Meetings, Expositions, Events and Conventions: An Introduction to the Industry.* Pearson.

Fenich, G.G., Scott-Halsell, S., and Ogbeide, G.C. (2012). *What the Millennial Generation Wants in Their Meetings and Events.* Chicago: Professional Convention Management Association.

Goldblatt, J. (2008). *Special Events: A New Generation and the next frontier.* Hoboken, NJ: John Wiley and Sons.

ABOUT THE CHAPTER CONTRIBUTORS

Andrew Kirby is the program director of the BA (Hons) International Events Management undergraduate degree at Regent's College London. Before entering academia, Andrew worked as an international event manager for over twelve years for a variety of international organizations including an IT consultancy, an electronics manufacturer, and a professional industry association. Andrew has a particular research interest in the use of sporting venues for conferences, meetings, and events and is unsurprisingly a keen Manchester United FC fan.

Jeff Papis is a senior lecturer in event management at Regent's College London. His academic experience goes back to 1992. Jeff has worked for cultural centers in Brazil and in the United Kingdom and has organized a variety of events, including conferences, graduation ceremonies, music festivals, and other social events. Jeff has a particular interest in event design, corporate events, and strategic event planning. His hobbies include BMX racing and computers.

Planning and Designing the Environment

CHAPTER **8**

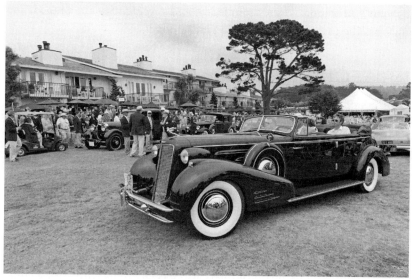

The environment is critical for outdoor car shows such as the Concours D'elegance.
Jamie Pham Stock Connection Worldwide/Newscom

Chapter Objectives

Upon completion of this chapter, the reader should be able to:

- Determine/make plans for types of speakers, entertainers, performers
- Determine sources of speakers, entertainers, performers
- Determine methods of choosing speakers, entertainers, and/or performers
- Secure contracts and communicate expectations
- Determine and develop plans for staging and technical requirements
- Develop admittance and credential systems
- Establish crowd management strategies
- Determine risk management plans

Chapter Outline

Introduction

The Event Requirements

The Event Location

Determining Speakers

Contracts and Agreements

Staging and Technical Requirements

Crowd Management Strategies

Managing Event Risk

Summary

Key Words and Terms

Review and Discussion Questions

References

About the Chapter Contributor

Sponsors have been the most critical component to growing the Motoring Festival now recognized as one of the Southeast Tourism Society's Top 20 Events. The rich data that Dr. John Salazar and USCB has gathered and provided from the event has been an essential factor to the growth of the sponsorship program and in driving our marketing effort. The quality and breath of information has become the benchmark for demographic data used in measuring the impact of destination events.

Carolyn Vanagell
President
Hilton Head Island Motoring Festival & Concours d'Elegance

NOTE: Dr. John Salazar is the chapter contributor.

INTRODUCTION

For an event to be successful, event professionals have many details to consider in the planning and designing stages. The mission of the event is at the center of planning and designing and the spine from which the event is built. The details of the event location, speakers/entertainers, and crowd management practices must consistently align with the **event's mission**. When the mission and the logistics are aligned, the event professional has the ingredients for a successful product.

THE EVENT REQUIREMENTS

Successful organizers of meetings, events, and conventions must strategically plan and design each event and align that strategy with the purpose and resources available from the client. Getz (2007) presented a typology of planned events based primarily on their purpose and program. The categories identified in the typology are: Cultural Celebrations, Political and State, Arts and Entertainment, Business and Trade, Educational and Scientific, Sport and Competition, and Private Events. Each event in the typology is created to accomplish an economic, cultural, societal, and/or environmental objective.

Meetings, events, and conventions are hosted for a variety of purposes. Meetings that educate a community's local nonprofit organizations can greatly differ from the annual gathering of a corporation's board of directors. Special events with strong commercial support, such as the Lollapalooza traveling music festival that generates revenues for both entertainment companies and the local community, will have planning and design characteristics that vary considerably when compared to a municipal Earth Day Festival intended to educate the local citizens on environmental conservation practices. Conventions that train and develop employees from Fortune 500 companies will diverge from practices used to train and develop government employees. Consequently, understanding the mission and purpose of each event as well as the organizers' available financial resources is imperative in planning and designing the environment.

Events require extensive planning, and the execution of a successful event endeavor involves teamwork among various departments, agencies, and small businesses. Event professionals manage three resources: time, money, and people. She continues to point out that professionals must orchestrate the three resources within a given period in order to produce an event that achieves the goals of the client. Therefore, each meeting, event, or convention begins with a mission.

Event author David Getz asserts that the experience of the attendees is the primary mission of meeting/event management. The mission should identify the goals the organization is attempting to achieve. Creating a mission will keep the organizer focused on the outcome of the effort. GolfDigestPlanner.com states the mission should be precise and measurable. Fenich (2012) states that objectives should be SMART: Specific, Measurable, Achievable, Relevant, and Time frame (p. 163). An example of a mission statement relative to the opening image of this chapter might read:

> *Our Car Show on July 4, 2014 is meant to raise $250,000 for the Boys and Girls Club of Hilton Head Island and to enhance public awareness of the antique car hobby.*

After the mission is established, branding the event is a strategy that will keep the organizer on task to accomplish the event's goals. A **brand** is a name, term, sign, symbol, design, or a combination of these elements intended to identify the goods or services of a seller and differentiate them from competitors. While branding an event might be a little different when compared to branding a product or service, the intention of branding an event is primarily the same. The focus of event branding is to effectively synthesize the elements while keeping the event unique and memorable. It is important that a brand be incorporated into an event in an organic way and not in a staged way. Once the mission and the branding of the event are clear, organizers can then move forward to determine the types of speakers, entertainers, and performers (SEPs).

THE EVENT LOCATION

When choosing the location to host an event, the event professional must be concerned with various logistical details. The original mission of the event can actually dictate the location. For example, a convention organized for a national corporation that requires its employees to travel might be best hosted in the nation's midsection if the employees are equally distributed throughout the United States. A central location for a national gathering might be best in cities such as Chicago, Illinois, or St. Louis, Missouri. Additionally, having a centrally located meeting will keep average travel costs low and will eliminate the coast-to-coast travel cost as well as travel time incurred by those who live on either the West or East Coast.

Event locations can also be directly impacted by transportation accessibility. Whether it is travel by auto, rail, and/or air, the mode of travel dictates where an event can be held. For example, just recently the 30th Olympic Games were hosted by London, UK. London contains two international airports and an extensive rail system; the city of London has a public transportation system servicing the 8+ million residents. The transportation infrastructure and access to international travel is a defining characteristic for hosts of major international events. In the United States, Washington, DC is a popular convention destination because it too has two major airports, good highway access, and is a rail hub. Bangkok is hosting more conventions due to its central location in Southeast Asia.

Other relevant characteristics that influence the location choice of meetings/events are the hospitality services available to the event attendees. The event planner must consider the locations' services and if the services adequately meet the expectations of the attendees. Attendees traveling and meeting at the local or community level might have differing expectations when compared to attendees who travel for international events. Senior citizens have different expectations of a destination than, say, millennials. Exceeding the attendees' expectations is extremely important and directly relates to the success of each event.

One of the primary hospitality services that will influence event attendee satisfaction (post-arrival) is the choice of venue. A 2 million square foot convention facility teeming with attendee activity is exciting for major national association conventions. However, such a large facility hosting a smaller local community meeting will be costly, and the unused facility space would be cold and unwelcoming for any attendee. Further, if the smaller event is using the venue at the same time as a large convention, the small event may be overwhelmed or may get less service. A smaller local and regional meeting might be best suited for hotel convention/meeting space that can cater to both large and smaller groups. A community's local hotel oftentimes has dedicated meeting space for smaller events. A very small event, such as a dinner meeting of the local Rotary Club, might be better suited to a private room in a restaurant. The restaurant chain, Maggiano's Little Italy, derives a significant portion of its revenue from meetings and events, and many locations employ a full-time meeting and event professional. It is imperative that the event professional match the size and needs of the group with the size and services available at the venue. The two operative questions event professionals must ask themselves are (1) who are they (the group) and (2) why are they here (what are their goals and objectives for the event).

A second factor that influences the event location can be the choice of available lodging in the community. Depending on the event, the attendees, and the intended outcome of the organizers, a community with a diverse lodging inventory may (or may not) be appropriate. For example, if the event will attract attendees who need different types of hotel service, a community with a hotel inventory that has various types of lodging products would be an appropriate location. However, if the event is intended to build esprit de corps among its members, a hotel that is large enough to accommodate the membership under one roof as well as adequately host the meetings and subsequent breakouts might play a larger role when choosing the event destination. Some event professionals prefer meeting on cruise ships for this reason. Smith Travel Research (STR) provides regularly updated data on room inventory and price (ADR) in most U.S. and many international destinations. Other factors that influence the event destination choice include access to food and dining options, attractions and other special events, as well as transportation throughout the local community.

The consulting firm Fenich & Associates LLC has developed an extensive database that includes over sixty different destination attractiveness metrics, such as the size of the convention center, hotel inventory, Average Daily Rate (ADR), occupancy (OCC), restaurants, airlift, cost of meals, recreation opportunities, spectator sports, climate, and so on. They have gathered this data for over 140 destinations in North America and can thereby make comparisons and evaluations for event professionals. The firm has also developed mathematical models that ascertain the magnitude of convention business a given destination should be seeing, given its relative attractiveness (consult their website for additional information).

DETERMINING SPEAKERS

Determining SEPs may seem like a daunting task. However, if the organization's mission and brand strategy are clear, identifying the presenters and entertainers becomes less complex. Event managers manage time, money, and people. Understanding the client's financial resources when organizing presenters and entertainers will help dictate the ability of the event professional to hire and/or recruit the appropriate presenters or entertainers. Even if financial resources are limited, there are strategies that less-funded events can utilize to hire and/or recruit the appropriate personnel. An example of the latter is the use of university faculty members for speaking to groups in the same locale as the university.

Various methods of recruiting presenters and entertainers can include the utilization of speaker bureaus, industry experts, university experts, entertainment agents, and directories. Using speaker bureaus provides planners with access to various speakers and entertainers. The speaker bureau will have direct knowledge of speakers and entertainers that address specific topics or that have a specific focus on event agendas. For example, a bureau may be aware of a celebrity who has a certain passion for raising funds for elementary education and will offer to speak on the need to support school fund-raising at a reduced fee. The American Program Bureau, the Premiere Motivational Speakers Bureau, the Washington Speakers Bureau, and the National

Geographic Speakers Bureaus are examples of bureaus that can locate speakers for business, university, and education purposes. However, bureaus may have extensive fees for booking their speakers and therefore may not be financially practical when choosing a speaker for an event. The "speaker fee" or "honorarium" can depend on a number of different factors, including the type of organization and nature of an event (for profit vs. not for profit), how far a speaker has to travel, length and number of presentations, and demand for a speaker's services. Additional expenses such as travel and lodging are not included in the honorarium.

Industry experts can also be identified as possible speaker talent for a meeting or special event. Industry experts can be found via book publishers because some experts are prolific authors. Additionally, industry experts can be found through professional associations, media interviews, and newspaper and magazine articles. Certain experts might be able to be contacted directly, but some might require to be contacted only through their publisher. However, industry experts may also charge fees for their speaking engagements so it is important that the event professional understand the financial resources available to them when booking the speaker. To the contrary, university faculty and researchers might be national, regional, or industry experts who are competent speakers and can be affordable options for events hosted by nonprofit agencies or lower-budgeted events.

Other methods of finding speakers and/or entertainers include utilizing talent agents, professional associations, and entertainment directories. However, the event organizer must be fully aware of the budgetary constraints that exist when recruiting from those entities as well. Planning an event is akin to running a business. At the end of the day, you will be left with a profit/loss statement that lists the event's income and expenses. The event manager needs to be sound in their approach to financial management.

When selecting SEPs for the event, it is important to remember the mission and brand strategy of the event. Staying focused on the purpose will help in identifying the right individuals that will lead to success. Conceptually, the event professional is the conduit between the event host and the SEPs. Consequently, it is important to consider feedback from various parties prior to making these arrangements. Feedback from the event sponsor will provide insight on their specific mission as well as the budget available for booking speakers and talent. Should the event host organize a board of directors to oversee event quality, the board members can also provide direction on the speaker and the specific content that needs to be presented. If the event is being organized for political and state, business and trade, educational and scientific, and sport and competition, members of affiliated professional associations might offer insights on specific individuals that would enrich the event. Professional members might also be a direct source for speakers and talent. For example, medical doctors holding membership in the American Medical Association (AMA) might be respected professionals in the discipline and could be appropriate speakers for an annual AMA convention. Often, members of the professional associations and societies are well aware of individuals truly admired in their field and are aware of the professional respect that they command from their peers. Another source of feedback that will help in selecting appropriate event talent is an entertainment agency. Entertainment agencies are cognizant of the interests and demands of the clients they represent and would have an understanding of which individuals are trending upward or downward. In short, the feedback you receive from the event sponsor, event board, professional memberships, and entertainment agencies should be carefully examined prior to arranging a contract with the speaker, entertainer, or performer. When booking entertainers, an agent rather than a bureau may be the source and the party with whom to negotiate.

With entertainers it is a good idea to listen to a recording or, better yet, to see a live performance prior to booking.

Program length will depend on the goal that the event host is seeking to achieve. For education and training programs, presentation and speaker length might be dictated by the type of training that occurs. For example, speaker-facilitated workshops that require more engagement from the audience can run significantly longer compared to a 45- to 70-minute standup presentation without audience participation.

When considering the length of time for entertainers, event professionals must consider the entertainer's programs as well as the guidance provided by the entertainment agency. When organizing musical entertainment for festivals and/or special events, the planner must consider the purpose of the entertainment. Musical entertainment for background and ambience is different than entertaining for dancing and musical enjoyment. The different purposes will dictate the stage placement of the musicians, the sound level, as well as their engagement with the audience.

Methods of compensating SEPs can vary. Speakers can be compensated based on a prearranged speaking fee that s/he normally charges per engagement. However, not all event hosts can afford to pay the set fees, so some event professionals may offer to pay a reduced fee speaking stipend that is the same for all speakers. The event host can also offer to make and pay for the travel and lodging arrangements for the speaker as a way of incentivizing the speaker. Compensating performers and entertainers can differ from the speaker arrangements because **compensation** can be based on different methods as well. For example, the set fee that the entertainment agency arranges and normally charges per entertainer/performer is possible with a portion of revenue from event sales being added or part of the total compensation.

When finally choosing SEPs, event professionals should consider the needs of the event as well as the direction provided by event committee members. Many events will organize an event committee that is responsible for selecting speakers and entertainers. The committee members can provide great insight when finally choosing speakers/entertainers. A list of questions to committee members to consider for speaker/entertainer selection could include the following:

1. Is the speaker/entertainer's background aligned with the mission of the organization and the event?
2. Is the speaker/entertainer affordable to hire for the event?
3. Will the speaker/entertainer have additional requirements above and beyond the fees paid, such as lodging, travel, and meal provisions?
4. Will the speaker/entertainer provide an experience that adds value for event attendees?
5. Will the speaker/entertainer have **staging** and equipment requirements that might exceed the planned speaker/entertainment budget?

CONTRACTS AND AGREEMENTS

When organizing **contracts,** event professionals should consider three things: (1) for whom something is done, (2) when will it be done, and (3) who will do what. The contract with a SEP is a one-time arrangement whereas if the agreement is broken, the cancellation of the speaker/entertainer can lead to an inadequately organized event. Hospitality law author Stephen Barth says that when nonperformance by a vendor will cause a negative effect on the hospitality operation, it is critical that language be included in the contract to protect the operation. Below is an example of an entertainer nonperformance clause. The example below is an agreement between the entertainer and a hotel.

> The Speaker/Entertainer/Performer recognizes that failure to perform hereunder may require Venue to acquire replacement entertainment on short notice. Therefore, any failure to provide the agreed upon services at the times, in the areas, and for the duration required herein shall constitute a default which shall allow the Venue to cancel this contract immediately on oral notice. The Speaker/Entertainer/Performer and/or his/her agent will be liable for any damages incurred by Venue, including without limitation, any costs incurred by the Venue to secure such replacement entertainment.

Contracts between event organizers and SEPs should be as specific as possible to eliminate any opportunities for miscommunication. Event managers should follow the following concepts:

- Ensure that all contracts conform to local, state, and federal regulations.
- Determine the time frame for final execution.
- Prepare original for each signer and use the signed originals as the official document.
- Create a separate checklist to track the approval process for all written agreements.
- Identify arbitration and dispute resolution methods.

After the contract is agreed upon, the event organizer and SEPs should be in constant contact with each other to ensure that all of the SEP requirements are being met. If travel arrangements are embedded in the agreement, the event professional should clarify the travel details no later than two weeks prior to the event. If the SEP requires presentation or stage equipment requirements, these details should be solidified no later than two weeks in advance as well.

While many of the previous details are important when dealing with SEPs, other details about the mission of the event as well as the attendees can help the SEP in organizing their presentation or show. It is extremely relevant to communicate to SEPs the objective(s) of the event as well as the demographics and psychographics of the attendees. Demographic characteristics refer to details such as attendee age, income, and education level, while psychographic characteristics refer to the value systems, motivations, and/or personalities of the attendees. Describing the event and attendees in great detail will help the SEPs tailor their presentation to the audience. The more appropriate the content is aligned with the audience, the more satisfied they should be with the event. The audience details also provide the SEPs with information that will help them understand the culture of the audience as well as the appropriate attire. After all, a "wardrobe malfunction" as occurred with Janet Jackson at the Super Bowl would not be appropriate for a children's event.

During meetings and conferences, event professionals should attempt to evaluate speakers via attendee feedback. Feedback mechanisms, such as session evaluations and conference surveys, can give event professionals insight on the appropriate or inappropriate speaker selection. Session evaluation forms can include session satisfaction evaluation items such as: (1) the speaker's presentation style, (2) content appropriateness, (3) ability to engage the audience, and (4) willingness to recommend the speaker to other conference attendees. These items will help guide the event professional in making speaking arrangements for future conferences.

STAGING AND TECHNICAL REQUIREMENTS

Staging and technical requirements for events can greatly vary. In order to determine the staging and technical needs, the event professional must balance the mission of the event with the needs of the SEPs. The size and height of a stage depends on the available space within the event venue, the number of attendees, and the type of presentation or show. For example, a special event fund-raising dinner might have musical entertainment that is needed for background music as well as a dancing post-dinner function. However, the primary mission of the event is to focus on fund-raising activities and the presentation of speeches. Consequently, the musical entertainment staging might be positioned separately whereas a smaller musicians' stage is set off to the side of the venue. However, when fund-raising, the master of ceremonies' stage is up front and at the center of the audience's view. Below are some example checklist items for staging:

Staging Checklist
Room size essential
Entrance and exit awareness
Fire exits and signage
Ceiling measurements high and low points
Ceiling facility for hanging props/mobiles
Side walls facility
Stage floor surfaces
Building of wings
Stage height, width, and depth
Room access time
Carpet and flooring
Available fabrics for ceiling and stage

Additional consideration should be given to the setting and décor of the event venue. Setting and décor can help brand the event, and it can be utilized to theme the venue and make a more favorable impression upon the attendees. While event professionals and staff can arrange the setting and décor, many professional decorators and designers can be contracted to prepare the venue. Exhibition Service Contractors (ESC), such as Freeman and GES, are the most widely used. The setting and décor can be as important as the speakers/entertainers chosen for the event.

Recently, the safety and securing of lighting, equipment, and staging has come under scrutiny. In 2011, at the Indiana state fair, fifty-eight people were injured and seven people were killed as a result of a stage collapsing due to high winds. In 2012, a stage collapse in Toronto, Canada, injured three and killed one person. The Toronto stage collapse is still being investigated. However, both of the tragedies pale in comparison to the 2003 Station Nightclub fire in West Warwick, Rhode Island. The fire killed one hundred people and was the fourth deadliest nightclub fire in U.S. history. The fire started as a result of the pyrotechnics used by the entertainers, and the investigation revealed that the club owners were not aware of the pyrotechnic plans. However, the band asserted the owners were informed. The three tragedies demonstrate the need to understand the equipment capacity and, in the case of the Station Nightclub fire, the need to be aware of the entertainer's special effects requirements.

The Unplanned Fireworks

George G. Fenich, PhD was attending a convention being held at the Opryland Hotel in Nashville. Live entertainment that included indoor pyrotechnics was staged in one of the atriums. The fireworks element began and, subsequently, Dr. Fenich was quite impressed when some of the fireworks traveled away from the stage and over the heads of audience members. Dr. Fenich was less impressed when one of the live palm trees behind him burst into flames as a result of being impacted by the fireworks. Luckily the hotel fire staff was able to quench the fire quickly: AND the show went on!

CROWD MANAGEMENT STRATEGIES

Providing adequate attendee access as well as providing a secure venue for the attendees should be the priority of an event professional. Appropriate venue space and the flow of attendees throughout the space can have great impact on the attendee's satisfaction with the event. Depending on the mission and objectives of the event, the venue space can have more open access or controlled access with minimum exit and entrance points. Open event access can be used to promote the free flow of attendees throughout the event as well as maintaining the open flow of attendees through the event's exits and entrances. This method is often used when no admission fees are charged to the attendees, and the intention of the event is to encourage the attendees to move freely from vendor to vendor or function to function. Controlled access is often used when entrance fees are charged, and controlling access is important to revenue collection. Minimizing access points will allow the event organizer to control people flow and help guarantee that entrance fees are collected.

Crowd Issues at the Haj in Mecca

The **Hajj** (Arabic: حج‎ Ḥaǧǧ "pilgrimage," also spelled **haj**) is the largest annually occurring pilgrimage in the world and must be carried out by every able-bodied Muslim who can afford to do so at least once in his or her lifetime. It takes place in the holy city of Mecca. As of 2010, about three million pilgrims participated in this annual pilgrimage. Crowd-control techniques have become critical, and because of the large numbers of people, many of the rituals have become more stylized. But even with the crowd-control techniques, there are still many incidents during the Hajj, as pilgrims are trampled in a crush or ramps collapse under the weight of the many visitors, causing hundreds of deaths.

SOURCE: http://en.wikipedia.org/wiki/Hajj, accessed December 2012.

Crowd management and **crowd flow** are extremely important to the satisfaction levels of the event attendee. Appropriate flow begins with understanding the facility's capacity, attendee estimated counts, and the schedule of event activities. Facility capacity is often dictated by a maximum capacity established by the venue and/or local fire department officials. However, maximizing a venue's capacity might not be the best strategy when hosting an event. While each event is different, the flow of people influences the pace of people moving throughout the event and eventually the attendees

Sign for Speaker. Photo by George G. Fenich

allotted time to view various venues and visit with specific vendors. An overly crowded event can lead to congested aisles and slow crowd flow, which can also reduce the number of event attendees.

Appropriate and effective signage can provide direction that eases congestion and increases the flow of attendees throughout the event. Appropriate signage will direct the attendee to specific event locations, gathering places, entrances, and exits. Signage should be placed at the entrance to an event to provide direction to the attendees. Additionally, event maps or kiosks can be intermittently placed at the entrance and throughout an event to reduce crowd congestion and reduce the need for the event professional to hire many additional employees or volunteers to field attendee questions related to exhibit locations. Effective signage can use color schemes and size to emphasize the location or relative importance of an event area. For example, if an organizer hired a celebrity speaker for a presentation at a national conference, it is important for the organizer to have signage that makes obvious to the attendees that the celebrity speaker will be presenting at a specific time. Making the signage obvious to the attendees will help in increasing the speaker's audience. Therefore, the effective signage should be larger when compared to other directional signs.

Crowd management and crowd flow are also directly linked to capacity levels of the equipment used to move attendees. For example, maximum occupancy of an elevator must be considered when moving people from one event floor to another. The same consideration must be given to escalators within the event facility. Event centers can describe the facility's capacity to move people when advertising their facility or convention center. For example, the Washington State Convention Center in Seattle, Washington, has their elevator capacities listed on their website and in collateral material, whereas event professionals can estimate the number of people that can be moved from one event floor to another. The elevator and escalator capacity are legal restrictions that are enforceable by state codes. Concern should also be given to stair access in the event that the elevators and escalators break down during the event.

Event organizers must also secure facility approvals (when necessary) prior to hosting the event. As convention centers have capacity requirements, so do open space municipal facilities. For example, outdoor publicly owned event locations, such as parks and recreation facilities, also have maximum capacity requirements and require municipal approval prior to the event. Often, the local municipality will have guidelines related to crowd, food, and liquor practices. Additionally, the facilities will also fall under the same local fire marshal code practices as the local event centers.

Crowd restrictions can be managed by queuing ticket sales, queuing lines, and identification methods. Festivals, events, and theme parks are now beginning to regulate the crowd flow by allotting a set amount of tickets sold and distributed during a time frame. For example, on Christmas Day, 2012, Disney World in Orlando (FL) was so crowded, officials stopped admitting people at 10 a.m. With this strategy, the event can better manage the crowd flow throughout the facility. Queuing lines also control flow and the event entrance as well as venues within the event facilities. Outside the event, the queue can help regulate the flow of entering attendees, while inside the event, properly placed vendor queues can reduce aisle congestion. Hotels and resorts attempt to control crowds not staying within their properties during special events and festivals through identification methods. For example, paying guests of a resort can be given an identification bracelet that indicates to hotel/resort employees that they have access to resort grounds. RFID tags are radio frequency identification tags that utilize a wireless system for automatic identification and tracking. RFID tags can also be used to manage the flow of event attendees throughout an event.

MANAGING EVENT RISK

Security and safety of attendees are extremely important to the perceived satisfaction levels of the event. Security and safety are not characteristics that are obvious to attendees when present. However, when absent, the lack of a secure environment can have negative impacts on attendee satisfaction. Smaller events hosted by municipal and nonprofit agencies often work with local law enforcement to ensure the safety of their attendees. However, the law enforcement agency must be informed far before the event to schedule the needed personnel. Larger events often contract with security

Restricting Hotel Access in New Orleans on Mardi Gras Day

Mardi Gras day in New Orleans is a world-famous event. The celebration involves hundreds of thousands of visitors converging on the French Quarter, drinking beer, and carousing. As happens after consumption of copious amounts of beer, revelers seek to find hotels where they can use the restrooms. However, not surprisingly, hotels do not want anyone other than registered guests using their facilities. Thus, they issue wristbands to individuals authorized to enter. Even the McDonalds restaurant on the edge of the French Quarter restricts bathroom access to paying customers. There are only two public toilets in the French Quarter—each at an opposite end. Finding a place to "relieve oneself" during Mardi Gras day has become so bad that a popular local song was coined and recorded entitled "There ain't no where to pee on Mardi Gras Day."

agencies for security and safety concerns. Contract companies can be used for specific tasks, such as bag inspections and other screening techniques.

When organizing the final event admission procedures, event professionals should consider the general admission criteria as well as event admitting policies that address VIPs, government officials, and special needs of attendees. The procedures should be

Inauguration of President Obama in 2009

The first inauguration of Barack Obama as the 44th president of the United States took place on Tuesday, January 20, 2009. The inauguration, which set a record attendance for any event held in Washington, D.C., marked the commencement of the first four-year term of Barack Obama as president of the United States. Based on the combined attendance numbers, television viewership, and Internet traffic, it was among the most-observed events ever by a global audience. Because of high demand and limited availability of the reserved tickets, some people planned to offer their tickets for sale through ticket brokers, Internet auctions, and classified listing services. Sales offers for tickets reached as high as $1,750 each for the reserved standing room section behind the Capitol Reflecting Pool, $5,500 each for the reserved standing room section in front of the Reflecting Pool and $20,000 each for the VIP section on the Capitol grounds. The inaugural parade route ran along Pennsylvania Avenue, N.W. from the U.S. Capitol, ending at the north face of the White House. During most of the parade, President Obama and First Lady Michelle Obama traveled in the new armored limousine because of potential security threats. No official count was taken of the number of people attending the inaugural ceremony, although multiple sources concluded that the ceremony had the largest audience of any event ever held in Washington, D.C. Government agencies and federal officials, who coordinated security and traffic management, determined the attendance count to be 1.8 million people. Amid the massive crowds that arrived at the U.S. Capitol for the inauguration, about 4,000 ticket holders were unable to gain entry to reserved areas on the Capitol grounds after security personnel closed the gates at the start of the formal ceremony. Many ticket holders were stuck in underground tunnels where pedestrian traffic was directed to and from the National Mall. NBC News dubbed one such tunnel "the Purple Tunnel of Doom," after the purple tickets that would-be viewers held. Others remained stuck in long lines as they waited to gain entry to the reserved areas. The inauguration took place in an era of enhanced security in the decade following the September 11 attacks. Security was so tight that every single portable toilet being brought in for temporary use by the crowds had to be inspected for bombs prior to installation and guarded between the time they were installed and inauguration day. Because of the size of the crowds expected in Washington, D.C. for the inaugural activities, planners raised concerns about public safety and security.

The police presence in the District of Columbia temporarily doubled, augmented by the addition of 8,000 police officers from around the United States. The police force was assisted by 1,000 FBI agents to provide security for the event, and the Secret Service Counter-sniper team was assigned to hidden locations throughout the area. The Transportation Security Administration had over 300 officers from its National Deployment Force on hand to assist the Secret Service with security inspections of attendees entering the National Mall. Ten thousand National Guard troops were on site, with 5,000 troops providing security duty in a ceremonial capacity and 1,300 unarmed troops aiding park police in crowd control at the National Mall. C Company of the 1-175 Infantry provided security between the first and second public viewing areas of the National Mall at the 7th Street, N.W. intersection, while the remaining members performed other security functions. The Federal Aviation Administration implemented additional airspace restrictions over Washington, D.C. between 10:00 a.m. and 6:00 p.m. on January 20, 2009. Secretary of Defense Robert Gates was chosen as the designated survivor to ensure continuity of the government in case of catastrophe, and he spent Inauguration Day at a U.S. military installation outside of the Washington, D.C. area. Obviously, many events professionals were involved in the planning and production of the inauguration.

written and communicated effectively to all staff and event volunteers. In the circumstance of government officials, high-security policies might have to be implemented in order to satisfy the security needs of the specific government official. Consequently, those policies might have to be implemented far in advance of the event. For example, if a major convention is hosting a country's sitting president or political leader, security clearances of event staff and volunteers should be completed months in advance of the event.

Organizers of conventions and special events should maintain risk management procedures for each event. **Risk management** is the identification and management of risk. Understanding, monitoring, and minimizing attendee risk will enrich the attendees' experience at the event. Additionally, managing risk should be the highest responsibility for each event organizer. For every event, a **risk assessment** is needed that focuses on managing the health and safety of the event attendees. Organizers should create a list of the possible attendee health and safety risks for each event. Consequently, each risk item should have a method to monitor, reduce, or remove that risk (for more in-depth insight, see chapter 4 on risk management).

SUMMARY

Event professionals face many challenges when planning and designing events. At the beginning of each great event are the mission and goals of the event. The mission and goals set the tone for the details that ensue. Having the event attended by global or local attendees also plays a role in the planning and design phases. The residential origin of the attendees can dictate the event requirements necessary to make the event successful (i.e., event location, event services, and hospitality services offered within the community). Details within the event need to be well thought out and carefully planned in order to manage the event's engagement with its attendees. Details such as signage, crowd flow, and admission policies have a significant influence on an attendee's satisfaction level. Lastly, each event professional must consider the safety and security for each attendee. Managing the risk level for each event should be of the highest concern by each organizer. The final goal of every event professional is to effectively plan and design each event to produce the best experience for the attendee.

Now that you have completed this chapter, you should be competent in the following Meetings and Business Events Competency Standards:

MBECS—Skill 17: Engage Speakers and Performers

Sub skills	Skills (standards)
H 17.01	Determine meeting or event requirements for speaker and performers
H 17.02	Develop selection criteria
H 17.03	Select candidates
H 17.04	Secure contracts and communicate expectations

MBECS—Skill 20: Manage Technical Production

Sub skills	Skills (standards)
H 20.01	Determine requirements for staging and technical equipment

MBECS—Skill 21: Develop Plan for Managing Movement of Attendees

Sub skills	Skills (standards)
H 21.01	Develop admittance and credential systems
H 21.02	Select crowd management techniques

KEYWORDS AND TERMS

Event Mission	Staging	Crowd Flow
Brand	Contracts	Risk Management
Compensation	Crowd Management	Risk Assessment

REVIEW AND DISCUSSION QUESTIONS

1. Why is the event's mission important to planning and designing a quality event?
2. What are the criteria that event professionals should consider while picking a venue?
3. What are some of the methods an event organizer can use when recruiting speakers and entertainers?
4. What are some of the details to consider when designing stage placement for an event?
5. What are methods of restricting crowds at an event?
6. Why is managing risk important in event planning?

REFERENCES

Fenich, G. G. (2012). *Meetings, Expositions, Events and Conventions: An Introduction to the Industry.* Saddle River, NJ: Pearson.

Getz, D. (2007). *Event Studies: Theory, Research and Policy for Planned Events.* London, UK: Butterworth-Heinemann1.

Barth, S. C. (2008). *Managing Legal Issues in the Hospitality Industry.* New York: John Wiley & Sons.

ABOUT THE CHAPTER CONTRIBUTOR

John Salazar, PhD is a professor and director of the Lowcountry and Resort Islands Tourism Institute at the University of South Carolina Beaufort. He is also the owner/consultant of Effective Measures Group that provides specialized consulting services to the hospitality and tourism industry.

Site Planning and Management

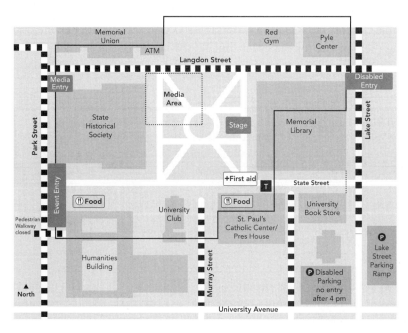

"Obama Event Map" from University of Wisconsin Madison. Used by permission of University of Wisconsin System Board of Regents.

Chapter Objectives

Upon completion of this chapter, the reader should be able to:

- Review the nature, scope, complexity, and fiscal requirements of the event
- Determine desired or demanded geographic location, type of **facility**, spatial factors, and operational logistics such as dates, duration, and cost of occupancy on site
- Develop site selection criteria, conduct **site inspections**, and evaluate potential sites
- Select the **site** that best caters to the needs of all, involving stakeholders of the event

Chapter Outline

INTRODUCTION

Site planning is the art of arranging **structures** and shaping the space in between (Lynch and Hack, 1984). Selecting the right site for the event is one of the most critical stages in site planning. The right event site offers attendees the best experiences physically along with being environmentally convenient and a pleasant event atmosphere. There are various elements that must be taken into account when selecting and planning the most suitable site for the event. In this chapter, three key areas for site planning and management will be covered: first, site **specifications** deal with the overall logistics and operational requirements of site planning and selection; second, site identification reviews various stages in order to select the most appropriate site for the event, starting from reviewing in-depth research in potential sites; developing site **selection criteria**; inspecting and evaluating potential sites; and selecting the best site for the event; finally, the layout of the site is designed along with reviewing space requirements, location, and floor plan.

> The chapter contributor has heard Barb Parsec say, "As I introduce and discuss each key component of planning an event, this time 'logistics,' I will start with the same three elements of *Developing a Time Line, Developing a Budget, and Establishing a Resource Listing.*"

SITE SPECIFICATIONS

Selection of an event site requires identifying the needs of all stakeholders, such as planners, sponsors, attendees, and service providers. When all their needs have been considered, the event professional must review and identify their specific resource availability and requirements for the successful delivery of the event. First, the professionals have to take a look at what resources are available to stage the event. One of the core resources that a hosting company must take into account is its financial stability. In order to assess the financial stability, the company has to develop the budget for the event.

Budget

The budget for the event is a blueprint for the professionals to make a decision on whether they have the financial resources to host the event. Without sound financial support, the event can't be feasible enough to move onto the next stage of planning. Dependent upon the nature and purpose of the event, generating profits is not always an ultimate goal for the event. For example, if one is planning a meeting of the board of directors of a company, profit is not the overarching goal: Communication and decision making is the goal. There are no revenues for this "event" but there are expenses. The same holds true for most "life cycle events," such as weddings: The goal is enjoyment and celebration not profits. Needless to say, developing projected revenue and expenditures based on the resources the event professionals have available will provide a clear idea of how the event must be run.

The budget is a process of financial estimation by which event professionals know how much they plan to spend and how they are going to generate revenue. Through this process, the professionals must identify each and every item of expenditure and income associated with running the event. This will highlight what is required to host the event and what should be included in the two sections (revenue and expenses). In revenue, typically, ticket sales and the number of attendees are listed, while in the expense, catering, entertainment, staging, technical requirements, staffing, and suppliers are included. Exhibit 1 is an example of the projected budget. Analyzing the financial resources for the upcoming event will help identify the type of site that can

EXHIBIT 1 Budget Planning

Description	Income	Expense
List all possible income and expense here		
Balance		

accommodate it and develop an operational and managerial checklist for the event (for more information on accounting and budgeting see chapter 6).

Profile and Image

Every event has its own characteristics to make it unique yet comparable with others. Its characteristics can be determined by its profile such as size, **venue**, target attendees, sponsorships, and auxiliary services along with the image or theme of the event. The profile is more related to the physical and tangible components of the event, while the image or theme is a holistic component of the event that draws the attention of target attendees.

The profile and image of the event are also key determinants of site selection. Among the various profile components, the size of the event is determined by the potential number of attendees that the event can accommodate. Charlotte, North Carolina was chosen as the location for the Democratic National (political) Convention because it is viewed as having the image of a city that is recovering from the recession of the early 2000s and as being vibrant. Dependent upon the number of attendees, the event can be categorized into the small (fewer than 200 attendees), medium (201 to 600 attendees), large (601 to 1,000 attendees), and mega (more than 1,000 attendees) scale. The purpose of the event is also highly related to site selection. For instance, if the event is designed to have community engagement, such as book readings, film screenings, and community dialogue, the event professional might look for a small venue to gather all interested people together. However, if the event is to promote the company's products, the site or venue can be located in a bigger city so that many people can easily access the venue.

Finally, the overall image of the event is a driving factor for selecting its site. The image of the event portrays its color scheme, graphics, and other materials that decorate the event. A golf tournament/fund-raising event, for example, is typically held in such a site/venue in Florida, California, and/or Arizona, which effectively achieves the event concept and image. Remember that the site must be determined by how well the venue/site suits the event and appeals to potential attendees as well as exhibitors.

Las Vegas Is the Best Choice

It should not be surprising that the Adult Video News, Best New Starlet Award is presented every January in Las Vegas, Nevada, at the AVN Awards ceremony. It is given to the porn actress whom the industry believes has displayed the greatest amount of potential and quality in her debut year. This award ceremony would not be held in Salt Lake City: It does not fit well with the community in Salt Lake but does fit with Las Vegas.

Facilities

Various event facilities are required to run the event effectively and efficiently. They include hotels, meeting rooms, banquet halls, restaurants, convention/conference halls, catering, and more, depending upon the profile of the event. When it comes to event facilities, the event professional must check the size, capacity, proximity of various facilities, and transportation systems. The site/venue should be near the airport, central station, or near the downtown area so that attendees can have easy access. For events with national and international audiences, the number of flights per day, or airlift, is important. As a potential venue, a hotel with conference rooms can be a good option as it provides catering service, staff, shuttle service from airport to hotel, and other additional services available along with good infrastructure for the event.

New York City, for example, is one of the most popular cities in the United States to host various events because the city itself easily accommodates the needs of event professionals, attendees, exhibitors, suppliers, and stakeholders. As a magnet of fashion, entertainment, dining, sports, finance, and shopping, New York City offers various facilities for the event attendees in order to cater to their needs.

Licensing

Licensing is a legalized approval that event professionals must obtain prior to launching the event. The required licensing for each event can vary by the type of the event so that the event professional must carefully review what licenses are offered at the site and what licenses are required or purchased by the organizer. If the event plans to serve alcoholic beverages, a liquor license is required and the event organizer must check all attendees' identification. In some venues, such as a restaurant, alcohol may only be served in the bar area which is licensed; in other venues all indoor space is licensed and in others the entire property is licensed. Thus, the event professional must be sure what space is covered by the license: An outdoor reception where alcohol is served is not possible if only indoor space is included in the license. Making things even more problematic with regard to alcohol is the fact that, in many locations, if the venue has a liquor license then alcohol cannot be brought in by the event organizer or attendees. Thus, private parties in guest rooms may not be legal.

A security license is also secured in order to offer a secure environment for the event. Security service organizations must hold appropriate general liability insurance coverage in order to protect the event. Generally, events are required to have security on site.

Permits are a form of temporary license. If the event is held in a nontraditional venue, such as a historic home, an occupancy permit may be required. Nontraditional locations may require a "temporary use permit" while holding a parade as part of the event will require a "parade license." There are many forms of required permits, and the event professional must look into what is required in a given location.

Adherence to "codes" may be thought of as a type of license. The event professional must follow fire codes that determine occupancy levels/number of people who can occupy a given room, whether flammable items, such as candles or pyrotechnics, can be used, whether material and products must be "fire rated," and so on. Zoning codes restrict how buildings and properties can be used. Codes in "historic districts" limit what can be done to the facades of buildings, including whether signs can be draped or attached. The event professional cannot give the excuse "I did not know."

Expected Attendance

The number of potential attendees of the event is one of the key factors to determine a site/venue for the event. If the site/venue is too small to accommodate the attendees, the site/venue will be so crowded that the attendees do not enjoy their time at the event. Whereas, if the site/venue is too big to cater to the attendees, the attendees feel that they are not part of the event. It is very important to fully understand the expected number of attendees and their profiles so that the event professional can tailor their event inclusion and event style to meet their needs, tastes, and event expectations.

In particular, the event professional must figure out how many attendees need special accommodation (such as people with disabilities). In the United States this is covered by the Americans with Disabilities Act (ADA), which covers virtually all public spaces. It requires that operators make all reasonable attempts to accommodate the needs of attendees with special needs. Not all countries have legislation equivalent to ADA. The event professional must ascertain what is required in a given geographical area. The special need that comes to mind most often are those who are physically challenged, such as those in wheelchairs. Ramps or lifts may be required and cannot simply be the "loading dock." Other special needs include attendees with visual impairments when large font programs, Braille documents, or even translators may be necessary. Attendees with special dietary needs must be accommodated, such as various types of vegetarian, kosher, and so on. (See chapter 10 on Food and Beverage for more details.) It should be noted that not all countries have the equivalent of ADA: Canada does not.

> An American with multiple sclerosis attended a conference in Vancouver, Canada. The attendee assumed policies like those under the ADA would be in place. Upon arrival he found that the hotel that had been booked could not accommodate people in wheelchairs, and he would have to stay ten blocks away from the convention center. However, there was no public transportation available that he could use to get from his hotel to the center—the only alternative was to "roll," rain or shine. Further, he required a small refrigerator in his room in which to store his prescription medication, but the hotel that could accommodate wheelchairs did not have mini-refrigerators. Ultimately the hotel bought a mini-refrigerator to place in his room.

Site Flexibility

The event site must be flexible in its space. Many events have the multiple functions and activities during the event so that the event professional can reallocate the space based on their needs and that of the function or activity. Not only the space but availability of the site/venue should be considered, including move-in and move-out time. When all functions and activities have been arranged outdoors, the event professional must have a contingency plan in case of rain.

Accessibility

Accessibility to the site/venue is typically limited to authorized personnel. However, the event professional must check with the site/venue manager regarding whether the professionals can access the site/venue during nonbusiness hours due to the event setup or decorations and whether the site/venue is well equipped for those who need special accommodations. The event professional is responsible for taking a tour of the site/venue (site inspection) carefully to check whether the site/venue is ADA compliant.

> The author was part of a site visit team for a national association representing operators of snow skiing resorts. A major aspect of their annual convention was the trade show, which entailed exhibiting some very large equipment. Further, the trade show was typically scheduled between other events. The site team visited a large, well-known hotel in California. It was located on the beach so that attendees who had been in snow all winter would much appreciate. However, the exhibit hall was in a converted garage with ceiling heights of about 7 feet and was located around the corner from the main part of the hotel—requiring attendees to walk the equivalent of two blocks to get there. The site team rejected the hotel for its annual convention.

Event professionals must clearly share the accessibility information with attendees, stakeholders, and exhibitors. The stakeholders and exhibitors might have unlimited accessibility to any gate as long as they have a key or pass available. However, attendees have limited accessibility to an event with a valid pass.

Accessibility is not limited to attendees. The event professional must consider access by trucks and tractor trailers that deliver exhibits and goods. Access on the show floor is also important in facilitating the setup and teardown of exhibits. That is why the newest designs in convention and exhibition facilities have all the show floor space on one level thus eliminating the use of elevators for the movement of crates, and so on.

> The Morial Convention Center in New Orleans has over 1 million square feet of exhibit space and is favored by event professionals because of its truck access. The entire back or river side of the building is lined with loading docks that make ingress and egress more efficient. This center even has a truck staging area across from the building to avoid truck traffic jams. Further, all the exhibit space is on ground level making movement of products easier. The center is almost one mile long, which requires employees to use bicycles and Segways to get around. It has enough "flat space" that every football team in the NFL can play each other within the center on the same day—and have space left over for fans.

IDENTIFY SITES

Event professionals are going to research several potential sites to determine the best site for their clients in order to offer a successful and memorable event. After reviewing the specifications of event features, event professionals develop a list of locations that can fit the needs of their clients. Dependent upon the type and scope of the event, event professionals have different selection criteria for a location and a venue. Identifying unique sites, locations, and/or venues that best fit the clients' needs is of utmost importance for the well-being of the attendees and for the success of the event. There are various locations or sites to be considered such as a small local community, suburban area, metropolitan area, or resort area. Along with the review of the location or the site, the venue has to be taken into account. Many options are available nowadays when selecting an appropriate venue for the event. For the small-scale event, a local restaurant with a private room would be a great option. A hotel with a meeting and conference room is also an option for a large-scaled event. The hotel can typically accommodate a registration area, a grand ballroom, as well as smaller breakout event rooms. The on-site catering staff can arrange for food and beverage as well as lodging accommodations for attendees.

Develop Site Selection Criteria

With the potential list of sites or locations, the event professional must develop the site selection criteria to choose the best site for their client. Site selection criteria are a barometer to choose the best site by comparing potential sites, weighting the sites, referring to the purpose and theme of the event, and ranking the sites. The following is a list of site selection criteria that can be easily customized to cater to the needs of each event's client.

   a. Size of the event
      i. How many people do you expect to attend?
     ii. Is the seating capacity suitable?
    iii. Are facilities large enough to provide a comfortable experience for those attending?
    iv. Does the site/venue allow attendees to move around without bottlenecks and delays?

   b. Suitability

      i. Does the site or venue fit the company's corporate image?

      ii. Does it give the correct impression for this particular meeting?

      iii. Will it appeal to the target audience?

      iv. Will the venue's staff add to the attendees' experience in a positive way?

      v. Is the layout of the site suitable for the event?

   c. Location

      i. Is the site/venue easily accessible to those attending?

      ii. Does the location offer the necessary road/rail/air links?

      iii. Is the venue/site suitable for any extra events/shows/excursions that have been planned?

      iv. Is the location quiet? In close proximity to accommodations if they are required? In a safe area?

   d. Availability

      i. Is the site/venue available on the dates required?

      ii. Are any extras, such as equipment, accommodation, and so on, available on the dates required?

      iii. How flexible are they if the event dates are changed?

   e. Facilities

      i. Does the site/venue have a variety of meeting rooms if required? An auditorium if necessary?

      ii. Can the venue offer a projector, electronic whiteboard, stationery, Wi-Fi Internet access, photocopying/fax service?

      iii. Can the site provide food and beverage services?

      iv. Does the venue have enough parking spaces?

      v. Will disabled delegates be catered to?

      vi. Do they have sports and leisure facilities such as a pool or gym?

   f. Cost

      i. Does the venue fall within the budget for the event?

      ii. What type of rates do they offer: 24-hour per delegate rate, individual room hire rate?

      iii. Can they offer any discounts?

      iv. Can the price be negotiated?

      v. Are there hidden costs?

      vi. When is payment required?

      vii. Is a deposit required and if so, how much and how far in advance?

      viii. What is their cancellation policy?

Conduct Site Inspections

An event site inspection is a must to make sure the event site offers all that the event professionals are looking for at a venue. What the site inspection requires is a visit to the site/venue being considered. Through the site inspection, the event professional can absolutely guarantee that the site is appropriate for their event. Typically, the event professional develops a site inspection checklist when visiting each venue to compare which one is the best fit for the event.

During the site inspection, the event professional must check how viable each facility is and how services are delivered to its attendees and clients. They must list all facilities that can be used for the event and potential services offered for the event. In particular, the meeting and convention center, venue, or hotel should provide a floor map with the detailed dimensions of meeting and function rooms. The Red Lion Hotel on Fifth Avenue in Seattle, for example, features 15,000 square feet of expansive conference, meeting, and event space for a business meeting, convention, or social event in downtown Seattle. With ten distinctive meeting and conference rooms, the hotel offers a comprehensive range of event options, layouts, and seating arrangements. The hotel's Emerald Ballroom accommodates six hundred banquet and reception guests. The hotel's capacity charts and floor plans are found on their website.

Evaluate Potential Sites

Potential sites for the event must be evaluated with regard to infrastructure of the area. Event professionals must have rough ideas of the number of attendees, their originating locations, and methods of transportation they use. The International Consumer Electronic Show (CES), for example, has been held in Las Vegas, Nevada, every January, hosts approximately 150,000 attendees from 150 different countries. In order to run this trade show smoothly and successfully, the event professionals must check the capacity of the city, Las Vegas, with tight cooperation with Las Vegas' Convention & Visitors Bureau, regarding the number of accommodations that can cater to the attendees, nearby airports, parking capabilities in the city, available public transportation, and accessibility to Las Vegas from different countries.

Think about potential sites for the CES in the United States. The event professional may consider several potential metropolitan cities for the CES, such as New York, Orlando, Chicago, Washington, DC, or Las Vegas, referring to their developed event selection criteria. First, the event professional reviews the number of attendees for the CES. Second, they can consider the originating place that the majority of attendees come from, international attendees and domestic attendees, in order to determine the most accessible site for the attendees. Third, the transportation must be considered: airline, car, public transportation, and so on, focusing on the airline hub, parking facility (free vs. paid), and any local public transportation.

Additionally, responding to green event practices, the event professionals must evaluate a potential reduction in the carbon footprint by gathering all CES attendees in one location. According to Carbon FootPrint, a person attending the CES from Seoul, Korea, to Las Vegas, U.S.A. by air generates 1.67 metric tons of CO_2. However, due to the CES, each attendee reports that he/she can save eleven additional trips, collectively avoiding more than 960 million miles in business trips. As a result of attending CES and consolidating trips, the estimated net savings in travel is more than 549 million miles.

After evaluating potential sites, the event professionals must rate the site based on the considerations reviewed before. Typically, the event professionals develop a table that can easily show which site can be most feasible to hold the big international event like CES. It is common to use a 1 (least affordable) to 5 (most affordable) scale. As shown in Exhibit 2, Las Vegas is the best suited city for the CES after evaluating all those options considered. In particular, Las Vegas is the only city that can cater to 150,000 attendees for the CES.

Select the Site

After reviewing all key options, the event professionals have to choose one site over other potential sites reviewed. In the process of selecting the site, the event professionals go through a series of negotiations to make the "best" deal for the event. If Orlando offers better room rates for attendees, for example, the event professionals may consider Orlando as a potential site for the CES. However, Orlando may require longer travel time for people coming from Asian countries. Attendees' travel time and room capability are weaknesses of Orlando over Las Vegas. Thus, the event professionals always think of what makes attendees happy and comfortable and what makes all parties involved in the event efficiently run the event. In the process of negotiating,

EXHIBIT 2 The Sample Rating Event Sites

	New York	Orlando	Chicago	Washington DC	Las Vegas
Accommodation	91,318 (1)	118,806 (2)	108,041 (1)	102,227 (1)	165,560 (5)
International airport	5	5	5	5	5
Accessibility from different countries	4	4	3	4	4
Carbon footprint	4	4	3	4	4
Total	14	15	12	14	18

NOTE: 1 being least affordable – 5 being most affordable
SOURCE: Travel and Tourism – US (2010). Smith Travel Research.

the event professionals revisit the purpose of the meeting, who will be attending, what the ideal location is, and what price ranges (room rate, facility rent, and so on) are affordable.

Attrition clauses, like cancellation, must be clearly specified in the contract in order to protect the integrity of the contract the event professionals have negotiated and the interests of the hotel if the event professionals fail to fulfill their obligation under the contract. There are various cases in the event that can be part of attrition clauses. First, what if the blocked hotel rooms by the event professionals have not been sold by the cutoff date? Second, what if the event professionals fail to meet food and beverage guarantees? And third, what if the event professionals fail to use other hotel services such as audiovisual, room service, and so on? Think about how the event professionals can minimize potential risks associated with these cases. The event professionals must have an ability to foresee their event accurately and thoroughly in a timely manner.

DESIGN SITE LAYOUT

The layout of the site/venue is an integral part of the success of the event. It also affects the overall atmosphere of the event as well as consideration of routes for emergency vehicles, power supplies, and topography. The organizer must carefully design and plan the layout in order to offer an enjoyable, comfortable, and engaging environment for attendees. If attendees feel the site/venue is cramped and hard to move around, they will have a bad experience with the event. This may lead to an overall bad evaluation of the event. When designing the layout of the site/venue for the event, various areas must be reviewed carefully in conjunction with the scale of the event. Dependent upon the scale of each event, the following requirements can be different. For each event, however, the following required components must be taken into account.

Space

Space for the events refers to the total required areas for both indoor and outdoor functions and activities to make the stakeholders engaged in the event interact actively, smoothly, and pleasantly. In order to determine required space for the event, the detailed specifications of the event must be shared between the organizer and the site/venue planner. They include the expected number of attendees, planned functions, activities, size and number of tables and chairs, or others.

Structures

Dependent upon the scale of the event, the structures are twofold: temporary and permanent. Many events have outdoor functions, activities, and ceremonies to make attendees engage in the event. For the outdoor features, the planners must install temporary infrastructure such as hard flooring to cover vegetation, chairs, tables, tents, lights, portable toilets, temporary cooking facilities, and so on. The opening event at the Meeting Professionals International Congress was held at the sports venue Busch Stadium. The entire baseball infield was covered in hard surfacing so that attendees could enjoy the atmosphere.

Utilities

Utilities used for the event refer to power, gas, water, sewerage, and broadband. As technology advances and more events are implementing environmentally friendly programs, the event professionals must check the technology-enhanced power systems and environmentally friendly power options of the site. First of all, the event professional must make attendees aware of the electrical system of the location, 110 V vs. 220 V. Most countries in North and South America, including the United States and Canada, use 110 V in their electrical systems, while most European and Asian countries, except Japan, use 220 V. If an appliance designed for 110 V is plugged into a 220 V outlet, it will burn out in an instant. The event professional must ascertain that adequate power is available.

> Al Copeland, the founder of Popeye's fast food chain lived in suburban New Orleans. Each year he would stage an elaborate light show at Christmas that attracted thousands of people to visit his home. However, the "show" required so much power that the local utility company could not supply it on the existing wires. Mr. Copeland had to rent two diesel generators in order to run his show.

The technology-enhanced power system is strongly related to the environmental or sustainable power option. For instance, if the meeting room has a light-sensing control, the meeting room remains dark if no one is in the room. Many event facilities, such as rooms, banquet halls, and other meeting rooms use low-cost fluorescent lights and a decentralized energy control system instead of a centralized system.

Today, high-speed broadband Internet service is a must. All event attendees carry their own Smartphone, iPad, and/or other types of mobile devices. In particular, if thousands of attendees at the event constantly use video instant messaging, video conferencing, the Internet, or VoIP, including Skype, at the same time, the event professionals must have multiple wireless Internet services available in order to prevent potential Internet outage. PSAV, the audiovisual company, recently developed a broadband calculator that event professionals can use to be sure there is enough capacity at a given venue to meet their needs.

> A session at the annual meeting of a professional association was held in the summer of 2012, and the focus was on the use of wireless technology. iPads were provided to many in attendance and others were given the URL for the website in order to connect with their personal smartphones, tablets, and PDAs. Within a minute or two of beginning the session, attendees were having difficulty with their connections: The number of devices in use in the meeting room exceeded the broadband capacity of the venue. The presentation crashed!

Parking

Parking space at the event is usually focused on the number of attendees. At least two parking options are available: valet and self-park. Many metropolitan cities in the United States, such as New York, Boston, Washington, DC, Chicago, San Francisco, and Los Angeles charge parking fees to even the event attendees. Las Vegas is one of the only cities that offers free self-parking—and that is only at the hotels and not the convention center. Access to parking is also an issue: Can attendees get in and out in a reasonable amount of time? Witness the famous music festival "Woodstock." The parking was so "inadequate" that attendees abandoned their cars miles from the site and walked in. Event professionals must also consider parking for trucks and other heavy equipment. "Parking" (storage) of crates and boxes used for trade show exhibits is still another piece of the puzzle.

Communication

There are land-based telephone lines, cell phones, PDAs, or walkie-talkies. Even though many attendees carry their own cell phones, the event professionals must have the land-based telephone because cell phones do not work inside many buildings. Also, the event professionals always test their cell phones and walkie-talkies in all areas to make sure all communication devices work at the event. For example, the cell phone of the author does not function/does not get reception in the building where he works—he must go outside to make a cell phone call.

Safety, First Aid

Safety is one of the most important components at the event. Safety for all people involved in the event and site must be guaranteed. At the event site, a designated area for first aid and emergencies should be available. In particular, local contact numbers for a hospital, police office, and the power utility company should be available.

Legal Requirements

The event professionals must know each country's legal requirements to handle alcohol and hire part-time and full-time crew members. Even though the legal drinking age in the United States is 21 years, countries in the world vary dramatically in the minimum drinking age, from birth to 21 years. Dependent upon where the event is held, the event professional must control offering of alcohol to the right people. Besides alcohol consumption, each country has set its own workforce regulations. In the United States, particularly, event professionals must follow all required regulations (i.e., EEOC, Equal Employment Opportunity Commission, OSHA, union rules, and so on) in the process of hiring crew members. There are a couple of interesting examples in resume writing between the United States and Asian countries. In many Asian countries, when job applicants submit their resumes to the potential employer, they have to provide their date of birth, their own picture, and gender, which is totally not a legal requirement in the United States.

Signage

Signage is a good communication tool that welcomes attendees and gives them a feeling of being part of the event as a participant. There are easels, sign holders, and banners to make all attendees connected with each other. However, event professionals have to decide where to place all signs and posters, what form of signage is used, how far apart each sign is placed, what sizes or shapes of signs and posters are needed, and what price for each sign or poster is reasonable.

These lighted signs were temporarily installed in a corridor while a convention was going on.
George G. Fenich

Service Contractors

As today's events are becoming more and more international, a variety of services must be available for international attendees. All of the international attendees are expected to command English well enough to communicate with other attendees. However, it would be a good idea to offer translation services for those who need help to communicate at the event. In particular, if people come to the trade show looking for potential business partners, the event professionals must consider this service seriously. Signs or posters available in multiple languages are an additional service for those who have limited knowledge in English.

Within the event site, the event professionals verify the locations of each required area and develop a preliminary site plan. While keeping the type of the event and the number of attendees in mind, the following areas must be identified along with space assignments in the site plan.

- Structures
  - Does the event need a temporary and/or permanent functional venue?
    - If the event needs both, how many venues does it need, temporary vs. permanent?
    - What activities will be held in the temporary/permanent venue?
  - Spatial assignment of event activity into the site plan
- Facilities
  - Identify names and locations of accommodations, meeting facilities, and other facilities involved in the event
- Services
  - Does the event need to offer translation service for attendees?
    - What language?

- ○ Does the event need child care service and special services for disabled attendees?
- Exhibit space
  - ○ How big does the event need exhibit space?
  - ○ Does the event professional need to contact a local convention center to hold an exhibit?
- Meeting or event program
  - ○ Does the event organization need separate meeting rooms?
    - If yes, how many rooms are set aside?
    - What is the size of the room?
  - ○ How many rooms are set aside for the event program?
    - What sizes of rooms are required?
- Attractions
  - ○ What are the nearby attractions that attendees can visit?
  - ○ Provide the directions of each attraction.
- Human and vehicular traffic
  - ○ Indicate pedestrian walkway and traffic directions (one-way or two-way)
  - ○ Indicate the potential places for signage
- Environmental implications
  - ○ List all participating environmental programs (recycling, carpooling, no hard-copy event programs, event apps, towel/linen reuse program, special incentive for those who drive a hybrid car, and so forth)
- Greening sustainability
  - ○ Use USB keys over printed handouts
  - ○ Replace bottled water with reusable water bottles
  - ○ Compost
  - ○ Donate leftover foods to food bank
- Security
  - ○ What security system does the event use?
  - ○ Should the event hire the security personnel?

SUMMARY

Selecting the most appropriate site for the meeting or event is one of the most important factors for the success of the event and the well-being of the attendees. The event site is a holistic environment. It impacts how attendees feel about the overall perception of the event and gives them an initial impression how their wants and needs will be satisfied.

Once the event professionals have determined the date, type, and purpose of the event, they then have to identify specifications and logistics of the event. This goes from budgeting, developing the event profile and image, to specifying all other operational logistics. After completing the whole process of the site specification, the event professionals are in the phase of developing the site selection criteria incorporating the needs of the key stakeholders of the event.

The site selection criteria must strategically define ease of access, affordability, and appropriateness to the specific event purposes. The well-identified site criteria capture what the event requires, how it portrays to deliver the memorable and unique event experience for its key stakeholders, and what it expects to achieve through the event. Typically, the event professionals review, compare, and rank the multiple sites based on the site selection criteria. Finally, they select the best-fit site for the purposes of the event and the needs of key stakeholders. The site selection criteria can be simple and short or comprehensive and long, dependent upon the type or size of the event.

The chosen event site must be inspected. The site inspection is a process to make sure the site is a viable place to offer the most memorable and unique event experience for its key stakeholders. Finally, it is time to design the layout of the event. The event professionals must determine what is required and what is not required to run a sound event.

Now that you have completed this chapter, you should be competent in the following Meetings and Business Events Competency Standards:

MBECS—Skill 22: Select Site

Sub skills	Skills (standards)
I 22.01	Determine site specifications

Sub skills	Skills (standards)
I 22.02	Identify and inspect sites

MBECS—Skill 23: Design Site Layout

Sub skills	Skills (standards)
I 23.01	Design site layout

KEY WORDS AND CONCEPTS

Facility

Site Inspection

Site

Structures

Specification

Selection Criteria

Venue

Site Layout

REVIEW AND DISCUSSION QUESTIONS

1. Define site planning. Describe the process that event professionals might follow while planning the most suitable site for an event.

2. What should be considered to develop site selection criteria?

3. What is the purpose of the site inspection?

4. List all required areas that should be reviewed in the process of designing the site layout.

REFERENCES AND INTERNET SITES

BOOKS

Hurt, J. (2011). Event & Meeting Planning, retrieved from http://jeffhurtblog.com/2011/02/01/meeting-site-selection-cheat-sheet-logistics/.

Lynch, K., & Hack, G. (1984). *Site Planning*, 3rd ed., Cambridge, MA: MIT Press.

ABOUT THE CHAPTER CONTRIBUTOR

Dr. Miyoung Jeong is on the faculty of the Department of Hospitality & Tourism Management at the University of Massachusetts Amherst (UMass). Prior to joining UMass, she taught at both Iowa State University and the University of Mississippi in the field of hospitality management. Her areas of teaching and research include hospitality operations, event management, and hospitality technology.

Food and Beverage Planning

CHAPTER 10

Event professionals have been organizing banquets since Roman times.
© Erica Guilane-Nachez/Fotolia

Chapter Objectives

Upon completion of this chapter, the reader should be able to:

- Determine target markets
- Develop a themed event
- Create an attendee profile
- Discover current trends in food and beverage

Chapter Outline

INTRODUCTION

A good deal of this chapter will focus on the role of the caterer. To be an effective planner/producer of meetings/events/conventions (event professional), one should understand the catering perspective. This allows event professionals to interact intelligently with caterers, food and beverage departments, and staff. It also provides insights to effectively monitor and evaluate food and beverage functions.

One of the first things to consider when planning a meal function is the reason for hosting it. Event professionals should ask themselves these questions: Who is the group? Why are they here? Is the meal function primarily to satisfy attendee hunger? Create an image? Provide an opportunity for social interaction and networking? Showcase a person, product, or idea? Present awards? Honor dignitaries? Refresh convention attendees and re-sharpen their attention? Provide a receptive audience to program speakers? The event professional should be informed about the reasons so that the appropriate menu, production, and service plans can be created.

SPECIFICATIONS AND GUIDELINES

Most hotels have a purchasing agent or department. They procure materials needed for production, including food, beverage, table linens, bed linens, lightbulbs, dishes, and so on. They develop specifications, check references, compare vendors, evaluate prices, negotiate prices and discounts, and discuss delivery schedules. In venues other than hotels, the event professional should identify if the venue has procurement and pricing models as just listed. If not, the event professional will need to develop them. For example, the event professional that is planning a religious retreat deep in the forest will need to have plans for acquiring every single element and food product necessary for the group because there is no one else to rely upon.

Most hotels use a system of **par levels**, which is the amount of food and supplies to always have in stock. Special orders for custom menus require more lead time for the purchasing agent to find and arrange delivery.

Usually the chef will prepare enough food to serve more than the guaranteed guest count. This overproduction is necessary to avoid running out of food. If the menu includes unusual foods that cannot be used in other areas or events, the client will need to pay a higher price to defray the extra food costs. With a standardized menu, clients may not have to worry about paying for overproduction. Chefs usually prepare for 3 to 5 percent over the guarantee, but this is negotiable.

The **guarantee** is critical. The event professional must pay for the amount guaranteed, even if that number of people do not show up. If a planner guarantees 1,000 people and only 800 show up, payment for 1,000 is still required. Payment for no-shows is called **attrition**. Generally, a planner gives an initial guarantee when the event is booked. A final guarantee must be made 48 hours in advance of the event, to allow the facility to order the food and call in staff. In some locations, where food deliveries are not available on a daily basis, a 72-hour guarantee may be required. In some cases, venues will allow event professionals to add additional attendees as late as 24 hours in advance, but they may not subtract from the final guarantee.

LABOR

Some menu items are very labor-intensive, particularly those made from scratch. It is not unusual for labor costs to be as much as one-third or more of a meal function's total price.

Labor is expensive in the food service industry. There are many hidden labor costs that are not readily apparent. There is a great deal of pressure to hold the line on labor costs. To control labor costs, a hotel may need to purchase more convenience foods, reduce menu options, eliminate menu items that require a great deal of expertise to prepare and serve, or charge the client more.

LABOR LAWS

Labor laws include provisions on hiring, firing, supervising, and so on. It is illegal to have minors serving alcohol. There are also laws against sexual harassment and discrimination against age, race, religion, and so on.

There is a federal labor law that stipulates hourly workers be paid time-and-a-half for all hours worked beyond 40 in a standard workweek. Union regulations vary from place to place, so if the hotel is a union property, be sure to check on the requirements. In union properties, workers typically receive time-and-a-half for any hours worked beyond eight hours in a single day.

The Las Vegas Culinary Workers Union is one of the strongest in the country. Their contract includes health coverage for workers, their spouses, and their children. They also have a culinary pension to provide the workers a steady source of income when they retire. They also provide members with down payment assistance to purchase a home. They have a voluntary 401K program. They operate a culinary training academy and offer a citizenship assistance program. Because employers pay into the pension by the hour, "steady extras" and part-time workers can qualify for benefits.

Steady extras are the first part-time workers (also called casual labor or on-call staff) to be called in and are also referred to as the **A list**. For larger events, the **B list** would be called in, and for very large events the **C list** would be called in.

Salaried workers must, by law, get paid a predetermined wage in a regular fashion. The advantage is the employee knows exactly how much they will be paid in every paycheck. The disadvantage is that they do not receive overtime and usually work many more than 40 hours per week.

STAFFING

Staffing is crucial in the service industry. The reputation of the venue (hotel, restaurant, convention center, and so on) rests on its ability to prepare and serve a consistent quality of food and beverage. Without the appropriate number and type of personnel, a venue cannot develop or maintain a first-rate reputation.

Customer satisfaction and repeat patronage are influenced primarily by food and beverage quality, service, sanitation, and cleanliness. An inadequate, undermanned, undertrained staff is incompatible with a successful food and beverage operation. Staffing is an ongoing activity because staffing requirements fluctuate widely. This is especially true for the group of employees who work part-time on very unpredictable schedules. There is a critical core of permanent, fixed-cost, full-time and part-time managerial and hourly staff members. Many of these people are career-oriented or otherwise satisfied with their current positions.

The majority of the staff consists of variable-cost employees who often tend to work for more than one caterer. The caterer must constantly cultivate new employees. This is especially important for hourly staff. A, B, and C lists can never be too long.

BANQUET EVENT ORDER

A **banquet event order (BEO)** may also be called an Event Order. It is created by the event professional or food and beverage provider and contains the following information:

- Date of Event
- Contact Information
- Billing Information
- Type of Event
- Guest Count
- Room or Location
- Time Line of Guest Arrivals
- Menu
- Ceremonies
- Presentations
- Toasts
- Room Setup
- Bar Setup
- Buffet Setup
- Table Sizes/Types
- Chair Sizes/Types
- Linen
- Glassware
- Flatware
- Dance Floor
- Stage, Lights
- Audiovisual
- Per Person Price
- Corkage*
- Type of Beverages
- Preferred Alcohol
- Additional Resources
- Labor and Staffing
- Cost Breakdown
- Signature Lines for Seller and Buyer

The BEO, once signed by both parties, is in essence a contract.

*Corkage is a fee that is charged per bottle when an event professional wishes to bring in their own alcoholic beverages.

REGULATIONS AND LEGISLATION

Liquor Laws

Liquor laws vary from state to state and even from county to county. Laws govern the times of sale, the days of sale, and the size of bottles sold. In many jurisdictions, alcohol can be served from early morning until late at night. However, in some jurisdictions, sale is more limited—say only after noon on a Sunday, whereas in New Orleans alcohol sales are allowed 24 hours per day, 7 days per week. In the latter, an individual can carry an open container of alcohol and consume it on the street. On the other hand, in some countries, the sale of alcoholic beverages is prohibited. In at least one jurisdiction, the sale of alcoholic beverages in public venues is limited to small, airplane-sized bottles containing one shot; sale by the drink is only allowed in private clubs. In European countries, consumption of wine by individuals under the age of 18 is permitted.

There are four types of illegal sales in all states:

- Sale to minors
- Sale to intoxicated persons
- Sales outside of legal hours
- Improper liquor license

Public Health

Event professionals and food and beverage providers must comply with safety and sanitation rules regarding the preparation, holding, and serving of food. An event professional is responsible for ascertaining that their food and beverage provider meets safety and sanitation rules.

MENU PLANNING

The director of catering or food and beverage and sometimes the event professional is often responsible for developing standardized menus (in cooperation with the chef and the food and beverage director), as well as unique menus customized for particular clients. The types of menu items a facility can offer depend on several factors. Before adding a menu item to a standardized menu or before offering to accommodate a client's particular menu request, the food and beverage provider needs to evaluate all relevant considerations that will affect the facility's ability to offer it and the guest's desire to eat it. Does the kitchen staff have the skill level to produce the item?

The demographics of the group attending the meal function must be considered. Average age, sex, ethnic backgrounds, socioeconomic levels, diet restrictions, where the guests come from, employment and fraternal affiliations, and political leanings can indicate the types of menu items that might be most acceptable to the group. Psychographics (the study of guests' lifestyles and the way in which they perceive themselves) can also be a useful indicator.

Age is often an excellent clue. Senior citizens usually do not want exotic foods or heavy, spicy foods, so excessive use of garlic, hot spices, and onions should be avoided. Avoid other distress-causing foods, such as vegetables in the cabbage family, beans, and legumes.

A senior citizen at a banquet was overheard complaining that the string beans were "too crunchy" and hard to eat. The beans were, in fact, fresh and sautéed as most people would like them to be. The issues for the seniors were (1) they were accustomed to eating canned string beans and (2) their teeth were in poor condition, so the senior had difficulty chewing.

Special Diets

Guests with special diets will influence the types of foods served. Some people cannot tolerate certain spices or peanuts (allergic reactions), sugar (diabetes), salt (high blood pressure, heart problems), fat (weight problems, high cholesterol), wheat, rye, or barley (celiac disease), or milk products (allergic reactions, lactose intolerance).

An acute allergic reaction to a food may manifest as swelling of the eyelids, face, lips, tongue, larynx, or trachea. Other reactions can include difficulty breathing, hives, nausea, vomiting, diarrhea, stomach cramps, or abdominal pain. Anaphylactic shock is a severe whole-body reaction that can result in death.

The eight common food allergies are:

1. Dairy allergy
2. Egg allergy

3. Peanut allergy
4. Tree nut allergy
5. Seafood allergy
6. Soy allergy
7. Wheat allergy
8. Carmine allergy

Some guests consume special diets for religious or lifestyle reasons. Some Jews require kosher foods; others may not keep kosher but will not eat pork or shellfish. Some devout Muslims may only eat halal (approved) foods. Some people will not eat red meat but will eat poultry and seafood. Many vegetarians (often called lacto-ovo vegetarians) will not eat animal flesh but will eat animal by-products, such as eggs and dairy products, but **vegans** will not eat anything from any animal source, including cream, eggs, butter, and honey. Accommodating some ethnic or religious requirements may create added expenses because of the need to hire outside specialized personnel (such as a rabbi to supervise kosher preparations) or to acquire special food items.

An astute event professional will provide the opportunity for each guest to indicate food preferences in advance of the event. This is often done on an event registration form where the attendee can check the appropriate boxes.

The Chapter Contributor Heard the Following Story from Alan L. Kleinfeld, MTA, CMM, CMP, CMM Advisors:

Some years ago, I was planning an annual convention for an Association of Unitarians in Phoenix, AZ. They are a politically liberal group and social progressives, so about 30 percent were vegetarians. I made this point very clear to my venues several times, and especially during our pre-con, to make sure that each meal had a vegetarian option. I should have suspected something was up when at the first meal function an attendee motioned me over to her table and showed me her vegetarian options: grilled tomatoes. That's right. A plate of nothing but grilled tomatoes is what this hotel took as a vegetarian option. Now imagine about a third of my participants all staring down at their plates at about the same time, trying to compute how this meal equated to a vegetarian dish. True, it was a vegetarian meal, but it lacked imagination, not to mention flavor. After talking with the venue, the next meal function had other options, like rice and pasta dishes with mushrooms and cream sauce. That was the last time I let a hotel decide what was vegetarian for me.

Planning the Menu

When a group is coming from a reception where heavy, filling hors d'oeuvres were served, the dinner should be lighter. If guests are coming from a liquor-only reception, then the meal could be heavier. If a group will be going to a business meeting immediately after lunch, order foods that will keep attendees awake. Protein foods, such as seafood, lean beef, and skinless chicken, will keep guests alert. Carbohydrates, such as rice, bread, and pasta, tend to relax guests and put them to sleep. Fats, such as butter, whipped cream, and heavy salad dressings, also tend to make guests sleepy, sluggish, and inattentive.

Politics can play an important role in menu planning. Serving veal to animal-rights organizations can anger guests because these groups believe that most veal is raised under inhumane conditions. Politically active groups may insist that the facility purchase and serve politically correct products.

Nutrition is a consideration for groups that will be at a hotel or conference/convention center for several days during a convention. Since virtually all meals during their stay will be consumed on the premises, special attention must be paid to nutritional requirements when planning menus.

Many people are avoiding trans fats, high-fructose corn syrup, sodium benzoate, and other unhealthy additives.

Whenever possible, have sauces and dressings served on the side so that guests can control their own portion sizes. Ask for fresh ingredients instead of processed foods that contain preservatives and other additives. A current trend is for the event professional to try to utilize products, especially fruits and vegetables, that are locally grown. This not only increases freshness, but cuts down on transportation costs and thus reduces the "carbon footprint."

FOOD COST

The venue should offer a variety of menu prices to suit its target markets. Prices must also be consistent with the target market's needs and desires. Caterers and food and beverage providers should be aware of ways to modify their standard menu, such as offering a less-expensive entree or removing a course.

The Formula

Food Cost Percentage = (Beginning Inventory plus Purchases minus Ending Inventory) divided by Food Sales.

Example:

$30,000 beginning inventory, $10,000 in purchases, $34,000 ending inventory, $20,000 in sales. (30,000 + 10,000 − 34000 = 6,000); 6,000/20,000 = .30 or 30 percent food cost.

RECEPTIONS

At receptions, plates can add as much as one-third to food cost.

Predinner receptions are designed to encourage people to get to know one another. Most conventions schedule an opening reception to allow attendees to make new friends and renew old acquaintances. If a reception is not scheduled and only a sit-down dinner is provided, then attendees may meet only the handful of people sitting at their dining table.

Stand-alone receptions are not predinner receptions. They are typically held during standard dinner hours and are intended to take the place of dinner. They allow attendees more time to have a drink, eat a little, and get to know one another. They can also be less expensive than a full, sit-down dinner.

The selection of food should include both cold and hot items. Food should have broad appeal.

DETERMINING QUANTITIES OF FOOD AND BEVERAGE

For receptions with dinner following, allow for about six to eight pieces per person. For receptions with no dinner following, anticipate approximately ten to fourteen pieces per person. If there are more females then males in the group, trend toward ordering ten pieces, but if the group composition is the other way around, plan for fourteen pieces.

Type of Reception	Type of Eaters	Number of hors d'oeuvres per Person
2 hours or less with dinner following	Light	3–4 pieces
	Moderate	5–7 pieces
	Heavy	8+ pieces
2 hours or less with no dinner	Light	6–8 pieces
	Moderate	10–12 pieces
	Heavy	12+ pieces
2 to 3 hours with no dinner	Light	8–10 pieces
	Moderate	10–12 pieces
	Heavy	16+ pieces

BEVERAGES

Understanding the purpose of the beverage function will give the catering sales representative an insight into the type of event desired. This information is invaluable when creating an exciting, memorable event. There are many reasons to schedule beverage functions. These events usually serve as a way for guests to socialize and engage in networking. A short reception can provide a transition period from a long workday to an enjoyable dinner.

A cocktail reception scheduled from 6:00 p.m. to 8:00 p.m. instead of a dinner should offer a variety and quantity of foods so guests can have enough to satisfy their appetites.

Spirits include distilled beverages, such as bourbon, scotch, gin, vodka, brandy, rum, tequila, and a variety of blends. Spirits can be consumed straight (neat), on the rocks (over ice), or as highballs or cocktails, mixed with a variety of ingredients.

Trends show that overall consumption will average three drinks per person during a normal two-hour reception period. Assuming that 50 percent of the people will order spirits, order the following quantities for every 100 guests:

# of Bottles	Type	# of Bottles	Type
2	Bourbon	1	Rum
2	Scotch	1	Brandy or cognac
3	Vodka	1	Tequila
1	Gin	1	Blended or Canadian whiskey

Wine consumption trends show that overall consumption will average three glasses per person during a normal two-hour reception period. Assuming that 50 percent of the people will order wine, order thirty 750 ml bottles for every 100 guests. Wine consumption trends also suggest that 30 to 40 percent of people will drink red wine, with the remainder preferring white.

Beer is classed as domestic or imported. Domestic beers would include Budweiser, Coors, and Michelob. There are also light beers, such as Bud Light, Miller Lite, or Coors Light. Imported beers would include Heineken, Corona, Fosters, Guinness, Stella Artois, Tecate, Sol, or Dos Equis.

There are also specialty beers from microbreweries. Food and beverage providers should know what is available in their area and be prepared to discuss these options with clients.

Kegs, or the smaller pony kegs, of beer would be appropriate for an outdoor tailgate, barbecue, or picnic, or where low price is a key factor. It is important to have the proper serving equipment and servers who are experienced with kegs so warm or foamy beer is not served.

Neutral beverages do not contain alcohol and include sparkling or still water, tea, coffee, nonalcoholic wines or beers, juice, sodas, and so on.

STYLES OF TABLE SERVICE

The style of service will often influence the types and varieties of foods the caterer can offer. The service styles that can be used for a catered meal function are:

Reception Service   Light foods are served buffet-style on a table. Guests usually stand and serve themselves. They normally do not sit down to eat. Food that will be passed on trays by servers during a reception must be easy to handle. Sauced items, which could drip, should not be served, but easy-to-eat finger foods would be appropriate.

Butlered Hors D'oeuvres Service   Food is put on trays in the kitchen and passed by servers. Guests serve themselves, using cocktail napkins provided by the server. This is a typical style of service used for upscale receptions. This style of service is only appropriate for finger food.

Buffet Service   Foods are arranged on tables. Guests usually move along the buffet line and serve themselves. When their plates are filled, guests take them to a dining table to eat.

Action Station Service   Chefs prepare and serve foods at a station in full sight of the guests. Guests are often allowed to choose ingredients. Foods that lend themselves well to action station service include work stations, pastas, grilled meats, omelets, crepes, sushi, flaming desserts, and Caesar salad. These stations are sometimes called performance stations or exhibition cooking.

Cafeteria Service   Similar to a buffet. Guests stand in line but do not help themselves. They are served by chefs or servers from behind the buffet line. This is a way to control portion sizes. Sometimes the inexpensive items, such as salads, will be self-service, and the expensive meat items will be served by an attendant.

Plated Buffet Service   Selection of pre-plated foods, such as entrees, sandwich plates, and salad plates, set on a buffet table.

Plated (American) Service   Guests are seated. Foods are preportioned in the kitchen, arranged on plates, and served by servers from the left. Beverages are served from the right. Used dishes and glasses are removed from the right. This is the most functional, common, economical, controllable, and efficient type of service.

Family-Style (English) Service   Guests are seated. Large serving platters and bowls are filled with foods in the kitchen and set on the dining tables by servers. Guests pass the foods to each other. Occasionally a host would carve the meat.

Preset Service   Food is already on the dining tables when guests are seated. Since preset foods will be on the tables for a few minutes before they are consumed, preset only those that will retain sanitary and culinary qualities at room temperature. Most common are bread and butter, but often the appetizer will be preset as well. For lunches with a limited time frame, occasionally salad and dessert will be preset.

Butlered Table Service   Foods are presented on trays by servers with utensils available for seated guests to serve themselves. (Often confused with *Russian service*.)

Russian (Silver) Service   Also called *Restaurant Russian*. Guests are seated. Foods are cooked tableside on a **rechaud** (portable cooking stove) that is on a **gueridon** (tableside cart with wheels). Servers put the foods on platters and then pass the platters at tableside. Guests help themselves to the foods and assemble their own plates. Service is from the left. (Often confused with *French service*.)

Banquet French Service   Guests are seated. Platters of foods are assembled in the kitchen. Servers take the platters to the table. Guests select foods, and the server, using two large silver forks in his or her serving hand (or silver salad tongs if the forks cannot be coordinated with one hand), places them on the guests' plates. Each food item is served by the server from platters to individual plates. Guests are served from the left.

French Cart Service   The type of French service that is used in fine-dining restaurants. Guests are seated. Foods are prepared tableside. Hot foods are cooked on a rechaud that is on a gueridon. Cold foods are assembled on the gueridon. Servers plate the finished foods and serve them to guests. This is the only style of service where food is served from the right.

Hand Service   Also called *Military service*. Guests are seated. There is one server for every two guests, and all guests at a table are served at precisely the same time. Servers wear white gloves. Foods are pre-plated, and the plates are usually fitted with dome covers. Each server carries two servings from the kitchen and stands behind the two guests assigned to him or her. When the captain gives the signal, all servings are set in front of all guests, and the dome covers are removed simultaneously. This is a very elegant style of service that is sometimes used for small gourmet meal functions. This style is sometimes called "*service in concert or synchronized service*".

The Wave   Also called *The Sweep or Waiter Parade*. This is a method of serving where all servers start at one end of the function room and work straight across to the other end. Servers are not assigned workstations. In effect, all servers are on one team, and the entire function room is the team's workstation. The wave is typically used in conjunction with plated and preset service styles. Large numbers of guests can be served very quickly.

There is a good deal of confusion between *butlered, Russian,* and *French service*, with even many professionals disagreeing over the exact interpretation. The key is to have the same understanding as the caterer so that there will not be any surprises. There are usually extra labor charges associated with upscale service styles.

For variety, mix service styles during a meal. Begin with reception service for appetizers, move into the banquet room where the tables are preset with salads, rolls, and butter, use French service for the soup course, use Russian service for the entree, and end the meal with a dessert buffet.

The following illustrates the importance of communication between all parties—planner, sponsor, and caterer:

I was a speaker right before lunch at one of our niche meeting industry associations at a major hotel in Las Vegas. They graciously invited me to stay for the lunch. I sat at a table and started chatting with my tablemates. We waited, and waited, and waited, but no lunch. I wondered what was going on. Finally, the servers started emerging and started placing these awful-looking plates in front of us. The food looked like it was thrown on the plates. I couldn't imagine what was going on. Everyone was bewildered. After the event, I ran into the director of catering in the pre-function space. Knowing him, I walked over and asked what had happened. He was beside himself. It turned out that the lunch was supposed to be served in red, lacquered bento boxes. At the last minute, the lunch sponsor saw the bento boxes were red and demanded the food be removed. The sponsor's color was blue, and their major competitor's color was red, and the sponsor would not allow the food be served in red boxes.

ROOM SETUPS

First, an appropriate function room must be selected in which to hold the event. Consider several things when making this selection. The major factors to consider are the appearance, location, utilities, and amount of floor space.

Most venues charge room rental rates that can only be negotiated if the group is very profitable. Sometimes room rental will be on a sliding scale, based on how much food and beverage revenue is generated.

Room dimensions, ceiling height, number of columns, exits, and entrances; the proximity, number, and quality of restroom facilities; the colors and types of floor and wall coverings; sound insulation; and lighting are important considerations.

The overall appearance of the room is important. Consider the following aspects of a room:

- Lighting
- Sound
- Color
- Wall treatment
- Temperature
- Smell
- Visibility
- Layout

The typical ceiling height in hotel or convention center function rooms is approximately 11 feet. In some areas, the building code may require 14-foot ceilings in public areas.

Columns are usually a negative in a function room because they can block sight lines for speakers or audiovisual presentations.

A lectern or head table should not be located near an entrance because the movement of those coming and going will disrupt the speaker. Have the room set up so the doors are off to the side so late-comers do not interrupt the presentation.

Room setups do not always occur indoors. Photo courtesy of SomersFurniture.com

Table placement at receptions also affects food consumption. An hors d'oeuvre table placed against a wall provides only 180-degree access to the food. A rectangular table in the center of the room provides two open sides and 360-degree access to the food, allowing greater food consumption.

With audiovisual presentations, minimize the amount of ambient light (i.e., unavoidable light seeping into a darkened room from around doors, draped windows, or production and service areas) that can wash out the colors in a presentation.

Event professionals should be concerned with:

1. Types of electricity available in house
2. Types of electricity that can be brought in
3. Maximum wattage available
4. Maximum lighting available
5. Number of separate lighting controls
6. Heating, ventilation, and air conditioning (HVAC) capacity
7. Closed-circuit TV, radio, and VCR system
8. Closed-circuit audiovisual system
9. Paging system
10. Number, types, and locations of:
    a. Electrical outlets
    b. Electrical floor, wall, and ceiling strips
    c. Phone jacks
    d. Dimmer switches
    e. Vents and ducts
    f. Built-in speakers
    g. Doors (Do they open in or out? Are they single or double doors?)
11. If the function will be held in an exhibit hall, a meeting planner will also be concerned with the number, types, and locations of:
    a. Gas hookups
    b. Exhaust fans
    c. Drains
    d. Water connections
12. Internet access
13. Wi-Fi availability

Space Planning

Local fire codes will dictate the maximum number of people who can be legally housed in a function room. Before making final decisions regarding room setup and aisle space, the event professional must check the local fire code for specific requirements.

Allocate about 10 square feet per attendee if seating is at rectangular banquet tables. If round tables are used, about 12½ square feet per guest should be allocated. These estimates will suffice if the venue is using standard chairs whose chair seats measure 20 inches by 20 inches. Adjust estimates if smaller chairs (seats measuring 18 inches by 18 inches) or larger armchairs (which usually have a minimum width of 24 inches) are used. Round tables are the easiest for the staff to service, and they maximize interaction among guests.

Aisles allow people to move easily around the room without squeezing through chairs and disturbing seated attendees. They also provide a buffer between the seating areas and the food and beverage areas. They are also needed for server access and maneuverability. Aisles between tables and around food and beverage stations should be a minimum of 36 inches wide. It is preferable to have 48 inches. The caterer should also leave an aisle around the perimeter of the room; while 48 inches is preferable, it should be at least 36 inches.

If the function includes dancing, the food and beverage provider can provide (or rent) about 3 square feet of dance floor per attendee. If they use lay-out squares, most of these types of portable dance floors come in 3 feet by 3 feet (i.e., 9 square feet) sections; plan on using one section for every three attendees. A 24 foot by 24 foot dance floor covers approximately 600 square feet of floor space; this would be sufficient for a group of approximately 200 attendees.

For bandstands, estimate about 10 square feet per band member. Drum sets usually require about 20 square feet. Large pianos, synthesizers, runways, sound boards, and so forth need additional space. Disc jockeys will need space to hold their equipment. Check the entertainment contract as it may set forth the floor-space specifications.

Bandstands and other similar attractions are sometimes elevated on risers. Stage risers come in many shapes and sizes. Their purpose is to elevate speakers, other entertainers, or audiovisual equipment so that a large audience can see what is taking place at one end of the function room. Most risers are 4 feet by 4 feet, or 4 feet by 8 feet, folding risers that can be adjusted to several heights. Risers should be set up with steps with attached handrails and light strips. A lawsuit can occur if a guest falls from an improperly set stage.

Head tables usually need about 25 percent to 100 percent more floor space than regular dining tables. If the tables will be placed on risers, increase the space estimate accordingly to accommodate the platform area, steps, and the need to spread the table-and-person weight properly over the stage. If using typical platform sections measuring 4 feet by 4 feet and 4 feet by 8 feet, connect a 4 by 4 and a 4 by 8 to have enough space to accommodate a dining table measuring 3 feet by 8 feet. About 48 square feet of platform space will accommodate approximately 24 square feet of dining-table space. The 48 square feet will accommodate four guests seated at 24-inch intervals. Twelve square feet per person is usually the minimum amount needed for head-table guests.

A raised head table for twelve people, plus a lectern, should be a minimum of 26 feet long. The rule of thumb is 2 feet per person, plus 2 ½ feet for the lectern. For more comfortable seating, allow 2½ to 3 feet per person.

To accommodate a reception adequately, allow about 5½ to 10 square feet of floor space per attendee. With 5½ to 6 square feet, people will feel a bit tight; they also will have more difficulty getting to the food and beverage stations. Consequently, they may eat and drink less.

Seven-and-a-half square feet per person is considered to be a "comfortably-crowded" arrangement. It is thought to be the ideal amount of floor space per person for receptions and other similar functions.

Ten square feet provides more than ample space for attendees to mingle and visit easily the food and beverage stations. It is an appropriate amount of floor space for a luxury-type reception. It is not an appropriate setup if a client is paying according to the amount of food and beverage consumed.

Remember to take into account space taken up by buffet tables, check-in tables, plants, props, and other décor when forecasting the number of attendees that can be served adequately.

Buffet tables need enough floor space for the tables and aisles. An 8-foot long rectangular banquet table needs about 24 square feet for the table and about 60 square feet for aisle space (if the table is against the wall); about 100 square feet for aisle space is needed if the table is accessible from all sides.

Allocate approximately two running feet of buffet table for each food container needed. To display three hot offerings, three cold offerings, and a condiment basket, set up a buffet table about 14 to 16 feet long. Two standard 8-foot rectangular banquet tables will require about 48 square feet of floor space for the buffet table and approximately 150 square feet of standard 3-foot aisle space surrounding the buffet table. The total allocation for this setup, then, is about 200 square feet.

A hot-beverage station will need about as much space as a buffet table. Bars will need more floor space because of the need to store backup stock, ice, and coolers to hold beer and some wines. Allocate enough working space for bartenders and, if applicable, cocktail servers. A small portable bar measures approximately 6 feet by 7 feet, or about 42 square feet. When considering the aisle and other space needed, allocate at least 150 square feet for the typical portable banquet-bar setup.

It is essential to communicate to the food and beverage provider exactly how the room should be set up. This can be included on the BEO. The BEO can also include designs generated by room layout software; these types of programs place tables, chairs, and other equipment into a meeting room. Free room layout software demos can usually be downloaded from companies that produce and sell this type of software, such as Meeting Matrix or Room Viewer. Using facility floor plans and other schematic drawings that show square footage, dimensions, doors, and other factors that may be important to the client, several visual plans can be developed using a basic template. Room size calculators on websites can help calculate the amount of space needed. The typical software program will draw a layout using industry standards as defaults (that can be changed) for such things as distances between rows of chairs or tables, aisle space needed, and the optimal angles that should be set to accommodate video presentations. Most of these software packages also will automatically generate standard seating styles.

The tables used should be the standard ones whose heights measure 30 inches from the floor. The typical types used in catering are:

1. 60-inch (5-foot) round: typically called a round of 8, or 8-top. It is usually used to seat six to ten people.
2. 72-inch (6-foot) round: typically called a round of 10, or 10-top. It is usually used to seat eight to twelve people.
3. 66-inch round: a compromise table size, it is designed to take the place of the 60-inch and the 72-inch rounds. It can seat eight to ten people. If a food and beverage provider uses this table, the facility may be able to minimize the different types of tables it carries in stock.
4. Banquet 6: a rectangular table measuring 30 inches wide by 6 feet long.
5. Banquet 8: similar to the banquet 6. It measures 30 inches wide by 8 feet long.
6. Schoolroom or classroom table: similar to the banquet 6 and banquet 8. It can be 18 or 24 inches wide and 6 or 8 feet long. It is used for business meetings where classroom presentations are made. Seating is usually on one side only. It can also be used as one-half of a buffet table.
7. Serpentine table: an S-shaped table typically used to add curves to a buffet line.
8. Half-moon table: half of a round table, or two quarter-round tables attached to make a half circle. Also referred to as a *half-round*.
9. Quarter-moon table: a quarter-round table. It is generally used as part of a buffet line.
10. Cocktail table: a small, round table. It is usually available in 18-inch, 24-inch, 30-inch, and 36-inch diameters. Use 30-inch heights (for sit-down service), shorter tables (for displays), or tuxedo (bar height) tables (for stand-up service).

The seating arrangement used will depend on the purpose of the catered event. Awards banquets, celebrations, theme parties, and so forth will influence the dining-room layout as well as the type of tableware, props, napery, floral arrangements, centerpieces, and other decor used.

A class speaker once told a story about an upscale dinner being held in the atrium of a museum that had a high dome ceiling. The planner decided to have white doves (birds) released after the people were seated. The doves would fly around the room and then back to their cages. They rehearsed it before the guests arrived, and it worked perfectly. The guests arrived in their tuxes and sequined dresses and were seated. Unfortunately, dinner was delayed because some VIPs had not arrived, and the heat started to rise. By the time they finally released the doves, they were dead and dying and fell like lead bricks onto the tables. Those still alive were flapping their wings, knocking over the crystal glasses. Pandemonium ensued. The planner's classic comment was, "But, it worked in rehearsal."

Bar setups are easier to plan than food events. Unlike food, alcoholic beverage service tends to be very standardized. Simple mixed drinks, wines, and beers are commonly served.

Attendees can draw 5 gallons of coffee from a single urn in 15 minutes; it is critical that the food and beverage provider provides adequate and speedy replenishment. Anticipate twenty 6-ounce cups of coffee per gallon. It takes twice as long to add cream and sugar as it does to pour coffee, so cream and sugar should never be placed directly in front of the coffee urns. By placing these items away from the urn, the line will move much faster.

From left to right, items should be placed in this order to facilitate the traffic flow at a coffee station:

- Cups and saucers
- Regular coffee
- Decaffeinated coffee
- Hot water for tea
- Tea bags, sugar, sweeteners, cream, lemon slices
- Spoons or stirrers
- Napkins
- Food (ideally this would be at the far end of a table or on a separate table)

Ask the food and beverage provider to place the items on the refreshment center menu, along with other utensils, plate ware, and silverware, on the other side of the food or on the food table. Try to maintain easy access to the coffee urns.

Buffets are generally faster and more efficient than table-service procedures, assuming there are enough buffet lines to accommodate the attendees quickly and efficiently. One of the potential disadvantages of buffets, though, is the possibility that some attendees will be finished eating while others are still waiting in line.

Lower-cost food items, such as salads and breads, should be placed first on the table so that the attendees' plates will be full by the time they reach the main course.

Buffet tables should not be set near doors or other entryways where they can cause traffic jams. If the buffet line will be longer than 16 feet, it should be two tables wide, i.e., about 4 to 6 feet wide. A long, narrow line is unattractive.

If floor space is tight, ask the food and beverage provider to use double-sided buffet tables. They can save as much as 20 percent of available floor space. They also tend to reduce leftovers because, when service slows near the end of the meal, the caterer can close one side of the line and consolidate all foods on the open side.

Whenever possible, beverages, such as wine, hot coffee and tea, and soft drinks, should be served at the table. This provides a bit of personalized table service that attendees appreciate. It also makes the overall service much quicker and more efficient.

Most meal buffets are usually set with one line for every one hundred attendees. This is based on the assumption that it will take one hundred persons about

20 minutes to go through the line. One line is one side of a buffet table; if there are two sides (double-sided buffet table), this counts for two lines.

If the food and beverage provider sets one food buffet line for every fifty people, they can feed the entire group in about 15 minutes. The first attendee will take about 5 minutes to go through the line. After that, there will be about four attendees passing through the line every minute.

Tabletop

The top of the table is the "stage." Once attendees are seated, they will spend the rest of the meal function looking at the table. The table presentation sets expectations for the meal and should reflect the theme. The linen colors chosen should not clash with the carpet or wall treatments.

Most catered events, especially dinners, have centerpieces on the dining tables. Centerpieces should be attractive and appropriate for the type of function booked. Centerpieces on dining tables should be eye appealing and never at eye level. They should not interfere with a person's seated sight line. Attendees should not have to have a conversation with a disembodied voice. For height, use an "epergne," a container with a slender center portion that does not obstruct the view across the table.

SUMMARY

The intent of this chapter is to provide the reader with an idea of how food and beverage functions are planned and executed by caterers. The following major topics were addressed: (1) typical menu planning considerations and how they affect menu development; (2) how the purpose of a meal function can affect menu development and selection; (3) typical service procedures; (4) typical types of meal functions purchased by meeting planners; (5) some of the major differences between on-premise and off-premise events; (6) determining the appropriate function room setups for various types of catered events including factors affecting space requirements for various types of setups; (7) staffing needed to execute various catering functions and the various departments that support the catering effort.

Now that you have completed this chapter you should be competent in the following Meetings and Business Competency Standards:

MBECS—Skill 8: Coordinate Food and Beverage Services (*Note: Only the planning elements of food and beverage service have been covered. Production or implementation follows in the book* Production and Logistics in Meetings, Expositions, Events and Conventions *by Fenich.*)

Sub skills	Skills (standards)
H 18.01	Determine food and beverage services requirements
H 18.02	Select [develop] menu(s)
H 18.03	Plan service style(s)
H 18.04	Select food and beverage providers

KEY WORDS AND TERMS

Par levels	A list	Vegans
Guarantee	B list	Rechaud
Attrition	C list	Gueridon
Steady extras	Banquet Event Order (BEO)	

REVIEW AND DISCUSSION QUESTIONS

1. Why are demographics important when planning events?

2. What is the role of the caterer in enriching the attendee's experience in an event?

3. What is the difference between banquet French service and French cart service?

4. What are the issues that the event planner and caterer need to consider while deciding on the menu?

5. How will the nature of an event affect food and beverage planning and management?

6. How does table placement at receptions affect food consumption?

7. How many attendees are typically seated at a 72-inch (6-foot) round table? What is an overset?

8. At a coffee station, why shouldn't you place cream and sugar in front of the coffee urns?

9. What is the ideal amount of floor space to allocate per guest at a reception?

WEB RESOURCES

Pinterest is a great resource for finding creative presentations at www.pinterest.com/pattishock

YouTube has many relevant videos at www.youtube.com /pattishock1

ABOUT THE CHAPTER CONTRIBUTOR

Patti J. Shock, CPCE, CHT, is a professor at the Harrah Hotel College at the University of Nevada, Las Vegas. She is also the academic advisor for the International School of Hospitality, a certificate granting school based in Las Vegas. She is widely published and speaks often at industry meetings. She has received many honors and awards, including the PCMA Professional Achievement Award (2005) and was named one of the 25 Most Influential People in the Meetings Industry by Meeting News (2002). She holds the Certified Professional Catering Executive (CPCE) designation from the National Association of Catering Executives and the Certified Hospitality Trainer (CHT) designation from the Educational Institute of the American Hotel and Lodging Association.

CHAPTER 11

Marketing of Meetings, Expositions, Events, and Conventions

Chapter Objectives

Upon completion of this chapter, the reader should be able to:

- Understand the Definition of "Marketing"
- Understand How Marketing Principles Apply to Meetings and Events
- Be Able to Identify Event Stakeholders
- Be Able to Identify and Characterize Torment Market Segments
- Be Able to Determine Appropriate Marketing Distribution Channels
- Be Able to Develop Marketing Strategies
- Be Able to Develop and Implement a Marketing Plan

It takes good marketing to get people to attend an event. © Alexey Lysenko/Shutterstock

Chapter Outline

INTRODUCTION

Plan an event and people will come. Right? Not necessarily. The most costly mistake in event management is not having an audience. No amount of lavish decorations, fine food, effective room design, engaging speakers, energetic entertainment, flawless audiovisual, or elaborate staging will compensate for an event that few attend. Despite all efforts to coordinate and manage a well-run event, if the intended audience does not attend or if the attendance numbers are too low, the event will not be deemed a success. It is impossible to underestimate the importance of event marketing and event communications.

Some events and meetings have minimal marketing or promotional requirements. For example, a corporate sales meeting, when employee attendance is mandatory, might only require an email notification. Social events, such as a wedding, birthday party, or an anniversary do not typically require extensive marketing. Events that depend on audience revenues and events that exist to create awareness require more extensive marketing in order to guarantee an audience.

In some organizations, event marketing efforts might be handled by an entire team of event professionals. They might also hire contractors who specialize in marketing, public relations, and promotional campaigns. In contrast, there are some organizations when an event professional has the sole responsibility for all of the event marketing efforts. In either case, it makes sense for the event professional to be involved in the marketing and public relations (PR) efforts to ensure that the event objectives are clearly represented and that there is a consistency in the meeting or event look, design, and theme concepts.

> In their online dictionary, the American Marketing Association defines marketing as: " *the activity, set of institutions, and processes for creating, communicating, delivering, and exchanging offerings that have value for customers, clients, partners, and society at large"* (American Marketing Association, 2012).

WHAT IS MARKETING?

To better understand what marketing is, it might be helpful to understand some of the accepted theories and principles of marketing. Marketing is typically thought of as the method promoting and selling a product or service. Using this definition, it might be helpful to think of events, conferences, or meetings as products, services, or offerings.

Using universal marketing theory, the event professional will start by examining what they are selling and identify the "**Four P's**":

1. **Product:** What kind of event are you planning? What are you marketing or selling? What is the end benefit to the people who will attend a particular meeting or event? What will they get emotionally, professionally, and physically?
2. **Place:** Where will the meeting, conference, or event take place? What is the location? Where is it being held? Is there a particular marketing appeal about the event destination? If it is a virtual event, what will drive them to attend online?
3. **Promotion:** What are the best methods of communication to reach the intended audience? Event professionals typically use: advertising (radio, television, newspapers, and Internet), public relations, direct mail, word-of-mouth, social media, and in-direct marketing promotions.
4. **Pricing Strategy:** What is the ideal ticket or registration pricing? If priced too high, the target audience might be dissuaded to attend. If priced too low, the perceived value and expectations of the event might be low. If it is a corporate event, price would be the cost: cost to put on the event, cost of travel to attend, and so on.

After analyzing the primary "Four P's," event professionals then need to look at two more "P's" to help them get organized:

5. **People:** In this case, people does not refer to the target audience (see below), but rather to the team who will actually implement the marketing plan and produce

or put on the event. It is important to make sure that the event professional has the resources needed to effectively implement a marketing plan.

6. **Process:** Process refers to the development of a marketing plan and careful examination of the effectiveness of the communication to the audience. Process refers to the steps that are taken.

In the early 1990s, the "**Four C's**" were developed in reference to consumer marketing. It might be helpful for an event professional to consider how those can be translated to meetings and events:

1. **Consumer:** By focusing on how the event fulfills the audience's needs and why the consumer should want to be there, the event professional has better success at gaining interest in the conference or event.

2. **Cost:** In deciding on a **price** to set for the attendance fee, the event professional needs to take into consideration both the income needed to produce the event and the attendee's perception of the value of the event to them. It is also important to take into consideration that, when deciding to attend a conference or event, the attendee also has other expenses, such as air transportation, hotel expenses, restaurant meals, parking, and even, if they are parents, child-care expenses.

3. **Communication:** Not only is the *method* of communication important for your intended audience, but the way in which things are communicated is also important. The choice of words, the grammar and spelling, the design and graphic layout, all tell a story that needs to compel your audience to attend. The event professional must keep in mind: (1) who is the group and (2) why are they coming.

4. **Convenience:** This "C" refers to considering how easy it is to register for the event and how convenient it is for the audience to attend. Things such as: timing of the event; the event location; how easy it is to sign up and pay and the date of the event—all relate to convenience. In today's busy world, convenience has become an important factor in an attendee's decision on whether or not to attend.

IDENTIFYING TARGET MARKETS

Two pivotal elements in planning a successful marketing strategy are to identify the **target audience** and to use the right marketing promotions (see chapter 12 in this book on promotions) to reach them. Determining who the ideal event or conference audience will be should be part of an analysis that is done in the initial program planning stages. Knowing who the desired audience is will help the event professional determine what type of marketing to implement.

By understanding a little bit about the **consumer behavior** of their **target market**, the event professional can identify the best way to reach them. Examining what motivates people to attend some events and avoid others is part of the analysis that helps to understand their response or buying behaviors. In this respect the event manager and the event professional need to become part economist, part psychologist, part sociologist, and part social anthropologist.

In the initial planning stages of the event process, the event professional should outline who the **event stakeholders** are (see chapter 5 of this book on stakeholder management). A stakeholder is one who has a stake in an enterprise. Typical event stakeholders are the producing organization of the event, the decision makers, the sponsors, the exhibitors (if the event has exhibitors), the organization membership (if the event is for an association or other membership organization), the beneficiaries (if the event is to promote a cause or is a benefit event), the participants (such as the speakers, presenters, volunteers, and performers), and, most importantly, the attendees or audience who will attend the event.

Some of the areas to consider when researching the consumer behavior of these stakeholders are:

Demographics of Stakeholders

These are the vital statistics of a specific population. What is their age? What is their marital status, their sex, their income, and their education level? What is their cultural or racial makeup? What profession and industry do they work in? What is their professional status? When marketing to exhibitors and sponsors (to entice them to purchase exhibit space or convince them to sponsor the event) there may be some additional demographic questions to consider: What kind of product or services do they sell? Where are they located, and what are their sales regions?

Psychographics

These are the personality traits of your stakeholders. What are their values? What interests them? What is their lifestyle? What are their delights, persuasions, attitudes, and perceptions?

If the event has exhibitors and sponsors, there may be some other psychographic questions to consider: What is the personality of the company? Who is the target market for their products or services, and what marketing messages do they wish to portray about their company?

Desired Outcomes

Each stakeholder will have something they hope to attain by participating in the conference, meeting, or event. A few examples of some possible desired outcomes:

- An exhibitor at an association industry trade show hopes to gain new customers for their products or services.
- The chief operating officer (CEO) of a business may wish to receive recognition from his or her peers by speaking at a large industry conference.
- The executive director of a charitable organization hopes for larger media awareness. that will help bring in donations for the charity that he or she represents.
- A college senior attending a Job Fair hopes to make valuable contacts that will help them land a fulfilling and lucrative job.
- A group of friends want to listen to good music, enjoy the company, have fun and forget about the troubles of the world for a few hours while attending a music festival.

By analyzing the event stakeholders, the potential attendees' demographics, psychographics, and their desired outcomes, the event manager and event professional will be able to create a target **audience profile** to help them gauge the best types of marketing for the event.

LOCATING THE TARGET MARKET

> A common mistake that new event professionals make is to assume that everyone will automatically want to come to the event.

While it may be true that anyone *may* wish to come to the event, it is important to define who is *most likely* to come, so that the event professional can concentrate their marketing resources in order to get effective marketing results.

Developing a target audience **marketing contact list** (or invitation list) is an important way to start. Association event professionals typically start with their association's membership lists. Collecting contact information for event attendees from one year to the next is another great way to build a target marketing contact list.

Lead generation techniques might be used to further develop a marketing list. Lead generation is a marketing term used to describe the development of consumer interest into products or services of a business. In event marketing, lead generation becomes **audience generation**. Examples of lead and audience generation might be: collecting business cards at an event; asking people who log onto a website to submit their name and email address; having people fill out survey cards, sign up for a door prize or sign in on a guest list with their contact information so they might be added to the marketing list for future events.

Event professionals sometimes purchase **marketing mailing lists** for targeted marketing campaigns. These vendors sell consumer lists, business lists, and other specialty lists for one-time direct mail or email usage. To maintain confidentiality of the list, the vendor requires that the event professional utilize a third-party company to distribute the mail (or email) and/or other event marketing materials. These mailing lists can often be purchased by set criteria, such as by region or job title. For example, an event professional who needs to build an audience for a 10K charity run in the San Francisco Bay Area might contact a mailing list provider to purchase the one-time mailing use of all of the subscribers in the San Francisco Bay Area to a magazine that has an audience of runners.

Other ways that event professionals determine where the target audience is likely to see or hear about the event is through personal observation. Where does the target audience conduct business or go to school? What other events does your target market attend? Where does your target market shop? What websites do they visit? What do they read? What online communities and social networking activities do they participate in? Sometimes government studies, chambers of commerce, trade periodicals, libraries, and media can be useful in research sources for locating the target audience.

REACHING YOUR TARGET AUDIENCE

Once the event professional has analyzed who their target market is and where to locate them, they need to ascertain the best way to reach them. In marketing, the term **reach** is the estimated number of potential customers who will see a specific type of promotional or advertising campaign. In some cases, the reach of the campaign will be determined by the limitations of the mail, email, or calling list. The event professional needs to analyze the extent of the reach to determine if that specific marketing promotion will be the most effective for their target audience.

In business, many organizations do surveys of sample target market audience members and by competitive research. By observing and asking questions of potential event attendees, the event professional can learn what is important to their audience and what is not. It is also useful for them to study what motivates attendance at similar types of events that the target market attends. Many event managers and event professionals find that reading the same publications and Internet sites that their target market reads is a helpful way to learn more about the audience and their needs.

TYPES OF MARKETING FOR EVENTS

Direct Marketing

Direct marketing is marketing by means of direct communication with consumers. When referring to events, the term "consumers" refers to your potential event attendees. Some of the more common forms of direct marketing for events include:

Mail Before the Internet, **direct mail** was the preferred marketing technique for promoting attendance at conferences and events. This included sending materials directly to an individual through the postal service. It was a costly and time-consuming method of marketing, but it is still very effective and is still commonly used for smaller meetings and events. Many organizations still use the postal service mailing for "save the date" postcards, letters, and meeting reminders. Invitations to VIPs, especially in a corporate setting, are best done in "hard copy."

The target audience must be well defined since the success of a direct mail campaign is dependent upon which mailing lists are chosen. Statistics show that a 3 percent response from a customer or mailing list is typical (therefore, in order to enroll 300 attendees, it would be necessary to mail 10,000 invitations). Direct mail to the members of an association has a much higher return.

Email   Email marketing has become the more predominant technique for direct marketing of events. The cost-effectiveness and ability to reach a wide audience makes email marketing very appealing. There are several good software programs that can help an event professional with bulk email distribution.

When sending invitations using personal email accounts, the event professional needs to consider the recipients' concern about receiving spam emails and getting computer viruses. They will also want to make sure the email reaches the recipient. Some items for consideration:

- A "catchy," but clear subject line that lets the recipient know what the email contains and peaks their interest into opening it.
- Using the BCC (blind carbon copy) address feature or the group email feature on an email program helps the recipient emails remain confidential to the others in the emailing list.
- Most email recipients have a spam blocker on their email program that will block emails from bulk email senders. Sending emails in individual small batches of 20 to 30 recipients will help circumvent the spam blocking feature. (The software programs that help manage bulk emails do this automatically.)
- The sender's name needs to be clear. Most email recipients will not open or will delete emails from email senders whose names they do not recognize.
- Most ISPs (Internet Service Providers) have a limit of no more than 70 to 90 names in a single outgoing email.
- Most email recipients are hesitant to open attachments, especially from unknown senders. Ideally the invitation information should be in the body of the email.
- If attachments are necessary, most event professionals prefer to send PDF (Adobe Acrobat) files instead of Microsoft Word documents. PDF files are less likely to be altered.
- The size of the email (and any attachments) should be no more than one MB (megabyte). High resolution graphics and photos can increase the email size to very large files that will stall, and sometimes stop, the receiver's email system. Graphics and photos should be reduced in file size before being included on an email.

Telephone   The telephone remains one of the best ways to connect with people on a one-to-one basis, and response statistics far exceed the response success of either direct mail or email. Sometimes that personal touch is necessary to encourage people to attend an event. Some event organizers organize a telephone tree, which involves having several volunteers divide up a phone list to make direct phone calls to lists of contact names. Some event professionals use third- party telemarketing companies or internal sales reps (ISR's) to help make phone calls.

For a telephone calling campaign to be successful, event professionals create a phone script for those who will call the target audience. A phone script helps callers use compelling language that will resonate with the potential guests. This phone script also functions as a sales pitch to help those making phone calls to remember all of the critical details such as date, location, time, and how to get tickets.

Advertising   An advertisement is a public notice. In most cases, advertising refers to paid forms of commercial advertisements (also called "ads"). The most common forms of commercial advertising are print media ads, such as newspapers and magazines; broadcast media ads, such as television and radio commercials; and online media, such as ads on websites and search engines, ads on social networking sites and web video commercials. Commercial advertising may also take many other forms: from billboards, to mobile telephone screens, bus stop benches, aerial banners and balloons, humans wearing signs (called human billboards), bus and subway train signs, and much more.

Because advertising can be expensive, event professionals want to target their advertising dollars to the people most likely to attend the event. Ads might be placed in relevant trade magazines, journals, or publications in order to provide exposure, not only for the event, but also for the organization. For example, if an event was targeted to an audience of event professionals, a few professional trade journals where the event might be advertised are: *Convene, Successful Meetings,* or *Meetings and Conventions* magazines. If the event had a target audience of bankers, the event might be advertised in the American Bankers' Association publication, *ABA Banking Journal.*

Some media outlets will offer **trade-out advertising** in exchange for a service that the event organization can provide. For example, an event manager for a large exhibition might trade exhibit space to a publishing company in exchange for an advertisement in their publication. A radio or television station might be willing to become an event sponsor to give them marketing exposure at the event in exchange for free advertisements on their radio or television station.

Many community events use posters or flyers (also called circulars, handbills, or leaflets) as a form of advertisement. Distributed and posted in public places where the target audience might assemble, this is often a lower-cost option to more expensive forms of commercial advertising.

Indirect Marketing

Also known as word-of-mouth marketing, **indirect marketing** is promotion using nontraditional and innovative means. Whereas direct marketing is marketing directly to your target audience, indirect marketing involves indirect communication about the event to create a "**marketing buzz**" about the event. Buzz is the sound that humming bees make; marketing buzz expresses the idea of people passing along the word from one person to another about a brand, product, or, in the case of event marketing, an event.

Social Media   Social media refers to all types of Internet communications. Interactive discussions on online news sites, blogging, online discussion communities, micro blogging, mobile technologies for communication, and social networking sites are all forms of social media. In prior decades, marketing for events meant one person calling their friends and telling them about something they were planning to attend. These days, word-of-mouth marketing tends to also involve social media.

The world wide web has become an effective way to connect people. The event professional might create a Facebook page, a Twitter Feed, a LinkedIn discussion board, or any other social media platform and then send a notification to others encouraging them to pass the word along to their friends. Social media marketing has become such a phenomena that many companies hire staff to manage social media platforms and to monitor social media dialog about their company's products or services.

Event professionals might also encourage further word-of-mouth marketing buzz and online social interaction by offering special discount tickets to their event, "pay for two and the third person is free" or "buy one, get one free" (known by the acronym **BOGO**) are common strategies to encourage people to invite their friends to an event.

CASE STUDY

TRASHed at the Coachella Music and Arts Festival in Indio, California

Eric Ritz, executive director of Global Inheritance uses YouTube, Flicker, Facebook, and Twitter to get the word out about their upcoming projects. He shared the following case study example:

Brief

The TRASHed Art of Recycling campaign is an ongoing recycling education program that redefines the way people view recycling and trash collection. Global Inheritance, a non-profit organization that inspires people to act responsibly and create change, arranges the artistic redesign of recycling bins, then integrates the recycle bins at high visibility events to encourage recycling and provide additional outlets for people to appreciate the artwork. Live paintings often occur at events in addition to the ongoing display of artist bins created beforehand.

What They Did

At the Coachella Music and Arts festival in Indio, California, Global Inheritance led a TRASHed project where they created an interactive art walk on the festival grounds to encourage participants to recycle. The 65-gallon recycling bins were designed by volunteer artists from around the world. Through social media networks, artists were informed of the contest and were asked to submit their designs. Following the festival, the recycle bins were then donated to a local school in the Coachella Valley.

Results

- Several thousand artists submitted designs
- Fifty artists were selected to design a 65-gallon recycling bin for the festival in 2012
- Eighty-five thousand people attending the festival were exposed to Global Inheritance through TRASHed
- Numerous blogs, social media posts, twitter feeds, and newspapers shared photos of the TRASHed exhibits, creating more awareness for Global Inheritance

Viral Marketing   Viral marketing is thought of as a marketing activity wherein insights about a product or service is disseminated on the Internet, just like a virus that spreads from person to person. The goal behind a viral marketing campaign is to get people to tell each other about something and then have those people tell even more people. Viral marketing for events can be difficult to implement and develop. Some of the most successful campaigns are those that get people to create something.

Guerilla Marketing   The term "guerilla marketing" was first entered into marketing lexicon by Jay Conrad Levinson in 1983 with his book, *Guerilla Marketing*. The term evolved from the concept of guerilla warfare, which refers to individuals who, as an independent unit, carry out harassment and sabotage during wartime. Guerilla marketing relies on unconventional and unusual approaches, usually in public places to get attention. Examples of guerilla marketing might include: a costumed character offering sample promotional items to the public; a random public performance; an unusual sign, billboard, or a flash mob (a group of people summoned to a designated location at a specified time to perform an indicated action, such as a dance before dispersing).

Guerilla marketing can be a fun and effective way to gain media attention. However, event professionals need to be careful about city laws and restrictions. The very nature of guerilla marketing is rebellious and nonconformist. However, when it comes to city zoning and ordinances, some guerilla marketing tactics could backfire. For example, there have been cases in San Francisco and New York where the city has fined organizations for not having a permit for their creative chalk art advertising on sidewalks.

Publicity   Publicity is an action that brings someone or something to the attention of the public through the use of nonpaid communication methods. For example, a public guerilla marketing technique, like a flash mob, might be a great way to get publicity. However, someone needs to notify the media that the guerilla marketing stunt is going to take place. A person who manages and generates publicity is called a **publicist**. A good publicist makes a living by getting to know the press and making valuable personal contacts that will help their clients gain publicity. It often takes years to develop a good **press list** of names and contacts that can be depended on to give exposure to their clients.

Public Relations   Public relations (or PR) is the art of convincing the public to have an understanding for and goodwill toward an organization, person, or event. Many large-scale event producers will hire public relations (PR) firms. Sometimes the event professional is responsible for public relations. Even an untrained person can learn how to garner some of this press publicity. Some of the more common PR activities include:

Press Invitation   The media (including newspapers, magazines, radio, and online news) is typically looking for newsworthy subjects—so the more compelling the event is to them, the more likely the press will be to attend. Event professionals or publicists need to send the first invitation to the media two to three weeks prior to the event and follow up with another invite two days beforehand. The invitation should include a "tip sheet" that gives the time, place, directions, and other details on the event and why it will be newsworthy. All invitations should be followed with a follow-up phone call to the press. If the event takes place over the course of several days, such as a convention, fair, or festival, the event professional needs to consider which activity of the event is most ideal for the press to attend. For example, the opening ceremonies with a celebrity keynote speaker might be more interesting and generate more press interest than afternoon educational sessions.

Press Release   Sometimes the best kind of publicity comes from newspapers, magazines, or the Internet. Print and online news media do not have enough staff or resources to be aware of all the possible news stories, so they rely on press releases to keep them informed about activities within the community and fill them in on news items that their reporters might not be able to cover. Press releases can also be sent to bloggers and other news reporting sources. Third-party media distribution agencies can serve as a distribution channel to the media, or the event manager can create their own press list for distribution.

   The press release should also include the name and contact information of the person sending the release. A press release has three parts: a headline; the body of the press release; and boilerplate. The headline should be succinct and interesting to get their attention. The body of the press release expands on the details and should be written as factual news, just as a journalist might write it. Some publicists or event professionals like to use a broiler plate. **Boiler plate** is a section of the press release after the story that tells about the organization or event. Boilerplate is an old news term that refers to standard text that is used repeatedly on multiple pages of a newspaper. It is a good idea to double space a press release that is being sent to newspapers and magazines to leave room for the editor's marks and should not exceed two pages. Online media sources do not generally need to have double-spaced press releases. Check with each publication to find out what medium is preferred for photographs (color, black and white, jpg, tiff files).

The following are some suggestions for writing a press release:

1. The first paragraph should include a dateline such as Chicago, IL (Chicago Daily News) December 1, 2013 Text of the first paragraph
2. The press release should be fresh, different, worthy and should appear in a timely fashion.
3. Whenever possible, the press release should provoke controversy. Controversy creates interest and responses from people.
4. The press release should start with a brief synopsis of the new item. Subsequent paragraphs can further develop each part of the synopsis.
5. The press release should be loaded with facts and details.
6. Press releases must be written in the third-person and not first person.
7. The total number of words in a press release should be targeted at 250 to 500 words.
8. The press release must be proofread manually and not simply by using spell-checking software.
9. Any contact information or URL links must be verified.
10. A press release should end with a hash tag symbols (###) to indicate the conclusion.
11. Remember the "Five W's plus H" in the press release: who, what, when, where, why, how.

The Public Service Announcement (PSA) An additional source of free publicity is the public service announcement, also called a **PSA**. This is a written script to be distributed to **broadcast media** for their newscasters or radio announcers to read on the air. In the United States, the **Federal Communications Commission** (FCC) mandates rules for the licensing of radio and television stations. One of the mandates of the FCC is a requirement to broadcast a certain number of PSA's. They will accept them in written form or in prerecorded in the form, such as an audio- or a videotape. They should be recorded in :20, :30, or :60 second "spots" and should be sent to the station two to three weeks in advance of the broadcast date. PSA's should be written so they can easily be read with double-spacing type.

CASE STUDY

The Cold War Modern Exhibition at the Victoria and Albert Museum in London, England

Molly Flatt, social business director for 1,000heads, a social media marketing and event company out of the United Kingdom shares this example of using social media, viral marketing, guerilla marketing, and publicity. "Events are in fact a huge part of what we do and very important in uniting people around a passion or brand and developing real emotional advocacy through immersive experiences," explains Ms. Flatt. The viral media efforts along with the event elements creating marketing "buzz" would be difficult to generate through paid advertisement.

Brief

1000heads was tasked with driving conversation among art and design communities about *The Cold War Modern Exhibition* taking place at the Victory and Albert Museum in London. The exhibition detailed the history of the Cold War and the art and culture that emerged from it. Primarily the activity needed to build intrigue relative to the exhibition, while bringing to life its essence.

What They Did

1000heads created and designed an Alternate Reality Game (ARG) for the exhibition called "7th Syndikate": a unique and immersive on- and offline experience that brought the exhibition to dramatic life.

Influencer Activation: 1000heads identified influencers from art and design communities,and contacted them with a cryptic email from a fictional spy organization called the "7th Syndikate" using espionage-influenced terminology and references to challenge them to become "Agents." Each influencer was assigned their own agent name and tasked with showing their allegiance by creating content on their own social media platforms and exploring the real world for ways to solve cryptic clues seeded on- and offline.

1000heads took the project further into the real world through reverse graffiti, stickers, and flyers in relevant areas of London. The culmination of the campaign was the "Big Reveal." They organized an in-character, fancy dress rendezvous for all agents where they were marched down to the Victory and Albert Museum and the Cold War Modern exhibition. On arrival guests were given an exclusive evening viewing of the exhibition and a chance to explore, discuss, and create content around the campaign themes and artifacts.

Results

- Seventy-five influencers engaged and created content throughout the campaign with thirty-five attending the "Big Reveal."
- User-generated content created across fifty different art and design social media venues.
- Marketing was seen by over 90,000 people online, equivalent to over 50 percent of actual monthly museum attendance.
- Double-page spread in the Evening Standard newspaper of the "Big Reveal" and other publications with a combined circulation of over 1,200,000, and no advertising space had to be purchased.

EFFECTIVE MARKETING COMMUNICATIONS

Another task of the event professional is to make sure that all of the messaging in the marketing campaign is coordinated. If the target audience receives promotional messages with different themes and styles, it will confuse them. Repetitive messaging and consistent design is useful in getting an audience to remember and sign up to attend the event. The best way to develop messaging is to identify what event qualities and features are most important to the target audience and then develop a message that reflects those qualities or features. The event professional starts by listing and ranking the most significant motivators for the audience to attend, and then focuses on two or three of the most important ones to develop a theme for communication with the target audience. Promotional materials should be informative, interesting, and invite positive responses. They should also have a **call to action**, which means that the message needs to tell the audience what to do next. "Call this number" "Register Now!" "Sign up" are all examples of a call to action.

The Brochure or Invitation

The invitation might be either a direct mail hard-copy invitation, or it may be a website version. When putting together the wording (or "copy") to be included in event marketing materials, the event professional needs to be sure to include the "Who, What, When, Where, Why, and How." The copy must convince the reader of the value of the meeting and elicit a response. Emphasize the personal benefits of attendance. Using phrases like "you will learn," or "you will gather new insights" help to show the event benefits.

The visual design of marketing communication materials is equally as important as the words chosen. Many event professionals will enlist the skills of a graphic designer. Effective graphic design helps set the tone and creates visual interest for the reader to want to look further. The appearance and style of marketing materials should vary based upon the different audience types and the message to be conveyed. The key to good design is consistency and readability.

Using Photographs in Marketing Materials

Photographs and pictures in marketing materials can help make your event more personal. As the old adage goes, "A picture is worth a thousand words." However, the event professional needs to be careful to obtain permission or copyright to use images. The Internet has hundreds of photographs available, yet even these photos may be licensed or posted for private use only. **Stock photography** are images licensed for sale or use and can be purchased online for reasonable licensing (also known as royalty) fees. There are also many sources of **royalty-free photographs** that are available for use without a fee. Many Destination Marketing Organizations (DMOs) and Convention and Visitor's Bureaus (CVBs) offer complimentary destination photos for event professionals and travel agents to help promote the event location. Sometimes photographers will give permission to use their photographs. It is always a good idea to check.

Photograph Resolution and Printing

Photos and logos that are copied from websites will often be blurred and fuzzy when used in print materials. That is because they are the wrong size, resolution, or file type. Images used for print require a much higher quality and resolution than those used on websites. Print resolution is defined by the dots per inch, also known as dpi. Pictures need to be 150 to 200 dpi for newspaper print and usually need to be 300 to 400 dpi for glossy type print. Commercial print resolutions might need to be as high as 600 dpi.

There are many file types including: tiff (tagged image file format), jpg (joint photographic experts group) and EPS (encapsulated postscript) files. Traditional off-set printing involves duplicating camera-ready copy through a printing press up to four times to create the necessary color separations. The plates print in four separate colors called CMYK for Cyan, Magenta, Yellow, and Black. These four colors combine to create the final color blends. Traditional offset printing may take longer, however, it can be the more cost-effective for a large quantity of print materials. Digital printing presses can be a faster way to have print materials produced. The event professional should work with their printer to determine the types of files, color types, and image resolutions that are needed.

EVENT MARKETING STRATEGY

Every event is a bit different, and every event may require a different strategy for capturing an audience. The experienced event professional starts by clearly setting marketing goals that align with the overall event goals. It can be helpful to document for stakeholders the marketing plan and to develop a **critical path** (see Chapter 3 in this book on project management for more details) time line for deliverables.

CASE STUDY

All Hands

Fund-raiser Sample Marketing Plan and Marketing Strategy

The San Francisco State University event management students will produce a fund-raising event at the Parlor Nightclub to benefit All Hands Disaster Relief. By producing this event, the students will gain hands-on experience in event management while contributing to a worthwhile, charitable organization. The SFSU students will promote event attendance through a student designed website, a Facebook page, social media outreach, press releases, networking with fellow students, notices on the nightclub's social media sites, distributing handbills, personal mass e-mail (**e-blast**) invitations, and coordination of a telephone calling tree.

The website will be detailed with information about the event and include photos and testimonials about All Hands Disaster Relief.

Mission

The mission of All Hands is to enable volunteers to provide assistance to communities affected by natural disasters. Started in 2005, All Hands has coordinated over five thousand volunteers in twenty-seven disaster relief projects worldwide, including Tohoku, Japan, after the devastating 2011 tsunami.

Marketing Objectives

- Reach over eight thousand students, colleagues, and friends by promoting the charity and the event
- Obtain an audience of three hundred people to the event
- To raise $3,000 in revenue at the event by charging $10 a person for admission
- Generate increased awareness of All Hands by gaining a 15 percent click through rate from the event website to the All Hands website

Target Markets

The San Francisco State University event management students have identified the following target markets for their event:

- SFSU college students
- Friends and family of the SFSU event management students
- Former All Hands volunteers in the SF Bay Area
- The Parlor Nightclub patrons
- Other nightclub patrons

Messaging

- Enjoy a night out while contributing to a good cause.
- Help the SFSU event management students succeed in producing a successful event.
- Mingle, socialize, network, have fun, and do good.
- Help All Hands support twenty disaster relief volunteers for ten days, providing services to over three hundred people.

Marketing Research

Ten SFSU event management students each conducted a survey of twenty of their friends and fellow college students to determine interest in attending. The student event team asked questions about location, date, event interest, and price point. With a 34 percent positive response rate to all factors from approximately two hundred people, it was decided that the three hundred attendance goal with a $10 price point was reasonable.

Strategic Alliances

The Parlor Nightclub generously offered complimentary event space and to promote the event on their website. SF Bay Area All Hands volunteers have agreed to assist with audience recruitment and post notices about the event on the organization's website. XYZ printer has agreed to print handbills at no charge, and SFSU instructors have agreed to allow event team members to make announcements in their classes.

Critical Path Time Line (for more information see chapter 3)

16 weeks out
Determine objectives and scope of the program
Determine target audience(s)
Develop marketing plan and schedule
Develop marketing budget (including print costs, pre-event letters, signage)
Recruit strategic alliance partners

14 weeks out
Develop the theme, messaging, and corresponding graphics, including event logo
Develop content for the website
Collect logos and marketing copy from strategic alliance partners

12 weeks out
Design promotional handbill and event poster (to include alliance partners' logos)
Develop an e-blast invitation list
Design website, Facebook page, and event RSVP process
Create networking/class announcement calendar and assignments
Provide All Hands and The Parlor with copy and event logos for their websites

10 weeks out
Design and send out "Save the Date" e-blast
Generate Facebook engagement and social media discussion about the event
Develop media contact list
Promotional handbill to printer
Develop poster distribution plan and assignments

8 weeks out
Write, rewrite, and proofread press releases and PSA's
Monitor Facebook, social media engagement, and event RSVP's
Poster distribution

6 weeks out
Send out press releases and PSA's
Monitor Facebook, social media engagement, and event RSVP's
Send out e-blast invitations
Begin networking and handbill distribution campaign (nightclubs, classes)

4 weeks out
Assess marketing strategy and realign
Monitor Facebook, social media engagement, and event RSVP's
Continue poster and handbill distribution
Media invitations mailed
Begin telephone calling tree campaign

2 weeks out
Third e-blast reminder
Follow-up calls to press
Monitor Facebook, social media engagement, and event RSVP's
Continue poster and handbill distribution

1 week out
Continued phone calls and networking campaign
Continued Facebook and social engagement
Reminder calls to positive responders to event

2 days out
Final e-blast reminder to event attendees

Marketing Assessment

How does an event professional determine if the marketing efforts were a success? Well, one would assume that if the event is a success and audience goals were achieved, then the marketing was effective. Yet, it would be if the marketing campaign was deemed to be unsuccessful, then waiting until the event date to find out could jeopardize the opportunity to shift the campaign and fix the problem. It is important that the event professional continually monitor results and marketing progress prior to the event.

Key Performance Indicator

In marketing industry jargon, a key performance indicator (KPI) is used by organizations to evaluate the success of a particular activity. By setting clear strategic goals, those goals become the performance indicators and against those goals there can be a measurement of the success. For example, in case study #3 (above), one of the strategic objectives was to attract an attendance of three hundred people. This number provides a baseline for a measurement of success. This is why it becomes very important to set numbers and percentages in the marketing plan.

Web Analytics in Marketing

As the discipline of online marketing has evolved, so has the sophistication of systems (or analytics) to determine its effectiveness. When deciding where to purchase advertising, the event professional considers where they are most likely to reach their target audience. In commercial advertising, the analytics to determine reach are important. The number of subscribers, the types of subscribers, and the publication distribution channels will provide the basis for the reach statistics in print media. Broadcast media uses rating systems to determine how many people are watching or listening to their broadcasts at any specific time of day.

The use of **web and media analytics** to locate target audiences on the Internet has become very advanced in recent years. There are often tools built into online advertising technology that can tell when a person has looked at a website. **Internet tracking cookies** are commonly used to measure an Internet user's search engine browsing history and the keywords used. Keywords are the words used by an Internet user when they do an Internet search. When purchasing search engine advertisements, the event professional can select the keywords associated with their ad or their target audience. They can then have their ad appear on the Internet users' search engine when keywords on the specific defined category is searched for.

For example, if an Internet user types in "hotels" and "Rio de Janeiro," the online advertising that particular Internet user will see will likely be about hotels or travel in Brazil. Internet advertising sellers can also give statistics about how many people looked up specific keywords. Most Internet advertising is charged on a "pay per click" basis, meaning the advertising purchaser will pay a fee for every time that someone clicks on the link to their advertisement. Because the costs can be difficult to control, many event professionals set a pre-determined maximum limit on the number of "clicks" that they will purchase from the online advertising seller.

Other Types of Tracking Analytics

Tracking analytics can also be used for flyers, posters, direct mail, and email marketing communications. The event professional will include marketing code numbers on the marketing materials with a specific call to action for the recipient to respond to. Some examples of call to actions might be "Use this coupon for a discount," or "Click here to see our event agenda." When the potential guest responds as a result of receiving the marketing materials and uses the code numbers on the marketing item or clicks a specific link on an e-blast, the event professional is able to gauge how successful that specific marketing campaign was.

SUMMARY

Event marketing can be a critical element to getting successful event attendance. Careful alignment of event goals and objectives with the marketing campaign is important, as is having a clear marketing strategy and analysis of the potential target audience. It is not enough to just plan an event and expect that people will come to it.

As audiences change, so do marketing strategies. An event professional needs to know what resources to use for a successful event marketing campaign. Event professionals should always be learning and exploring new ideas for useful elements and creative ideas to help improve their marketing efforts. Great marketers are always looking for inspiration and ideas to spark their imagination:

- Special advertisement with a great logo
- Creative flyer or invitation
- Interesting direct mail or promotional item
- Photographs from great theme events

- News report of a publicity stunt that garners attention.

Market to the right audience and the right number of people; extend the marketing reach with the right message and the right appeal; engage the audience prior to the event to get them excited about attending; recalibrate the marketing plan as needed; utilize all possible marketing types for the target audience; then they may very well come to your event.

Now that you have completed this chapter, you should be competent in the following Meetings and Business Events Competency Standards:

MBECS—Skill 26: Manage Marketing Plan

Sub skills	Skills (standards)
J 26.01	Conduct situational analysis
J 26.02	Define target market segments
J 26.04	Select marketing distribution channels
J 26.05	Develop integrated marketing strategy
J 26.06	Implement marketing plan

KEY WORDS AND TERMS

Product
Place
Promotion
Price
Target Audience
Consumer Behavior
Target Market
Event Stakeholders

Demographics
Psychographics
Audience Profile
Marketing Contact List
Lead Generation
Audience Generation
Marketing Mailing List
Reach

Direct Mail
Advertising
Trade-out Advertising
Indirect Marketing
Marketing Buzz
BOGO
Publicist
Press List

Boiler plate
PSA
Broadcast Media
Federal Communications
    Commission

Call to Action
Stock Photography
Royalty-free Photographs
Critical Path

E-blast
Web and Media Analytics
Internet Tracking Cookies

REFERENCE

American Marketing Association (2012).Definition of
    Marketing. Accessed at http://www.marketingpower
.com/aboutama/pages/definitionofmarketing.aspx,
December 2012.

REVIEW AND DISCUSSION QUESTIONS

1. What are the p's of marketing?
2. How should event professionals use marketing principles in event management?
3. Create an effective PSA.
4. What is a target market? For a meeting or event?
5. What are the marketing communication tools that event professionals can use to reach their target audience?

ABOUT THE CHAPTER CONTRIBUTOR

Loretta Lowe is a global event manager who believes in the power of human interaction. She is a senior event and incentives manager at Event Manager Freelance and an instructor of meetings/events at San Francisco State University. As a contract event manager, she has managed events for Nimsoft, Microsoft, Apple, Cisco, Sychron, Franklin Resources, Wells Fargo, Novartis, American Express, Fair Isaac, and many more.

Promotions Planning

CHAPTER 12

MPI engaged the actor Ben Stein as a speaker at their annual convention. This helped draw attendees and create publicity. Rick Steele/UPI/Newscom

Chapter Objectives

Upon completion of this chapter, the reader should be able to:

- Define promotions
- List eight different aspects of creating a promotional plan
- Assess promotional activities in terms of consumer decision making
- Identify three types of promotions
- Define the three types of promotions
- Differentiate between sales promotion, advertising, and publicity
- Know how to apply theories of promotions to each type to meeting or event

Chapter Outline

PROMOTIONS

Unlike personal selling, which is the fourth type of **promotions**, the other three categories are mass-market tools that send out a simultaneously targeted message to prospective consumers about events, conferences, and products. Promotions use many channels to distribute relevant messages of the products and services. With advances in technology, many new channels are being created all the time. These are needed to reach the target consumers during a given time period to meet both long- and short-term goals of a company. Depending on the objectives of the promotional activities, communications can inform clients about a new product, persuade potential customers that this event is the best one to attend, or remind past attendees that it was a great conference in the past, and they should come this year. These objectives are combined with goals relating to the demographic profile of the target market. The geographic dispersion, the density of the population, and the familiarity of the market to the product are some of the factors that aid in determining which media to use. Part of this decision is based on the media's **reach** and **frequency**. *Reach* refers to the number of potential people who receive the message. For example, local newspapers may have five thousand selected readers within a regional area but a television broadcast may reach a million people without discrimination. On the other hand, *frequency* refers to the number of times marketers want the same consumers to see the same message. So, a teaser message may be used once a month for several months to whet potential attendees' excitement about an upcoming meeting, exposition, event, or convention (MEEC), but as the MEEC approaches, the message may be broadcast once or twice a week to ensure that people know the details of time and location and remind them to make plans to attend.

PROMOTIONAL MIX

Promotional mix is utilized in order to attract a target market's purchase decision; to induce potential customers' purchase actions; to position a positive image of the company, event, product, or service on customers' hearts, minds, and spirits; to increase community awareness of the products or services; and to sustain the brand loyalty of the products and their services.

Traditionally, the **promotional mix** included personal selling, sales promotions, advertising, and publicity (PR). Personal selling is exactly as stated. This is one-on-one communication. It is considered the best and most effective technique because the seller can see how the person is reacting to what is communicated and then change tactics to be more convincing. Unfortunately, this is also the most time-consuming and the most expensive based on the expense per contact. For example, personal sales can be used with selling organizational consumers where one person represents many people or a large company as is the case when a Destination Marketing Organization (DMO) salesperson tries to "sell" a corporate meeting planner on using that destination for their next annual meeting. Another example is when working with pharmaceutical companies or medical associations; one person is the contact person so it would be advantageous to have a salesperson from the event work with the individual because the account is worth large amounts of money. This often occurs in hotel group sales. (More details are found in this book: Chapter 11 on Marketing and Chapter 13 on Sales Initiatives.)

Sales promotions are short-term techniques that promote and then remind attendees about meetings and events. Quite often, they are inexpensive items like rulers for consumer house and garden shows, rubber stress relief toys in the shape of the world for international companies or zip drives with company information on it. Advertising and publicity are designed to promote a single message simultaneously to a group of people. However, advertising controls the entire process from start to finish and pays the media (distribution mechanisms) directly. On the other hand, publicity creates circumstances where people, hopefully, will walk away with a positive perception, but the process is carefully planned and the media are not paid directly.

Size of Target Markets

Depending on the size of the target market, decisions regarding the selection of promotional strategies vary. For example, events like sports shows or concerts appeal to many different people, and there may not be a single consumer profile that fits. Therefore, for a larger target market, like an open-to-the-public event, an on-site showcase may consider using television advertising and/or a live radio broadcast as a promotional approach. A new variant is Convention News Television, which records elements of the meeting or convention and then broadcasts the recording on televisions in hotel guest rooms. This shotgun approach makes contact with different demographic and psychographic profiles of consumers and is worth the money for the number of people that it will reach. For a smaller local event with less money to spend, a local newspaper, billboards in the surrounding communities, and creative flyers are a less expensive alternative to reach the local target market.

Even if there is a set target audience, like a reunion or an association conference with a contact list, it should not be assumed that everyone on the list will come. In addition, it should be assumed that a percentage of the audience, even if they agree to come, will not attend.

The "Under-attended" Reunion

Four alumni were organizing a five-year high school reunion. There were 120 people in the graduating class. The organizers assumed that each alumnus would come and bring a spouse. Therefore, they told the resort that they would guarantee 240 guests. Of course, part of the contract required that the count must be within 10 percent of the guaranteed number (attrition clause) and any differences would be billed to the organizers. Unfortunately, only sixty alumni came and not all of them were married. What to do? They held a 50/50 raffle to try to get more money, but it was not enough. In this case, they were bailed out from their poor planning. Hearing about the plight of the committee, a single alumni stepped forward and not only wrote a check for the amount owed, but added more money to keep the party going for another hour.

Message Objectives

In order to disseminate effective messages through a promotional mix, identifying various expectations and creating motivating perceptions is vital. For example, during a car show event, using **AIDA** (attention, interest, desire, action) can aid in highlighting the impact of the promotions. First, an advertisement needs to attract *attention*, which is where an attractive female model can fit in since car shows attract a male audience. Once attention is achieved, the focus is on creating *interest* in the product by pointing out the features and benefits of the cars, trucks, or SUVs, all creating an *interest* in attending the car show. Next, it is important to have realistic expectations and understand what perceptions consumers have so that the message will achieve the *desire* in the consumer to attend the car show. The last step is to motivate the potential consumer (car show attendee) to take *action* by buying a ticket or planning a trip or going to the event. Sometimes this can take one message but if there are many different objectives, a series of promotions can be created. Keep in mind that each message should have a specific action that is accomplished. Should the message ask the consumer to go to the website and buy tickets or should the message create immediacy to get in their vehicle and drive over to the event now?

In order to promote a "certified massage convention," a promotional message could feature the new therapy-related equipment or the intangible excellence of improving one's knowledge and skills, or the maintenance of one's certification. The latter are sometimes referred to as Continuing Education Credits (CEU's). Depending on which objective is needed, these promotions could demonstrate the impact before and after purchasing and using the promoted products and services. Or possibly, the message could involve testimonials from other certified masseuses. By pointing out the benefits of going to the convention, these messages could motivate potential masseurs to register. When utilizing various promotional mixes, using the same or similar messages through images can reduce audience confusion.

Promotional Activity Budget

Deciding how much to spend on a promotional activity is a difficult task. The first step should be determining how much the event would cost. A break-even analysis assesses fixed and variable costs for an event to identify the minimum revenue that must be generated before a profit occurs. The formula is "revenue minus expenses equals profit" (see chapter 6 in this book on accounting and financial planning). The second step should ask: What is the minimum amount of profit (money left over after the break-even costs) the organizers want to make? This figure aids in deciding what price should be set for the event and how many sales or attendees are needed to reach the targeted goals. The budget can be based on three possible approaches: (1) past years' profits and budgets, (2) the competitors' pricing strategy, or (3) expected sales goals based on the percentage of increased revenue desired. Using a fundamental cost vs. benefit analysis can be a benchmark for event professionals to decide what strategic plans and approaches need to be implemented for the promotional tasks. Clarifying and setting clear goals for sales allows decision makers to determine how much money should be spent on promotions. It should be kept in mind that some "outcomes" of meetings or events are not tangible, such as in a medical meeting where the attendees gain knowledge but do not make sales. For instance, for an event that expects to attract twenty thousand attendees, it would be a good beginning investment if a previous contact mailing list of twenty-five thousand for a similar venture was used to spread the word. Contact lists usually imply that the people have asked about or have actually attended previous events that were similar; therefore, they are interested in the subject. On the other hand, to assume that all the attendees will come from one contact list would be unwise. Several different sources should be used.

Keep in mind that promotions are the tools used to communicate with potential attendees. It is easy to spend a lot on the event or meeting with the thought that the event must be spectacular for people to come—the *WOW factor*. However, if potential audiences do not know about the extravaganza, they will not come either. It is a careful balancing act.

Promotion Plan

No matter the size of the event, developing effective promotional plans can certainly assure the success. For each promotional activity, special requirements of strategic promotional plans need to be determined. The acronym SPECIAL is explained below:

- *S*pecify the target market segments
- *P*rovide goals for reaching sales revenues
- *E*stimate the cost and efforts of promoting the events
- *C*ost-share with partners
- *I*dentify the final evaluation methods
- *A*ssess all possible resources as promoting techniques
- *L*ocate long-term partners and sustain the current partnerships

Setting up the goals for evaluating the effectiveness of promoting events through experts' opinions, literature reviews, and comparative analyses are doable approaches to identify benchmark measures. Here are suggested step-by-step evaluation measurements of promotional effectiveness:

- Perceptions and attitudes of target markets toward the promoted events
- Visitations and expenditures of attendees before and during the events
- Experiences and satisfaction of participants toward the event promotional activities
- The effectiveness of each promotional activity in terms of meeting the goals and objectives of the events vs. the cost of promotional activities
- Possible measures could be positive changes in perceptions and attitudes, spending habits for sponsors' products, economic benefit to the surrounding area, and increased numbers of attendees or increased word-of-mouth

The ultimate objectives of promoting events is to inform potential attendees about the activity, persuade them that this is a good venture, and/or remind them that their involvement was worthwhile. Word-of-mouth about the event is the best promotion of all. As mentioned earlier in the chapter, the purpose of promotions is to AIDA: gain **a**ttention, generate **i**nterest, and create a **d**esire to take **a**ction. However, keep in mind that promotions can only sell the concept. The better the product and the more it meets the needs and wants of the potential consumer, the easier it is to convince people to buy.

Strategies to Stimulate Action: Urgency to Buy

Most people like to put off what they can do today so that they can do it tomorrow (procrastinate). As a result, it is important to develop strategies that can create a sense of urgency to take action. Using incentives to entice the target customers to act within a limited time will help create an effective strategic sales plan. Informing the target customers about a limited time offer, limited supply, or a great price deal will create a desire for immediate decision or purchase. Providing a bonus and extras to activate the buying power of the consumer and convincing them to act now has been proven as one of the most effective sales strategies. For example, early bird registration fees are less expensive than on-site registrations. Utilizing them will stimulate potential attendees into the action of registering before the early bird deadline passes. Finally, when your consumers are convinced to buy and act now, marketers and service managers need to make sure that the ordering process is as easy and convenient as possible.

Cross-Promotions

Incorporating potential partners into promotional campaigns can increase the budget, broaden the appeal of the event, and create mutually beneficial cooperative messages. In developing co-partners, discussions about providing in-kind monetary services and resources are important to assure that duplication of valuable time, data, and networks are not created. When copartners utilize cross-promotional strategies, it improves the branding of the event and expands the resources dedicated to the events. Cooperative advertising allows multiple companies to unite to create one message. For example, t-shirts for 10-K runs frequently have the event information on the front and all the logos of the participating companies on the back. This can attract a larger audience effectively with lower cost. Since most people do not throw out the t-shirts afterward, the reminder of the cause and fun lives on long after the event is over.

Sponsorship

Especially with the economic downturn of late, concerns and the price of everything going up, sponsors have played very vital roles in the MEEC industries. Sponsorship dollars make sports-related events, festivals, cultural events, fairs, conventions, and various events financially feasible. So long as the products, organizations, and events have a common goal or objective, they can unite to target a mutually beneficial audience and create effective joint promotions. For example, in sporting events, sponsors unite in creating sizeable purses so that the best competitors will enter. As a result, this creates a high-profile event with the best athletes, which draws large audiences, which in turn makes the publicity used more effective. This induces many sponsors to shift their donations and sponsorships to a market segment that can afford higher prices and can seek finer quality products and services. Another strategy, one used by meetings and conventions in the same industry, is "**co-locating**." This is when two organizations have their events in the same location on the same, or sequential, days. This creates additional drawing power for both events. Co-locating has been used for years by the Professional Convention Management Association (PCMA) and Event Service Professionals (ESPE, formerly ACOM). Discounted registration fees are offered to members of both organizations.

When seeking sponsors, it is important to think of the big picture. For example, with sporting events, athletes need clothes, equipment, food, drinks, medicines for injuries, and so on. Therefore, potential sponsors could be approached like department or sports stores, grocery stores, specialty food stores, beverage vendors, pharmaceutical companies, equipment manufacturers, and many more. In addition, other sponsors interested in linking their name to popular causes can be enticed by discussing how the event will improve their image and make them seem more humane to their consumers. Banks are interested in supporting fairs and certain sports (e.g., golf). Insurance and consulting companies are big supporters of meetings and conventions. Amusement parks, kids' toy vendors, and school suppliers are supporters of school-related programs and events. "FedEx Panda One" successfully transported two pandas from China to Washington, D.C. This special transportation highlighted the event itself and focused attention on FedEx as a major global transportation competitor. Coca Cola corporation has been a regular sponsor over the years for the Olympics. The positive link is used with sales promotions like cans and give-away products that have Olympic Gold winners as the image. The advertisements and publicity linking the winning mentality enhances the company image by uniting all the different promotional tools to create one positive message.

Partnership Opportunities

The benefits of using cross-promotions must start by finding the companies with similar goals and objectives for their products. Collaborative partners can experience win-win outcomes when they work together to share their main contacts of stakeholders and connections to their existing target markets. Some events and activity additions increase the effectiveness of adopting cross-promotions. For example, hosting breakfast gatherings, sponsoring charities and sponsoring speeches and public seminars can become highly effective approaches when pooling resources for different events. Event professionals need to be creative yet cautious about the image and the messages to make sure each sponsor agrees on the collective outcomes and perceptions. Communicate well with prospective partners about the benefits they can obtain when they agree to be part of the event.

Some suggested cross-promotions may include but are not limited to the following:

- Encourage the target market to try out products and services of corporate partners by providing free samples, coupons, and/or bundled products
- Give target markets products of collaborative partners as free samples or gifts
- Create opportunities for possible joint interviews when disseminating news of the event

- Mention partners' names when making announcements or sending press releases (done by IMEX America when they included the names of partners such as MPI, PCMA, and DMAI).
- Share advertising space with collaborative partners (often done by Destination Marketing Organizations(DMO's) when they include the names of hotels in their destination when creating an advertisement).

Invitation Letters

When sending out an invitation letter to participate in an event, the letter itself may serve as one component of the promotional mix—publicity. The press release lists important information about the event like

1. the purpose of the organized event
2. the names of organizers
3. the names of past and current sponsors
4. the names of advisory board directors for the events
5. the VIP status
6. the past event locations and highlights
7. the event location and directions
8. the time and date
9. the dress code
10. the main contact

The main selling points—the highlights of the event and the expectation of the participants—should be embedded in the text as part of the main motivation for joining.

Consumer Decision-Making

Many external and internal factors impact a consumer's purchasing decision. External factors or macro-marketing are things an individual person cannot control, like the economy, culture, technology, legal, or political systems. Cultural values change the way a person perceives what is valuable or worthwhile. What is happening in the economy? How secure do people feel about their jobs? These macro-marketing factors unite within a consumer to alter how they plan to spend their money and what they will buy when they do want a product. Demographic factors (income, gender, education, to name a few) are quantifiable data about a person. These aid in segmenting the population into more easily measurable markets so that promotional money is used to select the most effective and lucrative markets. However, demographic data cannot always narrow down the options enough. For example, many people watch football. There is no gender, income, age, geographic location, or any other demographic that can pinpoint who watches. Therefore, understanding psychographic factors (activities, interests, and opinions) allows promoters to create messages that can tap into the inner motivations in a consumer's thoughts.

Consumers can go through a five-stage process, depending on how familiar they are with the product. For attendees who frequently enjoy going to the event and are brand loyal, the decision is simple. Once they know the details of the event, they plan to go. The process goes from problem recognition directly to purchase. It would be great if all previous attendees would feel this way. However, people may have other interests and so they must spend more time deciding what to do. In this case, problem recognition is only the first step because they will be looking for more information about what else is available and then evaluating each alternative before making a decision on what to do. Thus, it is important for event professionals to not only communicate the details of the event but also communicate about ancillary activities, spouse and family programs, and attractions and activities in the destination. It is not by chance that Las Vegas, Nevada, attracts more conventions and attendees than any other locale in the United States. Knowledge of the five stage decision process can certainly assist event organizers when looking at how target markets think, seek, and act during their participation and purchase decisions. Recognizing these different stages can aid in creating different motivational messages to help possible attendees in making their decisions. Once the particular needs and desires are identified, marketers can create messages that tap into the needs and wants of their potential guests and increase sales.

Problem Recognition   The first step in consumer decision making is simple: The potential attendee must recognize that they have a gap between their needs and wants. That is, what do they have now versus what do they really desire. That gap in a person's needs and wants must be pointed out so that a potential guest realizes that they have a problem, hence problem recognition. Of course, the answer to their dilemma is to attend the publicized event. The challenge that marketers face is how they can assist consumers in transforming needs to desires. Again, the answer is simple: Provide informative and convincing messages within the promotional activities that will help them bridge the gap.

Information Search   When a decision is risky or a person lacks confidence in their ability to make the purchase, consumers seek information from various sources including personal contacts such as family, friends, and acquaintances. Or, they can search outside contacts like previous attendees, users' reviews such as blogs, consumers' ratings, and editors' choice. If these contacts don't provide enough information, the commercial sectors such as suppliers, dealers, retailers, wholesalers, salespersons, exhibition booths, or advertisements can provide additional data. As mentioned earlier, the more comfortable the consumer is with the decision, the less searching they need to do. First, they begin with what they already know from their experiences and memories. Depending on how much they can remember, a consumer might go to friends and family for help. If it is a question of professional information, data might be sought from coworkers, blogs, and industry reviews. If the person is still uncertain, then commercial sources are explored. If product attributes are needed, consumers will search advertisements or other commercial communications. Marketers may survey existing consumers to find out what sources their consumers used to increase their awareness of the products and services, where the sources were, and how they located the sources. By understanding the above information, marketers can obtain a big picture about where, when, and how to place their messages for the most effective use of their resources.

Usually personal experiences or others' experiences carry more weight. Because service is intangible, it is important to remember that guests maintain an image of the product in their mind because there is no tangible product that encapsulates the entire event or meeting. What people remember about the event becomes the product. That is because a service is consumed in a "moment of truth." This means that the interaction between the guest and the vendor happens in a moment and is perishable, it cannot be held in inventory, and there are "no do-overs" and thus no chance to repeat the experience. Bad impressions that are first impressions cannot be undone.

Evaluation of Alternatives   Once a consumer has gathered all the information they believe they need, they begin the process of evaluating all the alternatives. This can be comparing various conferences, meetings, or events to decide which are the best to attend, or it can be assessing various attributes of the event itself to decide whether the one conference is worth spending money on. Consumers weigh the importance of attributes such as price, quality, consumer services' effectiveness, brand, convenience of attending, atmosphere, location, and varieties of selections against their needs and wants.

Purchase Decision   Once the alternatives have been weighed, a decision is made. If the promotions have been effective, the potential consumer will turn into a purchaser by making reservations, travel arrangements, or registering for the event. However, it is also possible that a person can simply procrastinate and put off the decision until a later time. This is when incentives like early registration are necessary. In addition, while the potential consumer fully intended to buy, they may forget to take action. This is when a reminder promotion or a reminder message is a good objective. Finally, it is possible that they will decide not to purchase and that is when a persuasive objective could be used to explain all the benefits that attending a meeting, convention, or event will bring.

Post-Purchase Behavior   The level of a consumer's satisfaction is based on the gap between the perceived quality and value of the products/services received and the costs incurred. In the case of meetings and events, an attendee's needs and wants from a conference can be complex. Some want knowledge or recognition of the importance of the information provided at the event. Others want networking opportunities. Meeting up with friends once a year at conferences is another desire. When the quality and experiences are greater than the consumer's expectations, conferees are satisfied. When attendees are happy with their experience, they tell others and the positive word-of-mouth is priceless.

When consumers are not happy about the quality and experience of the products and services, filing a complaint, returning a product, refunding the purchase price, or making an exchange have been the most common post-purchase behaviors. For some severe occasions, lawsuits could be filed. Consumers' firsthand feedback and reviews on purchased products may impact the companies' future sales (or particular events/conventions' future attendance). Managers and marketers need to be in the hearts of their customers by understanding who the customers are, what the target customers like or dislike, what sources could be more accessible and useful for the target consumers, and what customers want for the services and follow-up. Only when managers and marketers can see the big picture can some negative situations be avoided and greater satisfaction and outcomes reported.

When a meeting or service is risky for an individual, more thought is taken on the outcomes. Marketers call this "**cognitive dissonance**." It refers to the post-purchase regret that a consumer can have when a purchase is risky for them. For example, did the meeting have a bad reputation but the attendee decided to go anyway? Public ridicule and "I told you so" or "you wasted company money" are threatening possibilities. Risk can also be expensive in terms of registration fees, location, or transportation costs. There are many forms of risk, and it is not always related to money. In these cases, it is important to communicate with attendees to remind them about all the positives of their experiences after they have returned home. Thank them for attending a great meeting. Congratulate them on their good decision to come. It is important to reinforce the positive reasons why they made the right decision to attend the MEEC. Thoughtful post-purchase follow-up, emails, or phone calls can enhance the image of the products and companies as well as extend to the consumers' enjoyment and satisfaction as a whole. This ensures a brand loyal attendee who becomes the best salesperson for future meetings.

The promotional mix provides a range of approaches to achieve the goals of the companies' sales for both short and long terms. Individually, sales promotions, direct selling, advertising, and publicity have their strengths and weaknesses. Depending on the objectives, a synergy can be achieved by combining all of them as they reinforce the message to a consumer's senses. Because promoters understand this, the lines of separation between the various promotional techniques have blurred over the years. Understanding which to use for the best effect requires an understanding of consumer behavior theory and how best to apply it to communications.

SALES PROMOTIONS

Sales promotions are short-term strategies designed to attract attention and remind consumers about the event. Sampling, rebates, contests, sweepstakes, and coupons are some of the tools that are used. People like to get "freebies." Sampling, contests, and sweepstakes are a great way for guests to try new things by reducing the risk of purchase because it is free. If they do not like the product, they just walk away. On the other hand, if they like the product, another sales promotion can go hand in hand with the trial. Free samples are used regularly at trade shows like the National Restaurant Association. Other trade shows conduct contests such as having attendees obtain "chits" or get "stamped" at every booth on the floor. Those successfully obtaining all are placed in a drawing for a prize. Rebates and coupons are great reminders that products they liked at the event can be purchased for a "savings" afterward.

ADVERTISING

Advertising and publicity communicate simultaneously to a mass market with one message. However, methods are distinctly different. Publicity puts out a message to the public but it does not control or pay the media directly. Advertising controls and pays for the message from conception of the message to delivery. The advertising agency plans what they want to say and how they will say it. Once the advertisement is created to specification, then all the media are evaluated for the best *reach* and *frequency*. Once the selection of a medium like television, radio, newspaper, and so on are decided, media are contacted to check how much each one costs for the given time frame, position of the message, and length of time. In television, position of the message could be the local 6:00 P.M. news during the second message space, or it could be a repetition of the same ad every break for the 6:00 A.M. morning report. On the other hand, the position of the message could refer to the second page of the first section in the middle of the page or a full-page ad in the June issue of *Meetings & Conventions*. If an event is for non-profit and considered to be for the public good, public service announcements (PSAs) can save the organization money. PSAs are inexpensive or free of charge for the media time and space for advertisements. For example, local media may be willing to run PSAs for a charity run.

In advertising, for example, to attract attendees to an electronics show in Las Vegas, the event professionals will design the exact message, layout (placement) from the headlines, copy, illustrations, and even the typography (typeface). The magazines cannot change anything about the ad. Then, marketers will pay electronics magazines directly to publish their ads, controlling what page, location on the page, and the issues when it will run. For various purposes of achieving promotional goals, advertisements may vary based on specific geographic areas, target audiences, and particular interests. Using the Internet, social media, newspapers, posters, electronic message boards, billboards, the exteriors of cars, television, radio, and event activities, these media are carefully determined based on whether the consumers are commuters, transit riders, or at home. Basic information, such as price and the benefits of purchasing the promoted products and services, can be presented depending on whether the marketer is trying to inform, persuade, or remind the consumers. Some advertisers may only use one single approach while the others may use multiple approaches for more effective outcomes.

Evaluating the outcomes of advertisements versus return on investment (ROI) has generated attention among companies and in the advertising industries. Generally speaking, proper and timely advertisements do stimulate sales, and they are proven to be one of the most important aspects of the promotional mix. On the other hand, the credibility of advertisements must be carefully evaluated for each message. Some individuals have become tired of "being fed unneeded" information through television commercials. However, creating a message that suggests a person has a gap between what they have and what they want is not necessarily a credibility issue and is a good audience for this purpose. Advertising is also good for giving a lot of data about a product for a person who is looking for alternatives during an information search. Radio broadcasting is also constantly filled with too many commercial messages. Hence, there is a satellite radio network that does not have any advertisements. However, advertisements on radios are good to attract attention for upcoming events with many repetitions to aid in consumer recall. When a DJ who has a positive commentary is added to the mix, credibility increases.

Direct Selling

As marketers become more savvy about communicating with their customers, new methods have been added. With computer networks and technical data mining, it is easy to obtain more information about potential attendees, like addresses and emails. However, in order to create a more personal touch to the promotional messages, information is needed, like birthdays, anniversaries, and preferences on hotels, food, and activities. For example, hotels may offer a free nights lodging on a couple's anniversary through a personalized letter or a restaurant might offer a "comped" dessert on someone's birthday using an email. Some may question the profitability of gifts. However, usually a couple will spend more than just one night at the hotel, but even then, they may purchase things at the gift shop or dinner in the restaurant, but they may just enjoy themselves enough so that they want to come back. Gifts make people feel special and this "good will" is important when developing brand loyalty. A gift that can be used and displayed in the office of a convention attendee, such as a clock, will expand the reach. And with technology, it is easy to keep track of individual preferences, and databases can insert a name and address to a letter at the proper time. The procedure is categorized as "direct selling" since the product and/or service providers are communicating directly with the consumers. During an on-site event, event organizers and booth representatives enjoy greeting their potential customers and run raffles and other games to obtain contact information of those participating. A simple example of this is having a bowl at a booth and asking anyone to drop their business card in so that they have the chance to win a gift. A recent development has been the use of electronic badge scanning of participants who stop at the booth. Even more advanced is the use of radio frequency identification (**RFID**) on badges with receivers in booths to capture attendee data. This information is used for subsequent follow-up selling as well as to track the ROI for the exhibitor. Mobile advertising has been questioned regarding the possibility of invading customers' privacy. When conference attendees are visiting each booth in a ballroom, a company booth can connect to each Smartphone to provide more details about the nature of the products, the location, and additional information about the company and its services or products. Coupons can be sent to a Smartphone. By scanning the customer's cell phone at the checkout point, discounts may be applied.

Social Media Outlets

Various traditional and advanced media including podcasting, mobile advertising, YouTube, and social media can reach mass target consumers. The MEEC industries can utilize media outlets through Internet technology by broadcasting their messages effortlessly as long as the message content is well developed and properly worded in advance. Messages may be created by independent producers and can be distributed with an affordable budget when social media and channels can be joined and clicked by the public easily. For example, podcasting could be downloaded by one click to a mobile device. The created messages could be heard and watched through video or audio files, be attached into a blog's file exchange, or generate followers and Facebook's "like" link. Podcasting could be a very good return on investment in terms of being capable of generating a high volume of listeners.

More and more groups have used social media to provide daily communications and activity news announcements. Many companies have benefited by the power of "word of mouth" when the advertisements are posted on Facebook or linked to websites. The Facebook site has generated its own sense of community. Blogs are also seen as the place where individuals can share their thoughts and event activities freely with global participation from others. Interactions among members can also stimulate the popularity of social media and enhance the visibility of advertisement and promotional activities. Customers also rely on other customers' product or service reviews. However, the accountability of reviews has been questioned since "fake" customers posted some reviews. More and more online brokers only give access of "customers" reviews to real customers who have purchased or booked products or services and have participated in events through the particular broker's site (e.g., Expedia).

Advertising Effectiveness

How can advertisements increase effectiveness and attractiveness? Touching the audience's emotional and moral needs could be one of the creative messages presented within an advertisement. Humor, fun, and positive connections to an audience's memories can also catch the attention of the audience. However, be careful about too many repetitions. People get irritated when a funny message is repeated over and over. By understanding that the audience is a frequent user of the Internet, technology can be the best delivery channel to develop. For example, placing advertisements in video games and on social media can be an effective approach to reach certain target markets.

The process of creating and producing the advertising messages is a paid, nonpersonal, promotional activity. Organizations and companies use newspapers, magazines, television, radio, billboards, mobile, and other social media for advertising. Although advertising has its credibility issues, overall it is very effective at conveying data. It is especially appropriate to use for attracting attention to an event or meeting or reminding people to attend a function.

PUBLIC RELATIONS (PR)

Public relations (PR) are similar to advertising in that they create one message to communicate to a large audience, all at the same time. It is different in that it does not control any part of the message nor does it pay the media directly. For example, in its simplest form, a local charity might send out a press release to all the media with all the information about the charity fund-raising event. It costs the price of the postage, and all the media have the relevant data. However, what the media do with the information is totally under their control. The television station may decide to throw it away because they do not see any newsworthy information that their viewers would be interested in. On the other hand, the newspaper editor may have a son who will benefit from the charity, and therefore he may want to help the fund-raising event in any way he can so he prints the entire press release in the paper. In either case, the charity can only hope that the media will adopt some or all of the information to pass on to their constituents but they could decide to do nothing.

Public relations could be seen as a third-party endorsement while advertising is more like a self-endorsement. PR focuses on image building by establishing relationships between the public and the committed companies and/or organizations. PR does not sell products and services directly for the committed companies and organizations, but its actions need to be in line with the goals and objectives of the companies and organizations. During a public relations campaign, creating effective materials include fact sheets, media kits, collateral speakers' highlights, as well as the arrangements of on-site marketing events. The main purpose of sending media kits (print and/or electronic format) is to facilitate getting accurate information to the press and to make it easier for them to use the information. For example, an event organizer may spend $3,000 for a one-eighth-page newspaper advertisement or s/he can choose to use a press and public relations agent to write editorial stories about the event. Or, a third option is for an advertisement to be run during the news show, which is going to air a story from the event. Celebrities are often invited to endorse certain missions and community services for profit or nonprofit purposes or a convention might engage a celebrity as a keynote speaker. The events and news surrounded by celebrity figures' images and speeches held in front of a newly dedicated association/center's exhibit venue could be seen as an event-within-an-event strategy that becomes a major public relations campaign and an effective public news announcement. A total communications management strategy would use both so that their message can be enhanced.

Compiling collateral materials, media news releases, an event-within-an-event, public service announcements, and public relations activities make every effort to promote the events, products, or services. Public relations campaigns feature stories for news releases, for holding marketing events, and staging press conferences. Reward programs, before and after testimonials, garner support from the community, provide favorable publicity from public figures, and support fund-raising. The appearances of invited public figures or street clowns certainly can draw visibility from the public and along the street. Many conventions invite the mayor of the city where the event is held to speak at the opening ceremonies. Obtaining the permits and/or meeting local codes can prevent unnecessary miscommunications when utilizing street promotion techniques, such as a small portable billboard carried by a clown, flyers handed to the public, and gatherings with celebrity figures at a local mall, children's hospital, or other featured locations. When public figures (city, regional, state, federal, and international leaders, among others) appear at special events, proper publicity with media involvement can certainly increase the credibility of the promoted event and generate significant public attention and interest. Positive images and reputations with accountability could be reformed through credible relations with stakeholders, customers, communities, and the media.

PR is a technique that creates images for its clients. Using tactics that do not pay the media directly is a very creative process because the message must be given in such a way that the audience will obtain an exact desired perception. Media events must be so exciting and newsworthy that all the reporters will want to come. Since reporters are invited to a lot of events, it is no small task to pique their curiosity or make it worth their while. As a result, public figures are always a good ploy because they bring their own appeal that draws the reporters.

SUMMARY

Promotions consist of four different categories: personal selling, sales promotions, advertising, and public relations (PR). Personal selling information has been discussed in other chapters (see chapter 13) so this chapter explores the different aspects of the other three. Because promotions are the different ways that marketers and event professionals communicate to their publics, there are many similarities that can be united in a general discussion before looking at the individual subsets. The size of the target markets, determining the budget, and sponsorships are important overall decisions that will determine the strategies for sales promotions, advertising, and public relations. When these are decided, the importance of each promotion will guide the percentage of the budget allocated to each. PR focuses on image building and establishes relationships between the public and the committed companies and organizations. There are merits and limits when using advertising or public relations. The two have varying approaches, but each aim at promoting products or services in an effective fashion. Both profits and nonprofits benefit from PR's connections to consumers. Advertising is a paid format that utilizes controlled messages to prospective consumers at a given time. When visitation to a destination declines and it struggles with its own destination image and branding, using advertisements to retain and sustain existing customer loyalty could be a difficult task. That is why PR is a better tool. Sponsoring a hospital or a charitable sports event is great for helping to focus attention on the more charitable side of a business. People tend to generalize their emotions from the hospital to the sponsor. For persuasion issues, advertisers are mov-

ing toward more subtle publicity. Television stars hold a can of Coke with the label showing during their show. The viewer cannot fast forward without missing part of their show so they generalize their emotion for the show to the displayed product. When watching a favorite television show, observe what products have labels as part of the show. Are they at the hospital fund-raising event? Does the star talk about the 10K run? Is there a picture of a restaurant or hotel in the background? Are they wearing a t-shirt from an event? On the other hand, radio DJs are very credible for their select audiences. They can become part of a person's "friends" because a listener is constantly bombarded by the opinions of the DJ on a daily basis. Usually all three are used in a total communications management (TLC) package to reinforce each other and adapt the messages to the strengths of each promotion.

DEVELOP SEQUENCE OF EVENT ACTIVITIES

Table 1 Specify Activity Procedures and Notes
The table gives a list of steps and guidelines in regard to hosting an event including the do and don'ts.

Activity	Notes and Steps
• To create and establish the goals of the events • To create specific event ideas that can best meet the goals	Event creation stems from the feedback and the need of customers, employees, and employers. Some events are treated as promotional events to promote the products/services in the mainstream markets while other events are planned to generate revenue and build up the visibility and networks. The planning steps should start as soon as the needs have been identified and confirmed. The event organizers will need to agree upon the format for the events. With planned events the initial focus is on what the vision and missions are, what the short- to long-term objectives are, and then set the deadlines for executions. State clearly the expected achievement from the event and if the event is free to the public or only for designated members and associations.
• To select the planning team members	Form a team equipped with proper skills and sufficient knowledge who are excellent at executing plans and events. The team should be a manageable size and highly organized. The team is well incorporated and representative among all members. Each member must know her/his responsibility and have the expertise to accomplish her/his assigned task. The whole planning team holds open communications and every member has the willingness to assist each other with teachable attitudes in a professional manner. Everyone understands what needs to be done, who is in charge of what by when, and why they have been given the responsibility.
• To generate a timetable that includes each activity's schedule and plan	Planning each activity with details by following a well-thought-out schedule with listed responsibilities can help each member of the planning team to undertake every specific task effectively. The team should meet on a regular basis for continuing reviews and support throughout the planning progress.
• To structure costs, pricing, and to search available funding sources	Establish possible financial supports through sponsorship and networks. Layout the baseline of each item's budget in order to provide a realistic price range. A realistic and doable budget is vital for running events without losing financial battles while reaching a positive revenue outcome.
• To check the needs for permits in hosting an event	Contact local officers to determine if obtaining a permit is a must prior to hosting the event at that particular location or facility. Reaching out to other organizers who have hosted events at the same location to obtain more details would be another good approach to prevent any unnecessary issues for the companies and the events planning team.
• To optimize the date selection	Check with other local or national events that may target similar groups of possible audiences. Be cautious about date selection and try to avoid any dates that may cause scheduling conflicts.

(Continued)

Activity	Notes and Steps
• To research and select a suitable site	Visit the list of sites under consideration to examine their facility, amenity, security, safety, and accessibility. Sufficient parking spaces should be available, adequate space for meetings and exhibitions is required, awareness of the cost of hiring on-site supportive helpers should be known, and what additional costs may be incurred. Ask the venues if suitable catering services and equipment would be available.
• To be aware of any legal liability	Check any legal obligations and policies. Identify in advance any related legal liability and obligations that are connected with the events. The policies relevant to cancellations, accessibility for people with disabilities, and risk pre-assessments are needed.
• To identify risk management and prevention	Assess potential risks and compile a prevention plan that can minimize the risks that are vital for the event planning team to make sure that a public liability insurance plan has been evaluated and will be purchased to take care of people at all levels.
• To provide a safe, secure, and healthy environment	Research each policy related to safety, security, and health, and identify what needs to be done prior to the event and how the policy can impact the events and attendees on-site. Ask for guidelines and tips prior to the events.
• To maintain transportation and logistics controls	Doable logistics arrangements and effective transportation plans can minimize complaints and inconvenience caused by parking routes, parking sites, or alternative means of transportation support systems. Proper signage and on-site staff will be helpful.
• To provide couriers and delivery arrangements	Also consider how your own supplies will be delivered to and from the event. Exhibitions need to be set up properly with clear and concise instruction regarding the logistics arrangement for supplies to be delivered to and from the events. Accessible parking, lift equipment for heavy goods, and available storage space are also needed at events.
• To develop plans for emergency situations	Check with the venue and host site to learn more about plans and the process of using fire equipment, evacuation practices, medical support, and an emergency phone and contacts. A guideline should be developed that clearly states what to do during emergency situations and how to do it.
• To provide emergency services	Contact professional emergency services for detailed guidance and advice. Establish a service contract and ask the professional emergency to be on-call.
• To utilize an account to track expenditures and revenues	To sustain an event effectively needs a balanced account. Establish a manageable account for each event and make certain that monitors spending carefully.
• To seek proper insurance coverage	Seeking proper insurance plans that cover employees, attendees, exhibitors, contractors, loss of valuables, and cancellation.
• Building alliances and liaisons with other partners	Create partnerships and establish a closer relationship with similar event sponsorship and turn competition into a knowledge-sharing platform when opportunities arise.
• To implement a doable marketing plan, website development, media identification, and event list for data publishing	Identify the goal, find the right partner/sponsor, execute an achievable marketing plan, and adopt various promotional mixes, advertisements, and prints.
• To establish relationships with sponsors, exhibitors, and media partners	Identify potential sponsors and determine if the sponsors fit the main purposes of hosting the events. Build a sustainable relationship and state clearly their benefits of serving as a sponsor.
• To establish booking data and to identify possible sponsors, speakers, and exhibitors.	Building a clear database to record bookings and contact information. Booking forms could be pdf files, hard copy, or online registration. Reaching out to current top-managers' contacts to identify possible sponsors. Research other similar events' exhibitors and retrieve names from the membership directory; potential sponsors and exhibitors may be identified and invited.
• To publicize and reach out to the target audience	Plan thoughtfully with strategic approaches to reach out to target audiences by using electronic (email, blog, social media, YouTube) and traditional media (posters, flyers, direct mail, press releases, newspapers, and magazines). Cross-promotional activities have been proven to be effective as well.
• To track the effectiveness of marketing, promotional activities, and public relations	Tracking the effectiveness of various approaches of marketing, promotional mixes, advertisements, and public relations to make certain that the target audiences are aware of the events and are enticed to participate in the events.
• To ensure the bookings	Confirm the event speakers and check the list of needs that will assist speakers to facilitate their speeches and/or workshops. If changes are needed, make sure an updated program needs to be delivered to the audience.
• To list all services and facilities	Layout the needs of operating and hosting the events. Check the availability of equipment and supplies including lighting, air conditioning, heating, accessibility, security, courier, presentation projectors, and speakers.

Activity	Notes and Steps
• To provide signage, programs, maps, and welcome packs	Providing a welcome pack that includes a program or brochure and a physical map for event activities with proper signage can certainly smooth the day and meet the needs of attendees and exhibitors.
• To develop a plan B for a rainy day	Developing a plan B for a rainy day is a must for outdoor events.
• To train and educate staff	Ensure each staff member knows to whom s/he reports to when there are situations and problems on the event day. Educating staff about all basic and professional manners and encourage them to strive for excellent services and present themselves with proper knowledge. A booklet or handout with a list of contacts and dos and don'ts will be necessary.
• To provide food, food, and more food.	Supply food through internal or external caterers. Follow the policy of food, safety, and health registration. Logistics for food delivery and on-site set up, and smooth pay transactions will ease the tension and increase the effectiveness of operating events.
• To plan onsite layout	Check the accuracy and proper arrangements for the layout of exhibitions and workshops. Follow up with the procedures and steps with on-site staff and managers to make sure they know their particular tasks. Check again to assure that couriers are in the correct area and catering is set up smoothly.
• To update and detail the accuracy of the event accounts	Detail and track the event accounts to examine if the event has generated revenues in certain areas and make documentation about how to make it a greater event next time.
• To select the date for the next event	Set and confirm the date for the next event as soon as possible for more organized arrangements in advance so the event's name and date can be listed in a timely manner.
• To highlight the events for the event sponsors, exhibitors, and board of advisory	Providing highlights of the events with facts, including the number of attendees, revenue summary, media press, photos, testimonials, and recommendations for future events, may sustain the partnerships. A thank you note can be included either in the beginning of the report or at the end of the report.
• To provide publicity for the success of the events	Brief the press regarding outcomes of the events and share the information or newsletter with the media to create positive publicity as soon as the events end.
• To establish post-event interviews and debriefing sessions to collect feedback	Acknowledge the planning team's efforts and collect staff's feedback to make a list of do and don'ts for future improvement. Meeting room's debrief sessions and comments on the pre-during/post-event will gather valuable information from the team for greater future planning.

Now that you have completed this chapter, you should be competent in the following Meetings and Business Events Competency Standards:

MBECS—Skill 29: Promote Meeting or Event

Sub skills	Skills (standards)
J 29.04	Coordinate [develop] promotions
J 29.01	Develop advertising plan
J 29.02	Develop cross promotional activities
J 29.03	Develop contests

MBECS—Skill 30: Contribute to Public Relations Activities

Sub skills	Skills (standards)
J 30.01	Contribute to public relations strategy
J 30.02	Contribute to publicity plan
J 30.03	Develop media relations

KEY WORDS AND TERMS

Promotions	Sales Promotion	RFID
Reach	AIDA	Public relations
Frequency	Co-locating	
Promotional mix	Cognitive Dissonance	

REVIEW AND DISCUSSION QUESTIONS

1. For each promotional activity, please list the SPECIAL requirements of strategic promotional plans that need to be determined.

2. What are the step-by-step evaluation measurements of promotional effectiveness?

3. What are the benefits of using cross-promotions?

4. Four major steps to obtain a target markets' attention are to stimulate their interests, to capture their desires, and to persuade them that their action can certainly assist event organizers to understand how target markets think, seek, and act during their participation and purchase decisions. Please illustrate the four steps in detail and state clearly what you would do to help your organization as a marketer.

5. A sense of urgency can stimulate actions. Explain what strategies will you develop to stimulate your customers' urgency to buy?

6. What are the purposes of using advertising?

7. What are the advantages of promoting events on live radio broadcast?

8. How can the AIDA model help in achieving promotional goals?

9. What are the factors that affect consumer decision making?

10. Why have many event organizers taken the advantages of utilizing public relations?

11. You are now an event and convention manager. Please develop your own sequence of event activities for one of your favorite events.

ABOUT THE CHAPTER CONTRIBUTORS

Dr. Rachel J. C. Chen is the director of the Center for Sustainable Business and Tourism at the University of Tennessee (UT), where she is also a professor in Retail, Hospitality, and Tourism Management. Dr. Chen has conducted various types of research projects in the areas of tourism, hospitality, and service management, including sustainable development, economic impact assessments, forecast model evaluations, tourist behavior analyses, and geographic information system (GIS) applications in business development. Her teaching interests include sustainable business, strategic management, eco-tourism, tourism economics, tourism analysis, event management, and marketing for hospitality and tourism. She serves as an associate editor, guest editor, editorial board member, paper reviewer, and track chair for twenty refereed journals and four national/international associations. Dr. Chen is a Fulbright Senior Scientist.

Kathryn Hashimoto, PhD is an associate professor in the School of Hospitality Leadership at East Carolina University. She holds two doctoral degrees, one in marketing and the other in curriculum and instruction, two M.B.A.s, one of which is in marketing and an MA in psychology. She teaches and writes in the area of marketing in the hospitality industry.

CHAPTER 13

Sales Initiatives in the Meetings and Events Industry

Chapter Objectives

This chapter provides the reader with an understanding of the following:

- Generally speaking, there are two types of sales initiatives in the meeting and event industries
- Recognizing the differences between a primary and secondary sales initiative
- Familiarity with the two sides of the primary sales initiatives depending upon type of client
- Step-by-step process to produce both primary and secondary sales initiatives

Meeting Professionals International (MPI) regularly incorporates a book and merchandise store or booth into their annual convention. George G. Fenich

Chapter Outline

TWO TYPES OF SALES INITIATIVES

Sales initiatives in the MEEC (Meetings, Expositions, Events, and Conventions) industry are growing in nature and depth partly due to changes in business paradigms and also due to diversification of product offerings within a brand. Current trends dictate that if meeting/event professionals are to maintain healthy, successful careers, they will need to be well versed in sales initiatives for meetings and events, but also for expositions and conventions. In order to best equip the event professional with the necessary tools to navigate the breadth of sales initiatives in the meetings/events sector, the following chapter will be divided into two sections. The first section will address primary sales initiatives, while the second section will address secondary sales initiatives. To distinguish between primary and secondary sales initiatives, primary sales initiatives are defined as those meetings/events where selling is the major purpose of the gathering. In turn, secondary sales initiatives are meetings/events where the major purpose of the event is not sales; thus, the sales features within the overall program become ancillary opportunities.

Primary Sales Initiatives

The parameter of primary sales initiatives for this chapter will focus on meetings, expositions, events, and conventions (for shorthand purposes, recognized as MEEC). The chapter will address the two most common scenarios for planners: (1) working directly for a client participating in MEEC or (2) working directly for the owner of the MEEC. Although these two scenarios are the two sides of the same coin, the preparation processes are not shared. The difference between these two scenarios is based upon the point of origin. In the case of representing a client participating in a MEEC, the focus is around sensory qualities of the product. How can you breathe life into the product by means of visual, auditory, tactile, olfactory, and taste? While representing a client who owns the MEEC, the focus will be around cerebral needs that answer who, what, where, when, and how. Once you have these two distinct perspectives in mind, the actual design processes will loosely resemble one another.

Before getting started on articulating the sequential planning steps for all major sales initiatives, it is important to first define those meetings and events that fall into this category. Although the following list is not exhaustive, it serves to provide examples of the range of sales events that exist in the business arena that will require a professional meeting and event planner to have skilled expertise: car shows, art shows, fashion shows, film premiers, boat shows, technology products, beverage sales, real estate development, equipment sales, and hair design showcases, to name a few. There are an endless number of products that exist in the marketplace that utilize MEEC to sell products either internally (**business to business**) or externally (**business to consumer**). Sales are the lifeblood of the MEEC industry, representing a multibillion dollar industry. In one way or another, sales initiatives will oftentimes be a topic that will require event professionals' consideration when producing a MEEC. In order to visualize the sales design process, please refer to the graphic to help the event professional approach the sales process to determine the correct design strategy to implement for the meeting or event. The first question to ask oneself, "Is the sales initiative the primary or secondary purpose of the meeting/event?" The second question to ask; "If the sales initiative is the primary purpose, then which side of the coin does the client represent?"

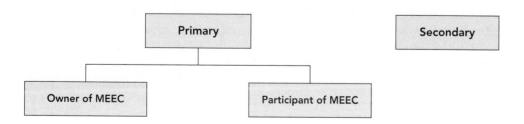

In essence, the meeting/event planner must respond to two questions before moving forward with preparing a strategy for the production process. First, determine the type of sales initiative the meeting/event will function as: (1) primary or (2) secondary.

Second, determine the population the client is serving: (1) **owner** of MEEC serves to build attendance, education, networking opportunities, and sponsorship deals or (2) **participant** in MEEC serves to build brand recognition, sales revenue, build database list, and extend market penetration.

Review Principles for Primary Sales Initiatives The first step in the process is to determine the most beneficial concept and design of the sales initiative. Begin with brainstorming sessions with the client and the client's marketing/public relation teams. This process will lead to the initial development plan for the sales initiative. The results of the collaborative process will answer how to best align the brand image of the client's company and product to the population of interest (exhibitors and/or attendees). In preparation for the initial client brainstorming session, Step I will illustrate the factors or elements the meeting/event professional will need to research prior to the meeting/event.

STEP I

Historical Data—It is important to know if the sales initiative being considered is a new product launch or if the event has been performed in the past. If the sales event is one that has taken place on previous occasions, then it is important for the meeting/event professional to be familiar with the historical information captured from the client's previous meetings/events. Pay special attention to former themes or the underlying story line of the event, the type of venue(s), marketing/advertising/public relations campaigns, budget, return on investment, production lead time, and whether the event was deemed a success or failure in the eyes of the client. Oftentimes, the client should have a production book (definition: a compilation of files placed in a three-ring binder, or electronic equivalent, that acts as a mobile tool kit to address contractual commitments, floor plan layout, staff names and contact information, on-site production time line, renderings, third-party information, hotel rooming list, and so on) created by the former meeting and event planner that articulates the full scope of the sales production from a historical aspect. It is advised, that the meeting/event professional request the production book for personal review of historical data prior to the first client meeting. Requesting a "copy" of the production book will position the event professional for success, as it will allow them to formulate the best sales initiative strategy to present to the client.

If, on the other hand, the sales initiative is for a new product launch, then the event professional will need to engage in blue-sky thinking (definition: open-minded thinking), offering multiple creative concepts that will align with the client's brand. In order to effectively engage blue-sky thinking, an event professional must research all of the direct competitor's previous meetings, events, and marketing and public relations campaigns to assist in formulating unique concepts for presentation to the client. Keep in mind that when preparing for the initial client meeting, the professional meeting and event planner will want to have multiple concepts ready for presentation (concept A, concept B, concept C, and so on) in order to offer viable options for all stakeholders

SWOT Analysis—This analysis tool is a strategic business planning exercise to evaluate strengths, weaknesses, opportunities and threats for projects and business decisions. The grid found below is the template to track all actual strengths, weaknesses, and all actual and potential opportunities and threats for any given meeting/event, in order to arrive at setting clear, achievable objectives.

Before addressing how to employ the SWOT analysis, it is important to first define each of the four attributes that comprise SWOT.

Strengths: The *internal* business elements that provide differentiating factors in the marketplace.

Weaknesses: The *internal* business elements that are considered vulnerabilities when competing in the marketplace.

Opportunities: The *actual* and *potential external* scenarios that exist that can be leveraged to enhance company performance in the marketplace.

Threats: The *actual* and *potential external* scenarios that can hinder a company's performance in the marketplace.

Starting in the upper left-hand corner, list in the "Strength" box all actual internal strengths. Once finished, move to the upper right box and list all actual internal weaknesses. Once complete, continue to the lower left box and list all known and potential external opportunities. Once complete, finish with listing all known and potential external threats.

SWOT Analysis Grid

	Helpful	Harmful
Internal Origin	**Strengths**	**Weaknesses**
External Origin	**Opportunities**	**Threats**

Once this exercise is completed, the event professional should have a total of four complete lists. Based upon the cumulative information contained in the full grid, the event professional can assess the business model to arrive at the strongest positioning for the client's company/brand to compete at the MEEC. Now that the overall objective has been pinpointed from the SWOT analysis, the event professional will use each item from each quadrant in the SWOT analysis to form a specific and actionable plan that will be delegated to the meeting and event team. For instance, each item listed in the strengths and opportunities quadrants will form the basis for how each bulleted item can be enhanced further to create a strong competitive advantage. Alternately, those items contained in the weaknesses and threats quadrants will become actionable items to minimize and/or improve prior to the execution of the MEEC. If the SWOT analysis is engaged in this format, the meeting/event professional will create a strong differentiation platform for the client's product, resulting in the most fertile chances for the client's objective(s) to be met based upon the direction revealed from the previous brainstorming sessions.

Consumer Behavior—This information will be provided by the marketing department from the client's company. The analysis will be derived from such sources as customer feedback forms, product surveys, and industry blogs. The consumer behavior profile will establish a general characterization of the majority population that purchases the client's product(s), allowing the professional meeting and event planner to develop a clear picture of how to best motivate sales at the MEEC. It will be important to review and understand the information contained in these reports, as the reports will provide key insights into the thinking and needs of the target consumer for the client's product(s). Another important element in the research process is to perform an exercise called "walk a mile in the consumer's shoes." The main focus of this exercise is to visualize how the target consumer currently thinks, feels, and behaves, along with what need does the product fulfill for the consumer? Once a clear characterization of the consumer surfaces, which is void of the event professional's internal thinking as a consumer, then the event professional can align the factual descriptions of the target consumer to the visualized sales environment that will be articulated through sight, sound, touch, taste, and smell. Next, it is important to "get out of your head space" and test characterizations revealed from the "walk a mile in the consumer's shoes" exercise. The second step of the consumer behavior exercise is to "test" the theories developed by the event professional. This process is known as testing premises: Gather a small population of four to six individuals to test market consumer behavior theories arrived at by the event professional. It is important to locate current customers of the client's product, possibly a few friends or business colleagues who happen to be actual consumers of the product, and for the event professional to engage them at the MEEC. Meet with these individuals to share with them the design idea formulated for the trade-show booth, retail area, or promotion of the overall convention. Questions to be considered at this time would be: What kind of presentations should be utilized to engage the audience? Should the program include interactive workshops? Is a trade-show floor the best environment to educate attendees? What tools should be utilized to convey and reinforce the product message? Who should serve as guest speakers?

By asking questions of this nature to the **test market** and listening to the feedback provided, the meeting/event professional will know definitively how to create traction with the target consumer. Lastly, confirm the consumer behavior theory and results depicted in this two-step exercise with the client's marketing department.

Demographics—**Demographics** is the study of human characteristics based upon gender, race, age, disability, region within the country, home ownership, and employment status. Information regarding the specific demographics of the target consumer will be supplied by the client's marketing department or from other sources of research. Just as performed in the exercise for the consumer behavior segment, the same steps will be taken again, specific to this demographic information. However, the main difference in this current exercise compared to the previous one will be a far more nuanced probing. Rather than simply focusing on the broad qualities of the majority population, the event professional will analyze smaller populations within the overall majority population. In general terms, this exercise may aim to reveal the compelling factors that are necessary to create a sale in, say, a person from the age range of 30 to 39 years of age, compared with the motivating factors for a person of the age range between 40 to 49, and so forth. The information gleaned from this analysis will be applied in numerous aspects. For example, the Communication channels for individuals ranging from 30 to 39-years-of-age is via Facebook and Twitter; while those individuals ranging in age from 40 to 49 years-of-age receive communication via direct emails and links to the company website where event updates are kept.

For each category of demographic information (age bracket, gender, target ethnicity, regions of the country, and so on), the event professional needs to aggregate the information so that the design and event concept will remain viable when targeting segments of the sales plan to each demographic category. Again, to help articulate potential questions that should be considered, the following is another example: What sales strategies and design factors will be employed to help motivate a sale from a 32-year-old male of Latin descent? What additional factors must be considered or eliminated to motivate a sale and resonate with a 21-year-old woman of Asian descent? Once all demographic information has been aggregated, the exercise will reveal multiple mini-sales strategies that are extremely specific to groups within the target consumer profile.

Now the event professional is in a position to marry the creative concepts (sight, sound, taste, touch, and smell) previously settled upon to each of the mini-sales strategies. For example, prior to the start of the MEEC, what promotional opportunities exist to reinforce the brand message with those consumers ranging from 20 to 35 years of age? Might it be possible to sponsor a nightclub event or distribution of inexpensive gifts at an evening event that would boost consumer demand for the client's product? Conversely, maybe a promotional event for those consumers in the age range from 35 to 50 years old would best be engaged with a brand message during a morning breakfast buffet. The way to create strong demand for the sales initiative offers infinite possibilities for pre-event, event, and post-event promotion and sales. The event professional's creative ability will be a strong asset when collaborating with the MEEC stakeholders. The event professional should show industry expertise by aggregating the demographic information as was described; it will lead the project to an even stronger sales strategy, resulting in far stronger revenue potential for the client.

Psychographics—Psychographics is the study of psychological characteristics found within the general population. The fundamental attributes studied in psychographics are personality traits, attitudes, personal values, interests, and general lifestyles. For the purpose of a MEEC, the psychographic analysis tool is a far more detailed analysis suited exclusively to a seasoned marketing executive, rather than a professional meeting and event planner. Currently, psychographic analyses married to meeting/event programs are not traditional scopes of expertise. However, a few thought leaders in the meeting and event industry are incorporating psychographic information into the design and execution processes of their meeting planning businesses. For this reason, psychographic segmentation is touched upon as another potential tool to support the event professional. Please become familiar with the nine psychological profiles contained on SRI International's website under VALS types to better understand the existing psychographic segments.

If, as a professional meeting and event planner, there is interest to establish a differentiated skill set, then it is recommended to fully engage the VALS psychographic profiles as another layer in addition to the consumer and demographic research. The general difference between the demographic research and the psychographic research is that demographics fall within the domain of marketing, while psychographics falls within the domain of branding. In essence, **branding** attempts to create a personality for a tangible/intangible product in an effort to create deeper connections with the consumer. The best and easiest way to arrive at a particular personality for a given product is to listen and note the descriptive words used by the client to describe the product. Examples are words such as happy, hip/cool, luxury, athletic, and so on. Then visit the VALS psychographic types to gain insight into which of the nine personality types align with those particular descriptive words defining the client's product. Information contained in the VALS profiles will help refine best practices specific to website design, communication styles, event content, trade booth stylization, technology preferences, and operational processes.

Stakeholders—Stakeholders are those individuals that have an active interest in the outcome of the MEEC project. Stakeholders can run the gamut from business owners, heads of departments, key sponsors, celebrity endorsers, board members, to name just a few (see chapter 5 in this book on Stakeholder Management for more detailed information). As an event professional, it is important to listen and note all visions held by the stakeholders for the event being produced, so that inclusion of stakeholder ideas can be assimilated into the overall design of the sales initiative. It is recommended that 51 percent of the ideas offered by the stakeholders be incorporated into the design and execution of the meeting/event. It is common practice among successful businesses to maintain the "buy-in" of stakeholders. There is no denying that the event profession-al's creative vision is important to the overall success of the meeting/event. However, remember that collaboration is a team effort, and, to keep the team (stakeholders) actively engaged in the overall sales initiative, it is important to create the feeling that each stakeholder contributed to the overall design of the sales initiative. Think of it like this: When someone recognizes you by name in a business presentation, don't your ears perk up and you pay closer attention to what is being said at the meeting? The same holds true in the collaboration process. If a portion of every stakeholder's ideas make it to the final sales design strategy, then each stakeholder will be more inclined to support the sales objective recommended by the event professional, more apt to attend event design meetings, and more apt to perceive the outcome of the sales MEEC in a far more positive light.

Competitors—Competitors are those businesses that sell the same goods or services within a defined population. It is extremely important to learn as much as you can about each of the companies that directly compete against the client's product. It will be important to find a unique format for the brand's communication message, look and feel of the sales booth, colors utilized in graphics, dress of the employees working the MEEC, video/digital branding, distribution methods of marketing collateral, ease of interfacing with the product's website, and entertainment methods used to draw in customers.

It is critically important to make sure that the client's sales initiatives are distinc-tive and memorable to the target consumers as they navigate their purchases within the sea of products that exist within the open market. Therefore, those elements that invoke the sensory processes (sound, touch, taste, visual, smell) will need to be original and distinctive to the client's product. If, after analysis, there appears to be too many common attributes between the client's sales design and a direct competitor's design, then there is a higher likelihood that the target consumer will lack the ability to have enough momentum to take action, the last step of AIDA. If the event professional cannot make an indelible impression on the public, then it will be almost impossible to move the public to make a purchase of the client's product, thus resulting in a fi-nancially unsuccessful meeting/event for the client. Therefore, never lose sight of Sales Rule #1—NEVER underestimate your competitor(s). Learn as much as possible about each of the product's direct competitors, plan for the unexpected, then create a sales strategy that is completely unique.

STEP II
Budget—The final step in the brainstorming process before a sales strategy is created is to understand the total budget that is available to produce the sales initiative. At this point in the creative process, the event professional will merge the previous seven steps with the total budget allocated to the sales initiative. A line item budget depicting all known costs will need to be created (for more information, see chapter 6 in this book, Financial Planning). Start by securing estimates from potential third-party vendors, determining the cost of labor, legal fees, transportation, drayage, catering, networking events, talent, equipment rental, marketing collateral, promotional gifts, video/audio production, set up and tear down fees, meeting/event planner's fee, and so on. Once a budget is created, it is recommended that a buffer dollar amount be added to the budget to cover potential fees that were overlooked in the creation of the budget. From here, the exercise will produce a total cost incurred to produce the professional meeting and event planner's vision. If the client's budget is less than what is needed to produce

the meeting/event, then it will be important to employ value-engineering strategies to comfortably reduce the design concept to match budgetary constraints. Keep in mind that opportunities may exist where certain products can be donated or sponsored, bartering may be employed, and discounted services via Guru.com can all help reduce the budget while maintaining the essence of the original sales strategy. Once the budget and the creative sales strategy are copasetic to one another, then the event professional has the "official" sales initiative that will be deployed for the client. From the standpoint of the planning process, the "official" sales strategy represents the midway marker in the full production process. It is recommended that going forward into the next steps of the production process should only be done to edit the sales concept to fit the remaining steps, rather than start from the beginning of the process due to a conflict. Stick to the concept plan and simply modify it to find the perfect fit to meet the client's objectives.

STEP III

Venue—At this point in the sales planning process, the event professional will want to shift into the role of a hypothetical real estate persona because Step #3 is all about location, location, location. Now that a strong sales initiative has been approved by the client, it is important to find the best location to showcase the client's product. The first aspect of location is to determine where the MEEC will be held. Depending on whether the professional meeting and event planner represents the host or participant will guide how much participation the event professional will have in this step. If the professional represents the MEEC owner, it will be vitally important to select a destination that satisfies the needs of the customer base, offers enough total hotel rooms to support the needs of the attendees, is easily accessible, is a diversified destination offering multiple entertainment options, and has a large enough venue to accommodate the MEEC needs.

If the professional meeting and event planner's client is a participant in the MEEC, it will be important to review the floor plan of the MEEC trade show floor to determine high traffic locations. Traditionally, end booths and those on major aisles are high profile locations as well as booths that are toward the front entrance of a large-scale MEEC. If, due to timing, it is impossible to secure a high traffic location for the client, then it will be critical to create manufactured foot traffic to persuade attendees to visit the client's booth. The best way to "manufacture" interest in the client's booth is to determine activities that will create a spectacle at the MEEC. Many planners utilize models, stilt walkers, hand-out fliers, advertisement within venue, dance teams, and spokes models to draw interest to a client's trade-show booth. No matter the type and number of spectacles created, it is important to create an actionable plan to boost foot traffic, rather than overlook this weakness. Even if the client has a high-traffic location, employing these options still makes sense.

Lastly, the meeting/event professional needs to have a clear viewpoint regarding the functionality and traffic flow patterns for the sales space based on the booth layout and design. Some of the questions that need to be asked are: How will the attendees interact with the sales personnel at the booth? How many open sides does the booth have for attendees to flow into the sales space? Is there enough space for equipment at the booth to conduct order taking? In particular, the larger the booth, the more questions should be considered before executing the design plans for the trade booth. Traditionally, larger booths will have the following design elements: lounge areas, mini-showrooms, and mini-offices for writing orders in the interior space while the perimeter space of the booth is used to field inquires.

Clearly, there are many considerations involved when determining the perfect location for the MEEC sales initiative. To become more familiar with design considerations for a sales space, such as merchandising, work areas, demonstration areas, and how to grab a consumer's attention; visit a local mall to familiarize oneself with current trends in retail presentation. The more crossover business practices that can be transferred from everyday retail locations to the trade show environment, the stronger the sales initiative will become.

Design—Design decisions are an important aspect of the sales initiative, as the design of a retail space and/or trade booth will need to have visual appeal to attract attendees to the space. A helpful metaphor to assist in the design phase is to acknowledge that the sales space is akin to a product "playground" for the consumer. To create a playful environment, it will be important to utilize sensory experience elements—color, fragrance, texture, technology, or music/sound. Employment of these devices will create a compelling space for the target consumer to engage the client's product. The main objective not only for the event professional, but also for the sales staff, is to create a welcoming sales environment that allows the target consumer to linger. As it is a proven fact in the retail industry that the longer a consumer spends time in the sales space, the more they buy, hence the more revenue is created.

Traditionally, the design of a retail or trade booth space will be handled by a third-party vendor that the event professional outsources to produce the tangible space. This is often done by a general services contractor like GES or Freeman. This can also be done by a specialty service contractors for elements like audiovisual, catering, cleaning, and so on. The latter can either be official contractors designated by the show management or exhibitor appointed contractors (EAC). However, before a designer is secured to build the trade booth, information needs to be garnered to assist the designer in his/her creative process. Therefore, it will be of utmost importance to learn as much as possible about the location of the meeting, event, exhibition; the site of the trade booth; and the distance between booths and direct competitors. It is important to capture information now that will address obvious design-related questions. Important pieces of information that will be invaluable to the pending trade booth designer will include, but not be limited to:

a. Budget
b. Square footage of space
c. Height of space
d. Sight lines of the space
e. What type of structure is allowed within the space?
f. What will be the walkway carpet color used by the owner of the MEEC?
g. What types of signage will be in the meeting space? Convention banners, bathroom facilities, directions, and so forth?
h. What will be the logo colors for the signage used by the owner of the MEEC?
i. What type of lighting can be used in the space?
j. Are exhibitors allowed to hang anything from the ceiling and what are the restrictions on doing so?
k. What are the fire marshal's requirements for allowable materials?

The design process requires an ample amount of input from the event professional in order to create a space that successfully articulates all the elements revealed in Steps 1 through 3. All of these aspects will be necessary details for the designer to know as thoroughly as the professional meeting and event planner, because he/she wants to create a functional space that begs attendees to slow down and step into the retail/trade booth space. Keep in mind when the initial consultation takes place with the trade booth designer, the strongest advantage an exhibitor has to create sales is based on the "live" component. Therefore, plan on including in the discussion how to incorporate imaginative features that cannot be found on the client's website or felt through the client's marketing collateral. The predominant objective in this step is to document all the necessary pieces of information to communicate to the booth designer, including how to three-dimensionalize the product, brand image, and consumer experience. Write everything down, communicate all ideas and important pieces of information in hard form and begin the external trail now, be it paper or electronic.

Implementation—This is the stage where the event professional can call in the troops to help articulate the vision for the sales initiative. Obvious calls to round out external partnerships to execute the sales initiative will be a trade booth/retail designer, graphic designer, video designer, audio designer, promotional product supplier, printer, furniture rental, lighting company, talent agency, website developer, uniform supplier, transportation company, equipment supplier, remote sales support equipment, and local bank for cash drop if necessary. At this point, the professional meeting and event planner can breathe a sigh of relief, as all due diligence is now complete, and the majority of the responsibility shifts to management and communications. In essence, this step of the planning process will transition the event professional from cerebral activities to communication activities. In previous production steps, the professional is focused on clarifying creative concepts best suited to the client's sales initiative. Now the event professional finds his/her major activities revolve around communication, feedback, the paper trail, and adhering to timeline demands. Therefore it is recommended to review all production details including update conversations with all third-party vendors at a minimum of once a week. Although it is easy to reassure oneself that communications have been crystal clear, anticipate misunderstandings as creativity itself; this is a very nebulous domain.

STEP IV

Sales Plan—Now after all these steps, the event professional arrives at the heart of the sales initiative, the sales plan. In this part of the process, two major components are addressed: (1) sales strategy and (2) sales tactics. **Sales strategy** is a business plan that states how a person or organization will sell products and services in an attempt to make a profit. **Sales tactics** are actions taken by a person and/or organization to implement the sales strategy. The sales plan will then be broken down into two separate groups of customers: (1) existing business and (2) new business. For both of these customer groups, it is important to determine a separate sales strategy and sales tactics for each population, resulting in two distinct sales plans. For both of the sales plans, spread the employment of strategies over three time frames: (1) pre-event, (2) event, and (3) post-event.

The focus of the sales plan is to determine quantifiable objectives that are measurable (**SMART** goals: Specific, Measurable, Achievable, Realistic, Timely). Consider, for example, benchmarks for revenue generation, i.e., gain over last revenue generation, number of qualified leads, sales territory, lock-in longer contract terms with existing customers (i.e., sales contract moves to a two-year contract from a one-year contract). The choice of measurables that will be utilized will be based on the type of sales event, previous historical methods utilized by the client, new objectives established by the client, and the research derived from previous steps. Once measurables and sales goals are determined for the MEEC, then it is important to blend the sales plan information with the marketing information previously collected to determine the sales tactics that will be employed to achieve sales goals.

Marketing Initiatives—In this planning phase, the event professional will utilize right-brain creative brainstorming techniques to determine the sales tactics to employ. Start by listing all possible methods that can be utilized to create a sale. These might include: contacting attendees via an eBlast prior to the MEEC event, social networking, advertising the meeting/event on the client's website, promotional mailers, offering preset appointments for attendees to meet with a sales representative, guerilla marketing, YouTube, and Pinterest. Performing this exercise will help determine the infinite opportunities that exist to help the client's product stand out in the crowd by creating a compelling "draw" to the booth/retail space.

It is also important to determine those activities that will take place on-site that will compel prospective **sales leads** to stop by the retail space/booth to familiarize them with the product. For instance, offering free samples, demonstrations, touch screens, video tutorials, spokes model campaigns, and hands-on trials can be employed. It is important to determine how to communicate the personality of the product to the target consumer. The more energy and dynamics the design employed in the booth and overall space, the more it will help create the human synergy between product and target consumer.

Lastly, don't overlook publicity and media coverage to help create a compelling booth/retail space. Work directly with the client's public relations team to determine media interviews, stock photos, customer endorsements, newsreels, press kits, video footage, and giveaways that might be used. Keep in mind the media components of the marketing initiative are not strictly confined to the onsite event/meeting. All of the marketing ideas resulting from the brainstorming session(s) will need to be divided into three time frames of deployment: (1) pre-event, (2) event, and (3) post-event strategies. It is very important to evenly spread the number of marketing strategies over the three time frames. An unbalanced marketing strategy with a heavy weight on the front end and a weak weight on the back end will prove to soften end results. In other words, don't take the chance of missing sales targets and forecasted revenue goals due to an uneven distribution of marketing initiatives over the full scope of the meeting/event.

Legal—The legal aspects that need to be considered in the preparation of a sales MEEC are too vast to be covered in a single chapter. The following list is a starting point for a meeting/event professional to explore while developing a sales initiative. Please be aware that this list is not exhaustive. It is important to secure legal advice from a qualified attorney in the state the sales initiative will take place.

   a. ADA compliance
   b. Child labor laws
   c. Union regulations
   d. Business license
   e. Sales tax license
   f. Business entity
   g. Sales permit
   h. Resale permit
   i. Fire marshal approvals
   j. OSHA regulations
   k. Copyright(s)
   l. Trademark(s)
   m. BMI, ASCAP, SESAC licenses
   n. Syncing rights
   o. Work-for-hire releases
   p. Liquor license
   q. Food handling certification
   r. Customs for importing international products

    s. Vendor contracts

    t. Indemnification

    u. Independent contractor contract

    v. Meeting/event insurance

    w. Talent release form

STEP V

Post—Keep in mind that "post" does not simply mean the "post-event survey." If a post-event survey is a tool the client wishes to utilize for the intended meeting/event, then the event professional should categorize this activity under marketing initiatives. "Post" for the purposes of this chapter, recognizes all activities that need to take place to wrap-up details of the meeting/event. These details may include determination of return on investment (ROI), creation of a historical file documenting the entire production of the sales initiative, return of trade booth/retail space to the client's headquarters or a third-party vendor warehouse, creation of a new SWOT analysis documenting observed strengths, weaknesses, opportunities, and threats of the meeting/event. All of these details are vitally important to document now in anticipation of next year's event. It is in the execution of these small details that separates the event professional from the competition. Consider all details, both big and small, that can be captured once the execution of the event has been completed. For instance, what elements of the forecast failed to be accurate? Were there noticeable deviations from descriptors of target consumer compared to on-site consumers? How accurate did the SWOT analysis prove to be? Were there changes to the budget that occurred that were due to miscommunication or some type of unforeseen error? What was your assessment of the working relations with third-party vendors and exhibit hall crew? What activities were done well compared to direct competitors? Was the production time line accurate, or would it be helpful for the client to secure an event professional earlier next year? Questions of this nature should be documented now with clear recommendations on how to improve the overall operation of the sales initiative.

In addition, it will also be vitally important to create a separate post-analysis that targets the profitability of the meeting/event. The information to be captured should include: quantify all new sales leads, revenue generated from MEEC, new sales contracts, expansion into new sales territories, media coverage, attendee feedback, client retention, and quantify the results of the sales strategy and tactics employed. For all the sales goals that were established in the brainstorming and execution phases of planning the meeting/event, the event professional will want to document not only the measurable numbers, but also his/her afterthoughts on the strategy and tactics. What could be improved? Where did the sales team excel? What were the weaknesses that occurred that could have been avoided? Are there numbers that may require clarification? Do not self-edit the post-analysis, include both large and small details of the sales initiative. Although this step may seem tedious, it will prove to be a competitive advantage in the way the client perceives the meeting/event professional.

Secondary Sales Initiatives

One of the emerging roles for event professionals is to strengthen the connection between a client's product and the brand identity for the given product. As far as the client is concerned, there are very few occasions in the annual business cycle for a product to have "live" time with the target consumer. The client requires the full breadth of leveraged "live" opportunities to gain the largest financial value. Therefore, not only are primary sales initiatives a strong marketing opportunity, but secondary sales initiatives can provide considerable incremental growth for a client. For the purpose of this discussion, the parameter for secondary sales initiatives that will be covered is limited to logo'd merchandise, auctions, talent merchandise, raffles, on-site bookstores, and all ancillary retail initiatives.

The first step in designing the sales initiative is to align the primary sales initiative to the secondary sales initiative. There is no need to reinvent the wheel; simply base the secondary sales initiative off of insights gained from the primary sales initiative. It will also be important to hit the same highlights and service style that will be articulated in the primary sales initiative. In this way, from the consumer's perspective, the secondary sales initiative is simply an extension of the primary sales initiative rather than a free standing off-shoot that is not mentally anchored to the client's marketing strategy. However, in some rare instances, a secondary sales initiative will not have a primary sales initiative to model after. If this happens to be the case for any given sales initiative, the event professional is managing, please refer to the steps contained in the primary sales initiatives to help produce the secondary sales initiative.

Review Principles for Secondary Sales Initiatives   As was seen with Primary Sales Initiatives, there are multiple steps or tasks that must be completed when developing secondary sales initiatives. They are as follows:

STEP I

Type of MEEC—It is extremely important to categorize the type of meeting/event for which the secondary sales initiative will be promoted. Determine if the MEEC is sales-based as in a trade show, convention, or symposium, or is the main motive of the MEEC educationally-based, or is the MEEC a gathering for fun (special event), concerts, sports events, or street fairs? Knowing the type of function the event professional will be participating in has a direct correlation to the methodology employed for the sales initiative. For instance, association meetings are usually driven by the education program and are more financially reliable and stable than corporate meetings and corporate meeting planning is far more random and sporadic, consisting of different types, sizes, and seasonality of meetings each year.

Space Requirements—Space requirements are based on sales volume for the specific location. However, space requirements can vary depending on the number of sales associates working the booth, size of the show, the targeted population you hope to engage, booth traffic, and types of sales activities. For example, assume that each sales associate on duty needs 40 to 50 square feet of exhibit space and your exhibit unit is the typical standard booth size, 10′ × 10′ (i.e., 100 net square feet). Then the exhibit booth can only accommodate a maximum of two sales associates at any given time. In addition, professional meeting and event planners need to calculate the average hourly booth traffic necessary to support the sales goals (e.g., 7 to 10 visitors per sales associate/per hour). Usually booths over 100 square feet provide consumers more room to roam, hence more opportunity to engage in a sale. Lastly, once the event professional has determined the number of sales associates needed to work the MEEC, it is important to schedule staff in shifts, if need be.

If the client of the event professional is an exhibitor, then a considerable part of the on-site production process will include the General Services Contractor (GSC). The GSC is responsible for all on-site needs including signage, carpeting, booth production, merchandising displays, hanging of lighting, and video/technology installation. The GSC will provide the event professional with a packet or website URL that spells out specific event information, forms, prices, and instructions for space requirements. Additional forms will be included for event professionals who require electricity, Internet connectivity, phone service, shipping information, and drayage fees. The GSC will help professionals keep close track of the crew on the show floor, including the I & D (Installation and Dismantle) companies, which may have been hired by the professional meeting and event planner. If the MEEC is held in a hotel, in addition to the space required for the primary sales initiative, be sure to list all meeting rooms and ancillary sales areas within the GSC contract. Ask the hospitality venue regardless if it is a hotel, convention center, restaurant, and if there are any unique issues that may impact both the primary and secondary sales initiatives of the meeting/event. This is particularly important when using nontraditional venues such as a parking lot or an airplane hangar. If the event is held in the United States, be sure that all sales spaces are compliant with the federally mandated American with Disabilities Act. For further details, including spacing requirements, please visit the website.

Product—The term *product* refers to the merchandise the event professional will be in charge of creating in a secondary sales initiative. It can range from donated auction items, client products, promotional materials, travel packages, books, webinars, and any number of tangible items. In order to be prepared for building and designing the secondary sales initiative, it is important for the event professional to view all products that will be showcased for sale. If the client is unable to provide the event professional with actual samples of the products comprising the secondary sales initiative, then it is suggested that digital pictures of each item in the sales lineup be obtained. Meeting and event planning is a highly visual creative process, and it would be a great disservice to attempt to design a sales initiative without holding, touching, and learning about the product(s) the event professional is responsible for building the secondary sales initiative around. For instance, the event professional may find after viewing the sales item(s) that the product lacks visibility, as it cannot be worn by the consumer. Therefore, the choice to include promotional products to support the secondary sales initiative would be advantageous. In this way the event professional gains the ability to reinforce the brand image and product name with the end-user. Also, using logo'd merchandise for meeting promotion is an effective advertising campaign, as it encourages awareness to prospective customers to attend the trade show or meeting next year.

Product Display and Supporting Atmosphere—The exhibit space for the secondary sales initiative can be as small as a ballroom in a hotel or as large as a hall in a convention center. Event professionals should try to consider the scale of the secondary sales space to determine how best to display products to optimize sales. One of the most important details of the merchandising display are the colors and graphics of the retail space. As was discussed earlier in the chapter, it is recommended to secure a third-party vendor who can create the structural retail space. When engaging the services of a specialist, oftentimes discussions will take place regarding the enhancement of the sales presentation. Specialty designs created from unique logos and designs, as well as stock imagery, create the overall atmosphere for the sales space. If the secondary sales initiative is within a trade show environment, the GSC can be of great assistance as the GSC maintains catalogs of designs that can be used to articulate the look and feel of the show space the event professional wishes to create. Traditionally, most of the designs offered by the GSC can be finished in an average of sixty days prior to the event date.

Video displays, LED lighting and screens, AV system and lighting, fabrics, balloons, and so on can create a supporting atmosphere for product display. Historically, AV was the primary means for creating atmosphere for meetings and events. Now however, LED's have overtaken a large part of the IT technology utilized at meetings/events. When utilizing LED technology, the planner is able to use multiple projectors to blend images and create new cutting-edge looks for the secondary sales initiatives. Also, line array speakers are more aesthetically pleasing than the original black box speakers. The ability to make changes electronically allows for last minute alterations to your cue sheet.

Lighting can provide illumination, especially at indoor events. One of the objectives of using lighting is to highlight and focus on the event decoration/decor and enhance the space. Lighting creates the mood of the event. For example, if gold-colored lighting for an event is used, the mood or tone can be luxurious. Spotlighting products sets a tone and can enhance a space with minimal décor.

Event professionals should work with design professionals who can develop the sales initiative's visual concept. The designer should provide concept development, the initial room plan, and preliminary sketches designed by computer aided design (CAD) software. A final rendering should be delivered that allows for feedback provided throughout the design process, a detailed list of deliverables, rental costs, and on-site supervision. The event professional must be cautious however, for misunderstandings regarding the scene designer's estimates of cost compared to the actual billing hours so that budget overages are not incurred.

Staffing—The ideal salesperson for the secondary retail space should be extremely knowledgeable about the products, have high energy, and be very enthusiastic about the client's company. However, staff should be trained before being exposed to customers. Staff training is extremely important to the success of a sales initiative. The event professional may prefer to hire an outside consultant to conduct the training or may develop the training program in-house. In either case, make sure to provide sales, plus guest service training, in order to prepare the staff to sell and function within the environment created. Also, staff must make sure to gather complete lead data and know what is the most critical information to gather so the client's marketing team can effectively follow up with sales prospects. In addition, think about how to evaluate the staff's performance. The number of leads, sales conversion, qualified buyers in the booth, signing up distributors, post-show recall of your booth/product, cost vs. return analysis, and/or ROI would be recommended measurements to use for evaluation. Again, staffing is very important because 70 percent of attendees remember what was promised and discussed at the retail space.

Signage—Signage can become a useful communication tool to increase awareness of the sales product(s). It can be achieved via digital delivery systems and projection systems. Before designing the signage, event professionals need to conduct research about the target consumer audience. Make sure to choose the right brand message to connect with the target audience. Once the correct message is crafted for the signage, reach out to third-party vendors or the GSC to create the signs. Keep in mind before ordering the signage, it will be vitally important to proofread the verbiage before it goes to print, as well as double- and triple-check your measurements for the size of the sign.

Other Requirements for Logistics—Planners must be aware of the power supply needed by each of the third-party vendors that will be contracted to fulfill the production needs of the secondary sales initiative. For instance, many contractors will require electricity for lighting, A/V, LED, and so on. Therefore, it is the responsibility of the event professional to ensure that there is an adequate power supply for the sales initiative.

Electricity is required for almost all aspects of a meeting/event. This includes, but is not limited to, catering, bands, DJ, A/V, heaters and air conditioners, lighting, chocolate fountains, games, and so forth. When considering how much electricity is needed, it is important to know the following equation: Volts $\times$ Amps = Watts. Most U.S. electrical circuits are 15 to 20 amps and the standard current is 110 volts, with up to 1650 watts per circuit. Therefore, it is the responsibility of the event professional to verify the number of outlets secured for electrical needs and that this number is suitable to the electrical demand placed on the outlets. Outside the United States, the standard is 220 volts—plug in your U.S.-made hair dryer, and it will burn out in a second!

Electricity can be found in hotel or venue rooms through outlets, power boxes, tie-ins, and the main disconnect. For outdoor events one is more likely to need generators. A generator uses a gasoline engine to produce electrical power. The only problem with a generator is that they are extremely loud, so if you are utilizing a generator for an outdoor event, make sure to place it next to another noisy area, such as the kitchen or, if possible, immediately outside the structure.

Financial Management and Price Strategy—For event professionals, revenue and expenses attributed to each event must be accurately tracked and recorded so as to determine the return on investment. The commonly preferred method to arrive at ROI for a sales initiative is through the Generally Accepted Accounting Principles as established by the Financial Accounting Standards Board. Once the event professional has an accounting system in place, then standard cost estimates are established, allowing the professional to practice cost control more effectively. Cost control involves determining the standard amount and cost per unit for direct material, direct labor and overhead costs, and managing these costs effectively. With the above system and standardized costs, event professionals can estimate the cost of materials, labor, and overhead. Thus, they can better estimate the cost of the final event as a whole. One important element that is often overlooked is the allocation of overhead expenses; this is very important for ensuring that a secondary sales initiative is profitable.

STEP II
Permits—Knowing what licenses and permits the business needs can be very confusing when planning a sales initiative at a meeting. It is important to list all of the required permits (e.g., alcohol and tobacco sales, special events, health permits, signage, zoning, sales taxes) and check with local officials to find out which permits the secondary sales initiative requires. Before selling one piece of merchandise to the consuming public, be sure to secure the necessary business licenses/permits that are required to keep the sales initiative operating legally, even if it is only for temporary purposes. One example is a temporary festival where a short-term liquor license is required in order to sell alcoholic beverages; it is not enough to hire a local bar or restaurant to provide and serve these beverages.

It is also important to obtain a sales permit for the sales and use tax in order to operate legally as a sales initiative. Keep in mind there are a few exceptions, depending on the nature of the business providing exemption from sales tax. In addition, when planners or exhibitors sell products at a MEEC, the local and state laws of where the venue is situated prevail over the sales transactions being conducted. In some states, if the sales initiative plan exists for less than 30 days, then the planner is allowed to apply for a temporary sales permit. Currently, within the United States, some states provide services on location at a trade show to make it easier for MEEC planners to obtain a temporary seller's permit that allows the sales staff to collect sales tax from consumers and report those amounts to the state on a regular reporting schedule.

Also, the permits needed for any construction (e.g., tents, stages, electrical) in cities vary. If the sales initiatives are not covered under the venue's permit, which is usually the case, then it will be incumbent upon the event professional to secure the necessary permits. Outdoor events require permits for tents, stages, electrical including generators, lighting, and so forth. Event professionals should consider the kinds of permits required for all aspects of the sales initiative. For example, professional meeting and event planners must get a permit from the appropriate government agency if selling food or other merchandise.

Sales Tax—If the secondary sales initiative occurs in more than one geographic subdivision (state), the declaration of tax will be reported to each subdivision prior to leaving the area for the next sales initiative site. Keep in mind that the U.S. Supreme Court has ruled on two different occasions that states cannot require businesses to collect sales tax, unless the business has a physical presence (or "nexus") in the state. Since the sales initiative is taking place in a specific location, the event professional needs to collect sales taxes as mandated by that city/township. Sales tax rates and rules are complicated and vary from state to state, city to city. In any case, consult the local sales tax collection agency in the state where the secondary sales initiative is being held to determine exactly what documents are required.

Intellectual Property (IP)—Event professionals need to gain an understanding of Intellectual Property (IP) laws including trademarks, copyrights, and patents for sales initiatives, including design of merchandise, premiums, Point of Sale equipment, video content, company logos, and taglines, to name a few. For example, trademarks are a specific type of IP laws that covers names, words, phrases, logos, and designs that identify and relate to a specific product. When researching possible business names or possible sales event names, it is recommended to visit the U.S. Patent & Trademark Office online. On the website, searches can be conducted to verify the intended name of a business or a sales event name is not currently in use. If a name for either is in "use" and has been secured with a trademark and/or copyright, depending on whether a logo is being considered, then use of those names would be deemed infringement. Therefore, in this case, the event professional needs to be sure to find a business name or event name that does not have a current trademark or copyright. Once it is confirmed a name is not in use, the event professional is free to file for a trademark. In order to get a trademark, submit an application to the U.S. Patent & Trademark office's website. In the interim, register a business name locally. However, it is not a substitute for a federal trademark, as the state registration will only reflect when the business name was first used for business purposes.

SUMMARY

As a future event professional, be aware that clients will seek out qualified professionals to organize sales initiatives—concept, design, organization, vendor relations, marketing, public relations, advertising, venue selection, risk management, and legal requirements. The event professional, in essence, is the ringmaster of the entire project and will collaborate with marketing, public relations, and vendors to manifest the client's vision of the sales initiative. To achieve a well-balanced sales plan on the client's behalf, it is integral for the communication skills of the events professional to be well developed. The difference between success and failure in the meeting and event industry most often rests on the event professional's ability to be proactive in their communications with all stakeholders (marketing, public relations, vendor, client, legal, technical crew, to name a few). The more the sequential steps become second nature to the professional when organizing primary and secondary sales initiatives, the easier it will be to maintain a high standard of communication to ensure a successful outcome for the client.

Now that you have completed this chapter, you should be competent in the following Meetings and Business Events Competency Standards:

MBECS—Skill 28: Manage Meeting or Event Merchandise

Sub skills		Skills (standards)
J 28.01	Develop product(s) design and specification	
J 28.02	Determine pricing	

MBECS—Skill 31: Manage Sales Activities

Sub skills		Skills (standards)
J 31.01	Develop sales plan	
J 31.03	Determine sales platforms	

KEY WORDS AND TERMS

For definitions, visit the American Marketing Association website, under Dictionary found within Resource Library or www.marketingpower.com/ResourceLibrary/Pages/default.aspx

Business to Business (B2B)	Test market	Sales tactics
Business to Consumer (B2C)	Demographics	SMART
Owner	Psychographics	Sales lead
Participant	Branding	
SWOT analysis	Sales strategy	

REVIEW AND DISCUSSION QUESTIONS

1. Explain the differences in objectives and planning between designing a primary and secondary sales initiative.

2. What resources would a meeting/event planner utilize to compile background information to assess the best primary sales initiative for a client? Include all resources that can be pursued to best understand historical data, SWOT analysis, consumer behavior, demographics, psychographics, stakeholders, and competitors.

3. Please address the common and differing points in planning a primary sales initiative from the perspective of working for a client who owns the MEEC vs. working for a client who is a participant of the MEEC.

4. When designing a secondary sales initiative, retail merchandising becomes paramount. Discuss retail merchandising efforts—staging, placement, promotions, floor layout, and so on—that can offer inspiration for the creation of a meeting/event secondary sales initiative.

5. Why are event professionals expected to be well-versed in sales initiatives in the MEEC industry?

RESOURCES

- AMC International—Point of Sale and Data Capture for Trade Shows
- Bump Technologies, Inc.—Mobile application designed for iPhones and Android phones. The Bump allows user to share contact information by simply bumping two phones together.
- Certain—Innovative Saas Event Management Platform
- Charity Auctions Today
- eSalesTrack—Cloud-based sales force automation
- Expo Tracker—Registration system, Networking center, Exhibit sales system, and so forth.

- File Maker Pro—FM Credit Card
- File Maker Pro compatible application—Hero—Manage your conference business
- Growth Capital Portal—SWOT algorithms
- MeetingMatrix—Connects venues with event planners
- Partner—Mobile POS systems
- Retail Anywhere—Ecommerce solutions
- SalesVu—The easiest way to accept credit cards
- Show Data Solutions
- Silent Auction Software

TRADE PUBLICATIONS

License Global
EXPO—Smart Meetings

B to B Magazine
Sales and Marketing Management

ABOUT THE CHAPTER CONTRIBUTORS

Soyoung Boo, PhD, holds two PhD degrees in tourism studies; her domestic and international experience in the event and meeting planning industries has gained her considerable recognition resulting in her current position as an assistant professor of Tourism Studies in the School of Business at The George Washington University located in the District of Columbia. Her research concentration reveals the psychological and marketing aspects impacting the special event and meeting planning industries. Dr. Boo has published numerous marketing, hospitality, and event-related academic articles in leading journals across the globe. She also contributes to refereeing several academic papers specific to the event and meeting planning industries. A most recent highlight of Dr. Boo's contributions to the event and meeting related industries can be found as a council member of the Convention Industry Council and is an entrusted advisor to the APEX Industry Glossary's Standards Review Council.

Christine LeClaire, CSEP, is the president of Studio Ennovate, LLC, a special event company originally based in Las Vegas, Nevada, with new headquarters in Washington, DC that has produced events and conventions spanning New York City, Boston, the Caribbean, and Las Vegas for 20+ years. Ms. LeClaire is a graduate of the University of Nevada at Las Vegas Hospitality Administration program specializing in event management and minoring in Theatre Management. She is currently working on her Masters of Business Administration at The George Washington University and can be found guest speaking at the university to undergraduates and graduates on meeting management. She has served as a board member for the Las Vegas International Special Event Society, and she speaks and writes regularly on the subjects of entertainment and the customer service experience.

Epilogue

Like the sun set, the reader is closing the last chapter of this book and is moving on to another place in pursuit of a career as an event professional.
© mizio70/Shutterstock

Chapter Outline

Introduction

Content Areas in This Book

  MEEC

Summary

Key Words, Acronyms, and Phrases

Discussion Questions

About the Chapter Contributor

Chapter Objectives

Upon completion of this chapter, the reader should be able to:

* Know what was learned in the preceding chapters of this book
* Know the scope and magnitude of the MEEC industry
* Know the various Knowledge, Skills, and Abilities (KSAs) that are necessary to be a successful event professional
* Know the tasks and activities involved in planning a meeting or event
* Identify those MBECS standards for which you have basic knowledge

INTRODUCTION

Meetings, Expositions, Events, and Conventions (MEEC, pronounced like geese) are a part of the larger field of tourism. This is an exciting career area. Regardless of the attitudes and interests of the potential MEEC professional, they should be able to find a satisfying employment niche in MEEC. Now that the reader has completed this book, it is expected that they have some knowledge of the MEEC industry. The operationalization of MEEC falls into only two categories: Planning and Producing. The reader now has in-depth knowledge regarding the tasks and activities involved in the planning of meetings and events.

CONTENT AREAS IN THIS BOOK

The specific areas or content of this book, to which the reader has now been exposed, comprise basic knowledge including:

* **Strategic Planning in Meetings, Expositions, Events, and Conventions**
  In this chapter you learned about the definition of strategic planning, articulating the purpose of creating a strategic plan for a

meeting or event, and identifying the four key steps in the strategic planning process.

- **Project Management**

  In this chapter you learned how project management is applied to meetings, expositions, events, and conventions. You learned about the historical perspective of project management as a business process, a description of project management, a comparison of project manager and meeting planner roles, the project charter, the project management plan, the project scope and work breakdown structure, and the plans and documents that comprise the collection of data throughout the project's lifecycle.

- **Risk Management**

  In this chapter you learned about risk management as it applies to planning or hosting a meeting or business event, analyzing the risks associated with the specific characteristics of a particular meeting or business event, how to develop a risk plan that addresses mitigation measures and contingency plans for identified and analyzed risks, and how to identify the relationship between liability and risk management.

- **Stakeholder Management**

  In this chapter you learned about identifying your stakeholders; determining the potential impact of stakeholders on meetings or events, and vice versa; stakeholders' relationships in terms of power, influence, and interest; planning stakeholder programs and activities; and managing stakeholder relationships.

- **Accounting and Financial Planning**

  In this chapter you learned about accounting responsibilities and evaluating return on investment and return on equity; defining, determining, analyzing, and construction of a budget based on organizational goals and objectives; establishing registration and other pricing for events; establishing budget review, cash control, and other financial procedures; and managing cash and cash flow.

- **Event Program Planning**

  In this chapter you learned about analyzing previous programs, embracing adult education learning styles, ascertaining attendee expectations, determining program components, legal and regulatory requirements, the development of cost estimates, garnering stakeholder support, determining requirements for each program component, developing a program agenda/itinerary, and developing personnel assignments.

- **Planning and Designing the Environment**

  In this chapter you learned about making plans for types of speakers, entertainers, and performers; sources of speakers, entertainers, performers; methods of choosing speakers, entertainers, and/or performers; securing contracts and communicating expectations; determining and developing plans for staging and technical requirements; admittance and credential systems; crowd management strategies; and risk management plans.

- **Site Planning and Management**

  In this chapter you learned about the nature, scope, complexity, and fiscal requirements of the event; the desired or demanded geographic locations; types of facilities, spatial factors, and operational logistics such as dates, duration, and cost of occupancy on site; site selection criteria, site inspections, and evaluation of potential sites; selecting the site that best caters to the needs of all involved stakeholders of the event.

- **Food and Beverage Planning**
  In this chapter you learned about food and beverage requirements, target markets, developing a themed event and creating an attendee profile with regard to food and beverage.

- **Marketing of Meetings, Expositions, Events, and Conventions**
  In this chapter you learned about the definition of marketing; applying marketing principles; working with event stakeholders; identifying and characterizing target market segments; appropriate marketing distribution channels; marketing strategies; developing and implementing a marketing plan.

- **Promotions Planning**
  In this chapter you learned about promotions, eight different aspects of creating a promotional plan, promotional activities in terms of consumer decision making, three types of promotions; differentiating sales promotion, advertising, and publicity; applying the above to each type of meeting or event.

- **Sales Initiatives in the Meetings, Expositions, Events, and Conventions Industry**
  In this chapter you learned about two types of sales initiatives in the meeting and event industries; the differences between a primary and secondary sales initiative; the two sides of the primary sales initiatives depending upon type of client; the process to produce both primary and secondary sales initiatives.

MBECS

As an industry evolves and matures, there is an increasing need among clients, employers, and governments to have a codified set of competency standards to which professionals must adhere. Until very recently no common set of knowledge, skills, and abilities (KSAs) existed for event professionals. This changed with the release of the *Meetings and Business Events Competency Standards* (MBECS). **MBECS** contains the KSAs required of meetings and events professionals. This content of this book is based on MBECS.

The table on next page contains all of the domains that make up the major categories in MBECS. The check marks (☑) identify those KSAs covered in this book and for which the reader should now possess the requisite knowledge. This provides a basis for determining knowledge gaps on the part of the reader.

This book contains all of the knowledge related to planning of meetings and events that is expected of people who are to be employed at the coordinator and at the manager level. It does not deal with the knowledge of planning that should be possessed by an event professional at the director or executive level. There is a companion text, *Production and Logistics in Meetings, Expositions, Events and Conventions* that covers material related to MBECS knowledge regarding producing meetings and events.

The content of these two texts plus the basic knowledge of MEEC that the reader is expected to have prior to studying from this book provide the reader with an understanding of the KSAs that are included in the **CPM-IS** and the corresponding exam. The "checklist" in this chapter indicates what the reader has learned in this text. The reader is encouraged to obtain the additional education and training that will allow the reader to complete this checklist and thus be prepared to Certified Meeting Professional (CMP) certification.

Table 1   Meetings and Business Events Competency Standards (MBECS)

Now that you have completed this book, you should be competent in the following Meetings and Business Events Competency Standards that have a check mark '√' beside them.

Domains/Skills	Checklist
A. STRATEGIC PLANNING	
1. Manage Strategic Plan for Meeting or Event	☑
2. Develop Sustainability Plan for Meeting or Event	☐
3. Measure Value of Meeting or Business Event	☐
B. PROJECT MANAGEMENT	
4. Plan Meeting or Event	☑
5. Manage Meeting or Event Project	☐
C. RISK MANAGEMENT	
6. Manage Risk Management Plan	☑
D. FINANCIAL MANAGEMENT	
7. Develop Financial Resources	☐
8. Manage Budget	☑
9. Manage Monetary Transactions	☑
E. ADMINISTRATION	
10. Perform Administrative Tasks	☐
F. HUMAN RESOURCES	
11. Manage Human Resource Plan	☐
12. Acquire Staff and Volunteers	☐
13. Train Staff and Volunteers	☐
14. Manage Workforce Relations	☐
G. STAKEHOLDER MANAGEMENT	
15. Manage Stakeholder Relationships	☑
H. MEETING OR EVENT DESIGN	
16. Design Program	☑
17. Engage Speakers and Performers	☑
18. Coordinate Food and Beverage	☑
19. Design Environment	☑
20. Manage Technical Production	☑
21. Develop Plan for Managing Movement of People	☑
I. SITE MANAGEMENT	
22. Select Site	☑
23. Design Site Layout	☑
24. Manage Meeting or Event Site	☐
25. Manage On-site communications	☐
J. MARKETING	
26. Manage Marketing Plan	☑
27. Manage Marketing Materials	☐
28. Manage Meeting or Event Merchandise	☑
29. Promote Meeting or Event	☑
30. Contribute to Public Relations Activities	☑
31. Manage Sales Activities	☑
K. PROFESSIONALISM	
32. Exhibit Professional Behavior	☐
L. COMMUNICATIONS	
33. Conduct Business Communications	☐

SUMMARY

This chapter is entitled "Epilogue" since it synopsizes the content and material covered throughout this book.

Now that you have completed this chapter, you should be competent in the following Meetings and Business Events Competency Standards:

MBECS—Skills 1, 4, 6, 8, 9, 15, 16, 17, 18, 19, 20, 21, 22, 23, 26, 28, 29, 30, 31

KEY WORDS, ACRONYMS, AND PHRASES

MBECS   CMP-IS

DISCUSSION QUESTIONS

1. What does MBECS represent?
2. How could event professionals prepare for the CMP-IS and the corresponding exam?
3. How do MBECS and CMP-IS relate?
4. How does the content of this book relate to MBECS?
5. The contents of this book are based on MBECS. How can these benefit event professionals?

ABOUT THE CHAPTER CONTRIBUTOR

George G. Fenich, PhD, is a full professor in the School of Hospitality Leadership at East Carolina University.

index